POSTCARD HISTORY SERIES

Will County

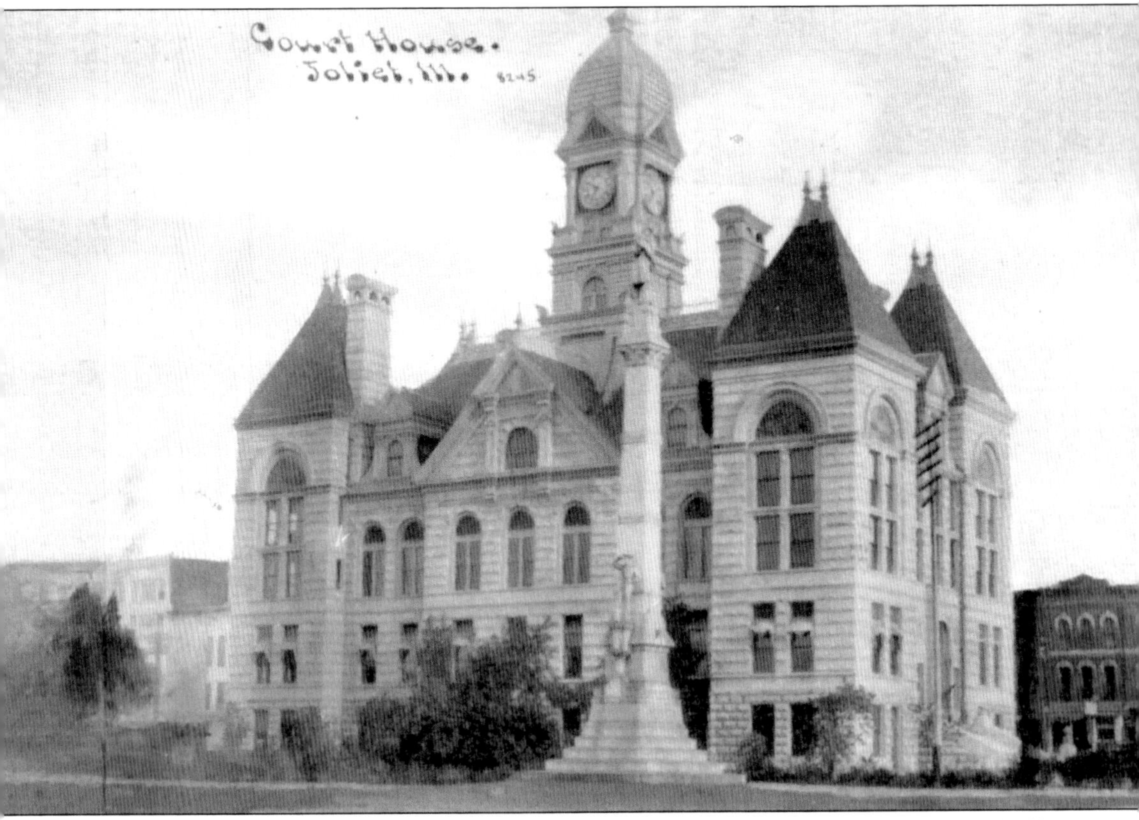

This postcard photograph shows the third Will County Courthouse from the corner of Jefferson and Chicago Streets looking southwest. Built between 1884 and 1887, the third courthouse was constructed from Joliet limestone and stood on the public square on west Jefferson Street until its demolition in 1969. The distinctive high clock tower, colonnaded front portico, and cone-shaped corner structures represent the Federal architectural style. John C. Cochrane, the architect of the building, also designed several other Illinois courthouses, including the Illinois State Capital in Springfield. (Courtesy of the Lewis University Canal and Regional History Special Collection.)

On the front cover: This postcard photograph shows a view of Lockport Street in downtown Plainfield looking west from the intersection of Illinois Street. Some notable features in this early-1920s photograph include the opera house building to the left with its unique alcove windows, cone tower, and a clock mounted above the windows. The small crowd on the corner is standing in front of Overman's Restaurant and Soda Shop. In the center of the photograph, the interurban railroad tracks running down Lockport Street can be seen. (Courtesy of Sam and Lynn Reichert.)

On the back cover: In 1885, J. R. Bowman entered the Chicago dairy market by purchasing the milk business of M. A. Devine. Six years later, he sold his St. Louis operation and moved to Chicago where he formed the Bowman Dairy Company. Over the years, the Bowman company expanded its markets outside Chicago and built large bottling plants on the south side of the city. One such plant was built on Wolf Road adjacent to the Rock Island tracks in Mokena. The nine men pictured in this postcard photograph are factory workers at the Bowman Bottling Plant in Mokena. (Courtesy of Robert Horras.)

POSTCARD HISTORY SERIES

Will County

David A. Belden

ARCADIA
PUBLISHING

ISBN 978-0-7385-6063-2

Published by Arcadia Publishing
Charleston SC, Chicago IL, Portsmouth NH, San Francisco CA

Printed in the United States of America

Library of Congress Catalog Control Number: 2009922405

For all general information contact Arcadia Publishing at:
Telephone 843-853-2070
Fax 843-853-0044
E-mail sales@arcadiapublishing.com
For customer service and orders:
Toll-Free 1-888-313-2665

Visit us on the Internet at www.arcadiapublishing.com

Contents

Acknowledgments

The publication of this book would not have been possible without the assistance and support of various institutions and individuals. The following area historical repositories, institutions, and individuals have provided help, material, and support from their collections for this book: Lewis University, Mary Ann Atkins and John Lamb; the Will County Historical Society, Lynne Mickle Smaczny; the Joliet Area Historical Museum, Kim Shehorn-Martin; Sam and Lynn Reichert; Michael Lambert; Tony Evans; Brian Weber; Erwin Klopfstein; Carol and Wehlan Triebold; Mike Arbanas; Robert Horras; Dave Zelinski; Dee DeGroth; Daniel Rozak; Bill Molony; Patricia Thomson; Missey Schumacher; Jason Carle; Marilyn McManimen; Richard Quinn; Minooka Community High School; Robert Williams; Kimberly Puckett; Dave DiLorenzo; Sherry Harris; Michael Denson; and Dr. David Middleton.

Several people have also been helpful with local histories, materials, and equipment, and to the following individuals I am very grateful: Carolyn Kinsella, Kathy Friant, Les Kern, Debbie Dobson, and Glenda Smith. I would also like to especially thank Robert Horras and Dave Zelinski for their time, assistance, and friendship in providing material and guidance on the early history of Mokena and Wilmington. The digitization of material would not have been possible without the generosity of EcoLab, Joliet Plant, and Candace Schlesser. A very special thank-you goes to Christine O'Brien for providing her time, help, and expertise in proofreading the text for this book.

The production and preparation of the material for this book would never have been possible without the dedication of numerous students in my local history classes. I wish to thank Ashley Avila, Michael Foltynewicz, Zachary Friant, Cody Hanchett, Joshua Horne, Ryan Koziol, Latrice McGaughy, Matthew Santillo, Erin Schuch, Elizabeth Celmer, Alexandria Griparis, Taylor Hartman, Alyssa Macuiba, William Mallady, Adam McAtee, Haley Musgrave, Kaitlin Olvera, Felicia Orsini, Amer Tanveer, Bennett Driver, Kasey Hegeduis, Holli Kirsch, Timothy Lofky, Emily Miller, Matthew Mytnik, Eleftherios Politis, Kimberly Ramsak, Joseph Waller, and Chelsea Bestow. A very special thank-you goes to Katie Kuta for her organizational skills and postcard selections.

Finally, I acknowledge the help of John Pearson and Jeff Ruetsche at Arcadia Publishing; my wife, Krystyna, for her patience and support while I worked on this book; and my late grandmother Mary, who sparked my early interest in history all those many years ago.

INTRODUCTION

The Local History Digitization Project at Minooka Community High School is designed to increase awareness of the area's local history and access to its historical collections. It digitizes collections from around the community, making them accessible on the Web site, www.localhistoryproject.org, and in a publication format. The scope of the digitization project includes postcards, photographs, genealogical information, area maps, plat books, newspapers and clippings, church records, telephone books, and school yearbooks, among others.

Over the past few years, the focus of the project's efforts has been postcard digitization. Postcards are one of the top collectibles worldwide, competing with coins and stamps. They can be very inexpensive, sometimes free, and take little space. Some postcards are very artistic and bring back nostalgic memories. In fact, just looking at vintage postcards evokes an earlier time in American history when life was much simpler. Each postcard is a snapshot of the past: a moment, a slice of social history frozen in time. Postcards provide a panorama of the events of the past century, including wars, sporting events, great exhibitions, and local fetes, to name a few. They can also show the development of rail, road, sea, and air transportation. Perhaps the most fascinating part of the postcard is the back side. Every postcard that has been mailed tells a little bit about its place in the bygone world. The picture, stamp, postmark, message, and address are part of the life of two people—the sender and the recipient—in the past. The intent is to show the historical and cultural aspects of Will County in this book. The postcards will provide the means to discover early towns in the county.

Many different aspects of Will County local history and life can be found in the picture postcards collection found in this book, including schools, businesses, sports teams, social gatherings, churches, public parks, homes, street scenes, and buildings. Because the history of Will County is so intertwined with the growth of the railroad, pictures of railroad depots and businesses located near the tracks are also part of the collection. These picture postcards form the basis for this book. The intent is to showcase an important component of the digitization project and, at the same time, celebrate the local history of Will County through postcards.

Of particular interest are the written messages found on both sides of the card. While the postcard did not serve as a medium for substantial messages, it did open a window to how people thought and communicated in the past. Longer, more intimate messages still had to be sent by ordinary, closed letters, but by the early part of the 20th century, the picture postcard became the perfect medium for short communications. When appropriate, the correspondences found on the postcards are included. It is also important to note that the first chapter (Joliet) is the shortest of all the chapters in the book. In order to showcase as many communities in the county as possible, and because the author has already published a book on Joliet, the decision was made to shorten the chapter.

Nearly 200 years ago, the land that is now Will County was covered by a vast prairie. Potawatomi Indians farmed, trapped, and traveled the area, which was at the crossroads of their land trails and river routes. In the late 17th century, European fur traders arrived and also began to take advantage of the abundance of muskrat, beavers, and other creatures. Trade slowed substantially by the 1820s, as hunting and the enclosure and tilling of the soil depleted the fur supply.

In 1826, Jesse Walker established the area's first permanent white settlement, Walker's Grove, near the present town of Plainfield. Most newcomers relied on agriculture, milling, and trade for their subsistence. On January 12, 1836, the state of Illinois responded to the residents' petition and formed the county of Will, combining parts of Cook and Iroquois Counties. The Illinois legislature named the county for Conrad Will, a member of the first nine general assemblies. Later that year, the three commissioners of the Will County board held their first meeting in the county seat of Juliet (later Joliet).

Six months after the county was formed, workers broke ground for the 96-mile-long Illinois and Michigan Canal, which connected the Chicago River with the Illinois River. The man-made waterway helped to boost the economy and put many new towns on the map. In the mid-19th century, mining augmented the county's economy. In 1864, while drilling for water, William Henneberry unintentionally hit a rich vein of coal. Soon thereafter, speculators arrived, and by the early 1880s, coal mining had reached its peak in Will County with seven companies operating mines, employing 2,180 men and producing 700,000 tons of coal annually. During this period, limestone quarrying also boomed. By the 1880s, Joliet had adopted the nickname "Stone City," shipping tons of limestone to Chicago for use in the construction of the water tower and residences and businesses throughout the city.

By the early 20th century, the economy of the region began to change as manufacturers and refiners opened and operated sites in the area, and Will County experienced a new industrialization. Although industrialization began to decline by the 1980s, the population of the region began to expand and today is known as one of the fastest-growing counties in Illinois.

A few final thoughts . . . People of every place and time deserve a history. Only local history satisfies the need to remember the most routine matters and the most intimate parts of one's life. Local history allows the reconstruction of the everyday lives of those who lived before, along with their goods, machines, tools with which they worked, and the groups that they were a part of in the community. Local history helps recapture how they experienced the world they lived in and how it can be better understood today. While every community has stories to tell, there are too few devoted historians to tell them.

Those few local historians are all driven to piece together a cherished, intimate, and routine past. They all cannot get rid of their curiosity with their community's past. Oftentimes, this curiosity does not allow them to write the critical local history that is required to understand the past. They lack a methodology or a complex hypothesis to help examine the past. Instead, they focus on the anecdotes, the stories, the details, and the particularities. Much like the local museums and historical societies, which collect and store all those long-forgotten objects from the past, many local historians run the risk of just focusing on the images and just reminiscing of the past. As the field of local history is, by nature, very fragmented, it may continue to remain so unless the present condition of local history research changes. While the local historians know, in detail, what contributions they have made by collecting, studying, and writing, it is hoped that books like this will help to renovate local history research and allow the talented amateurs to seek to understand what is truly happening to their home and community. Let these postcards invigorate one's desire to research the local history of his or her community.

One

Joliet

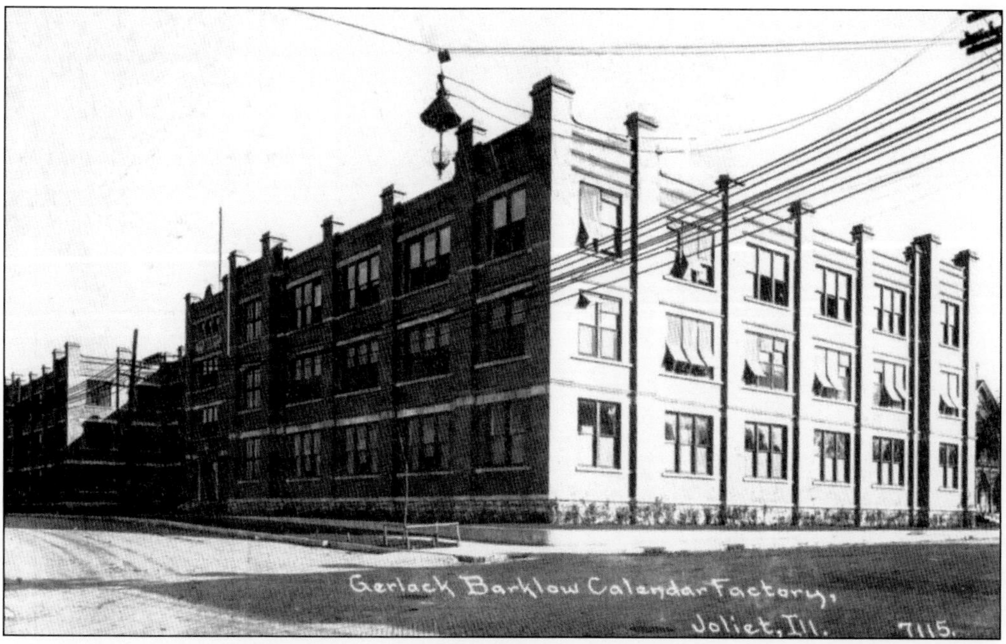

The Gerlach-Barklow Company was established in June 1907, and within a month, ground was broken for the company plant on East Washington Street, just east of Richards Street. The company, best known for its calendars, also manufactured postcards, greeting cards, booklets, and other advertising items. By the 1950s, the Gerlach-Barklow Company was among Joliet's largest employers with more than 1,000 employees.

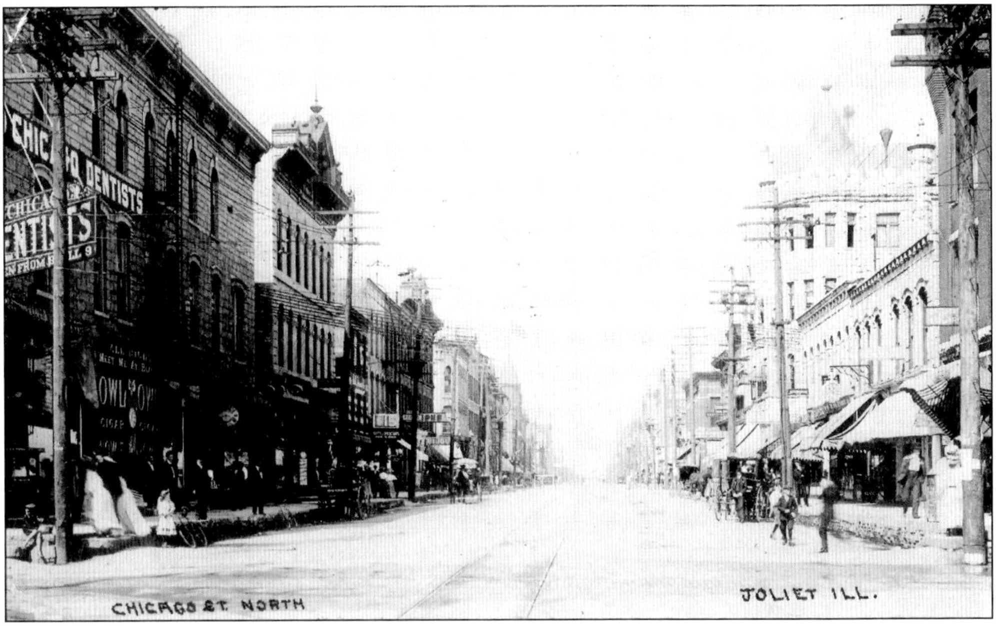

This *c.* 1900 postcard photograph shows the familiar intersection of Chicago Street looking north from Jefferson Street. The streetcar tracks in the middle, the horse-drawn buggies, and the overhead electric wires supported by wooden poles help to show life in an earlier time. The Harris and Foley Store and the Barber building can be seen on the east side of the street, and the Goodspeed and Munroe Block buildings are visible on the west side of the block.

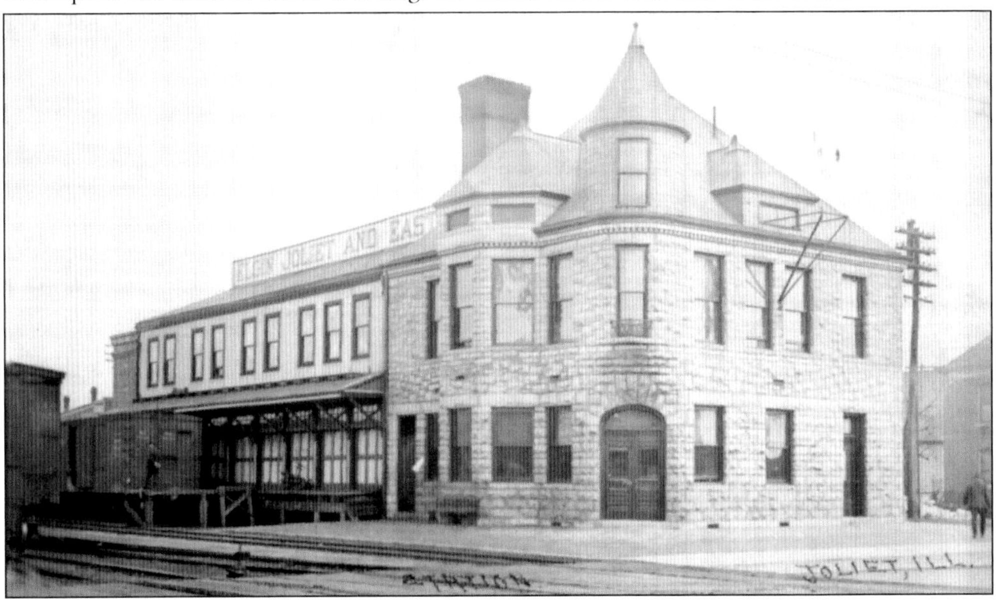

The Elgin, Joliet and Eastern Railway passenger depot was located on Clinton Street, just east of the tracks. The railway built the limestone building in 1892, and it functioned as a depot until 1907. In 1914, the building was used as a passenger station by the Joliet and Eastern Traction Company, which ran a streetcar business out of the building until 1923. From 1944 until 1986, Fitzgerald's Furniture used the building for its business. The City of Joliet owns the building today.

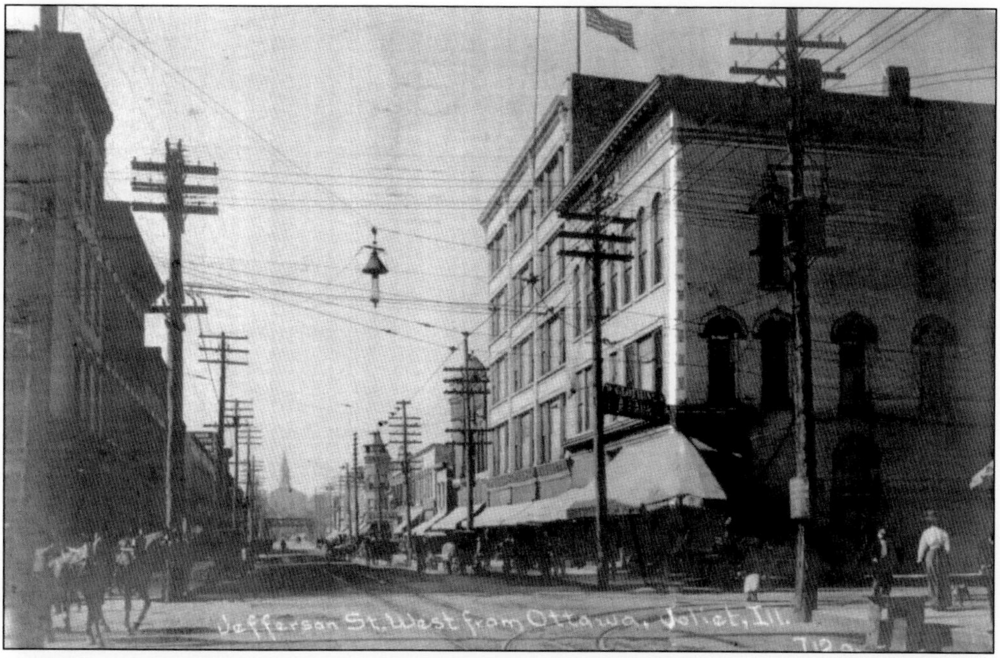

Looking west on Jefferson Street from the corner of Ottawa Street, a number of downtown landmarks are visible on the north side, including the D'Arcy-Hammond Block building, the five-story Boston Store with its rooftop flag, and the M. Calmer Dry Goods Company. Across the street on the left is the Will County National Bank. In the distance, St. Patrick's Church is visible.

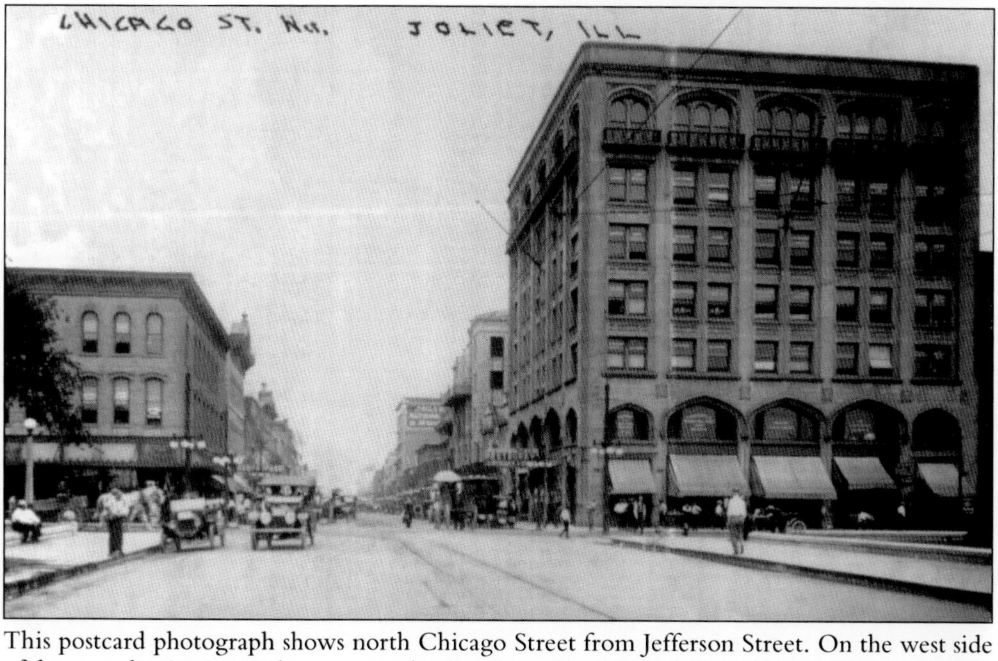

This postcard photograph shows north Chicago Street from Jefferson Street. On the west side of the street beginning at the corner is the Goodspeed building, followed by the Munroe Block. Across the street on the east side of the block is the Woodruff/Morris building with Schneiter's Restaurant sign in the foreground, followed by the Princess Theatre and the Barber building.

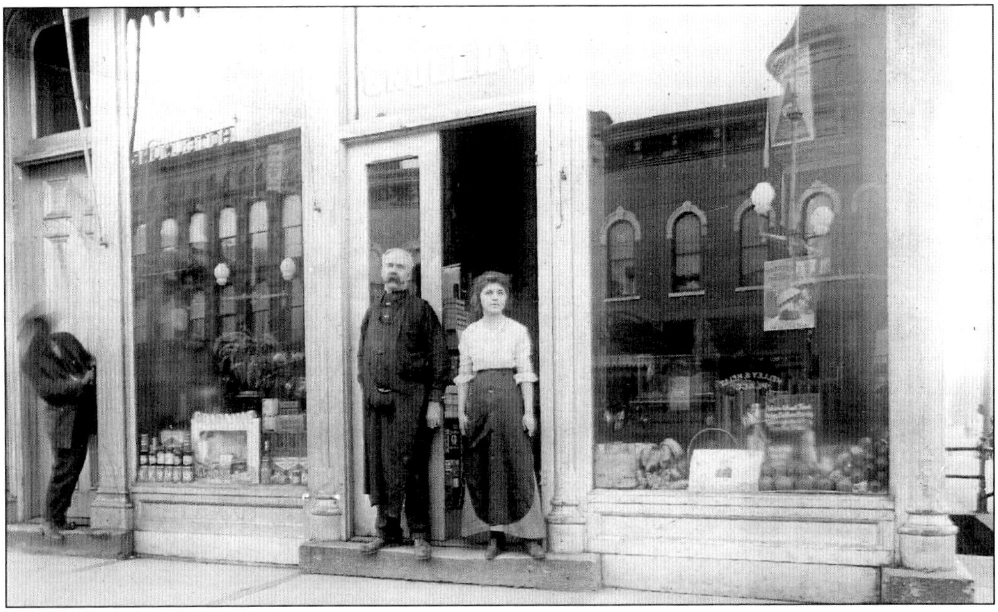

The Mahoney Grocery Store, located on the southwest corner of Chicago and Cass Streets, was established in 1867 and featured fresh fruits, vegetables, eggs, and other staples. The Mahoney family lived above the grocery store and owned five horses and a cow that were housed in the barn behind the building. Jeremiah Mahoney II and his granddaughter Evelyn Mahoney are pictured here in front of the store in 1914.

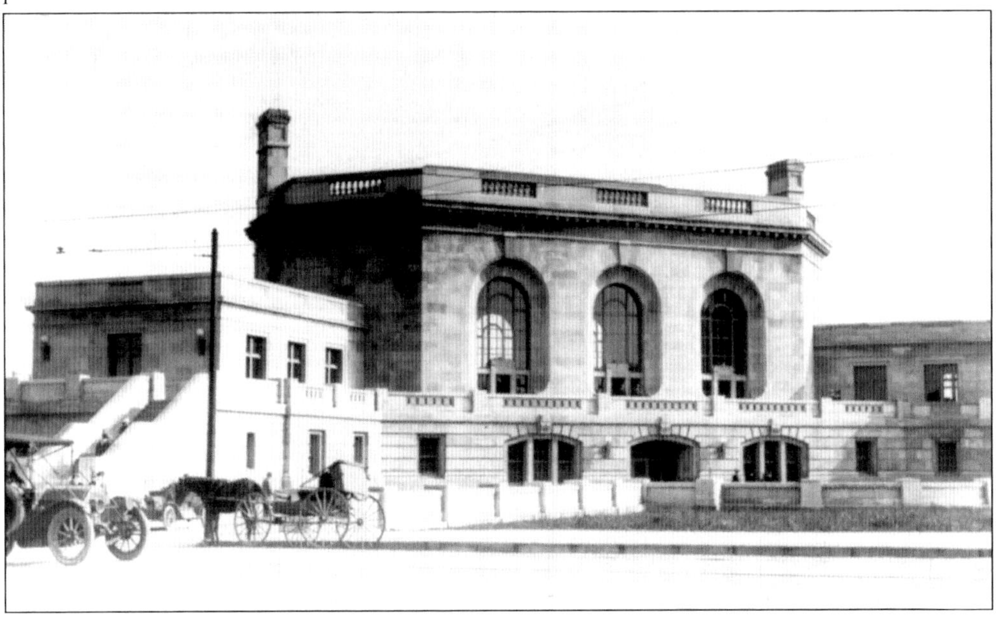

This postcard photograph shows the front of union station looking southeast from Jefferson Street. Built in 1912 by Adam Groth and Company for nearly $250,000, union station, with its neoclassical design, has served the city of Joliet for nearly a century. Stairs on either end of the station allow passengers to climb nearly 20 feet to the elevated level of the newly designed tracks. In 1991, that station was completely renovated as part of the City Center revitalization program.

The historic St. Joseph Church, located on North Chicago Street, was established in 1891 to serve the growing community of Slovenian immigrants who settled in Joliet at the end of the 19th century. The present church building, with its distinctive dual spires and silver hue, was built in 1905 from Indiana limestone. The postcard photograph shows the church looking southeast from the corner of Chicago and Clay Streets.

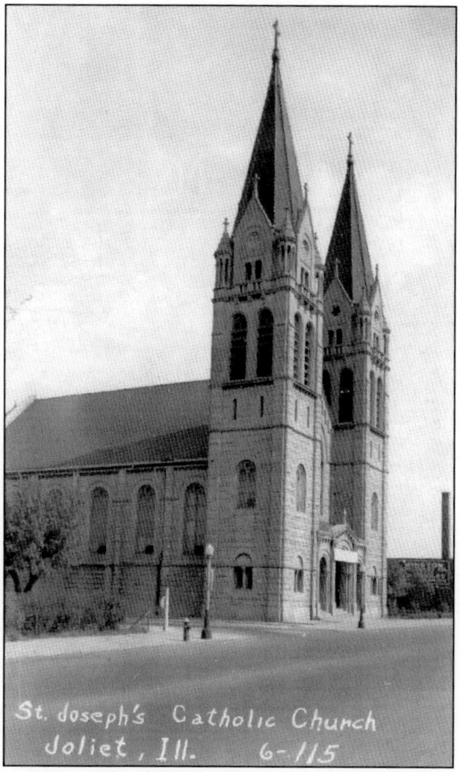

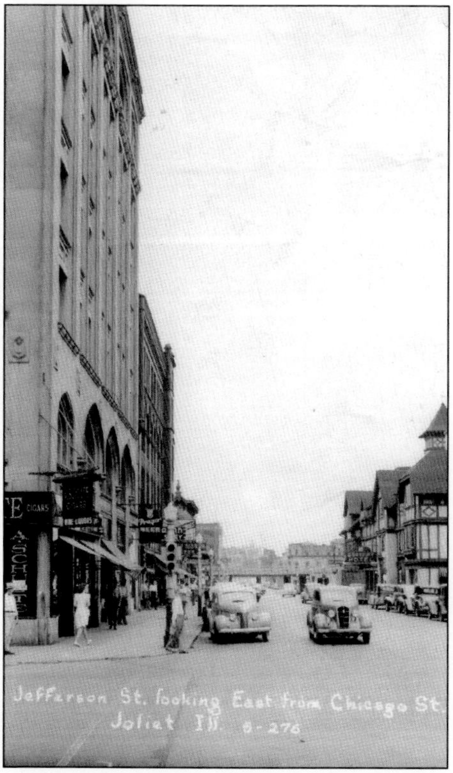

Looking east on Jefferson Street from the corner of Chicago Street, two downtown landmarks are visible on the south side: the old English-style Woodruff Inn and union station, built from smooth Bedford stone. On the north side of Jefferson Street, the seven-story Woodruff (Morris) building can be seen on the northeast corner, and the four-story Young building is just to the east.

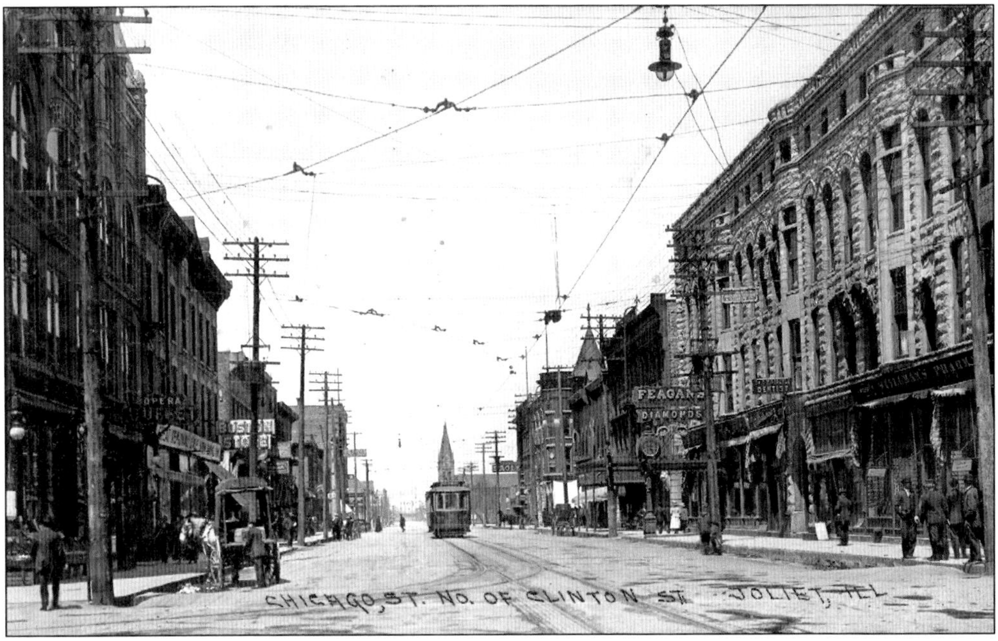

This is a postcard photograph of Chicago Street looking north near Clinton Street. The long limestone structure on the right is the auditorium building, which housed the city's first civic auditorium and functioned throughout the years as a cultural arts center for the community. For years, Stillman's Pharmacy operated out of the first-floor corner location on Clinton Street.

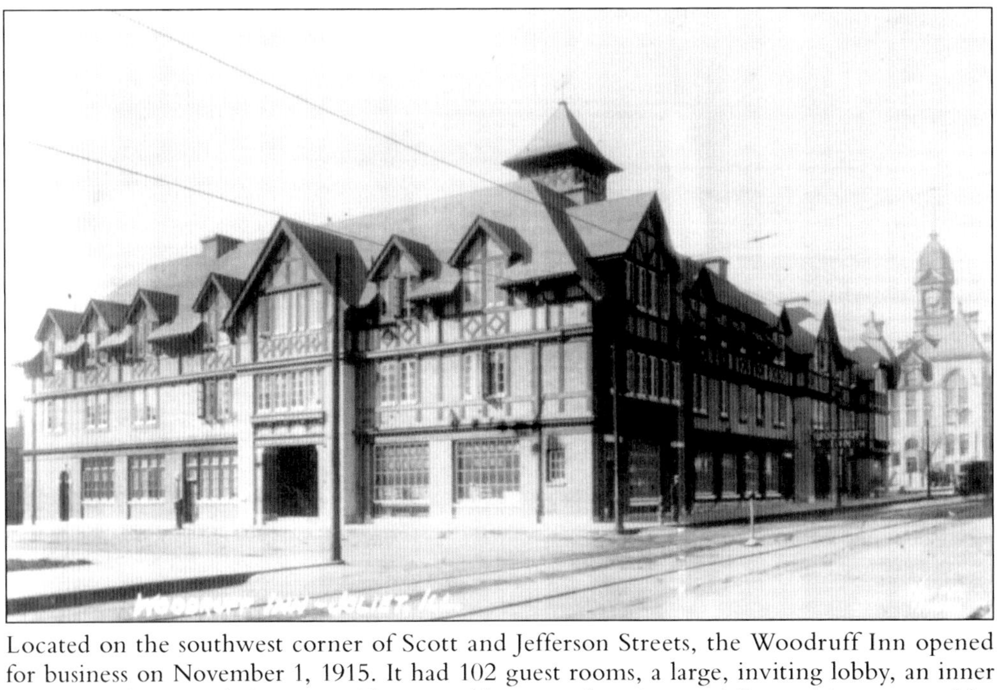

Located on the southwest corner of Scott and Jefferson Streets, the Woodruff Inn opened for business on November 1, 1915. It had 102 guest rooms, a large, inviting lobby, an inner courtyard that provided guests with an outside tranquil setting, and fine cuisine prepared by chef Marcel A. Pfister. The hotel was razed on December 21, 1971, ending an era as a distinctive downtown landmark.

Two

Lockport

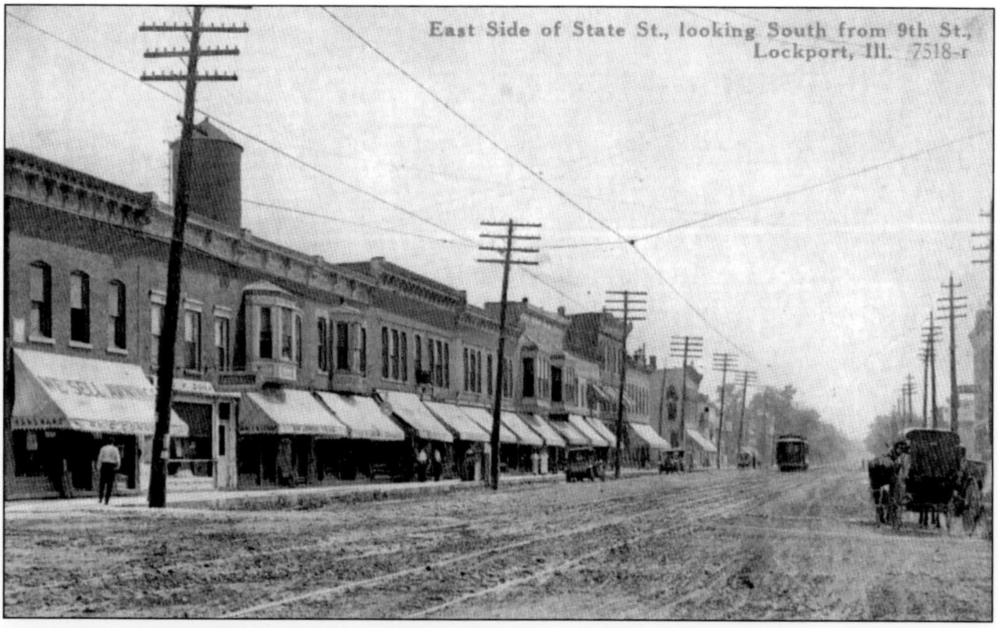

State Street has traditionally been the core of retail activity in Lockport, and many of the businesses operating on the street today are housed in the structures dating from the late 1800s. Some of the buildings are frame or brick, but most were constructed from limestone that was quarried locally. This picture postcard shows the east side of State Street looking south from Ninth Street.

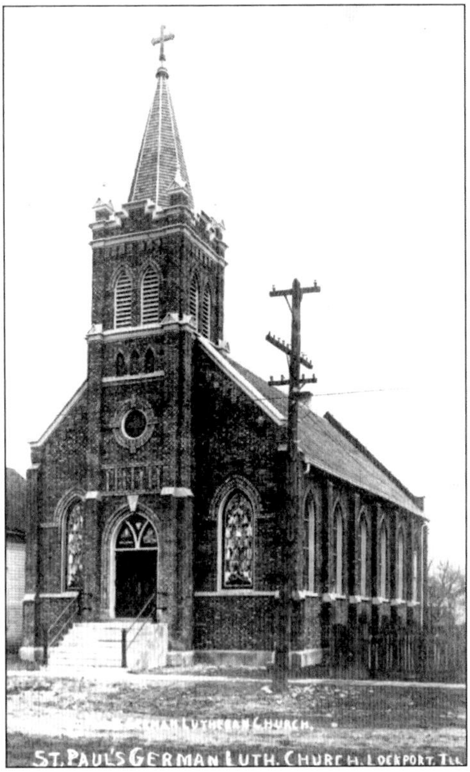

St. Paul's German Lutheran Church was officially organized on June 11, 1871. The founders of the church met in a frame building on Eleventh Street between Washington and Jefferson Streets. On February 25, 1912, the congregation decided to build a new church with construction beginning in early August. St. Paul's German Lutheran Church has served the community for over 137 years. This picture postcard shows a view of the 1912 church looking south from Eleventh Street.

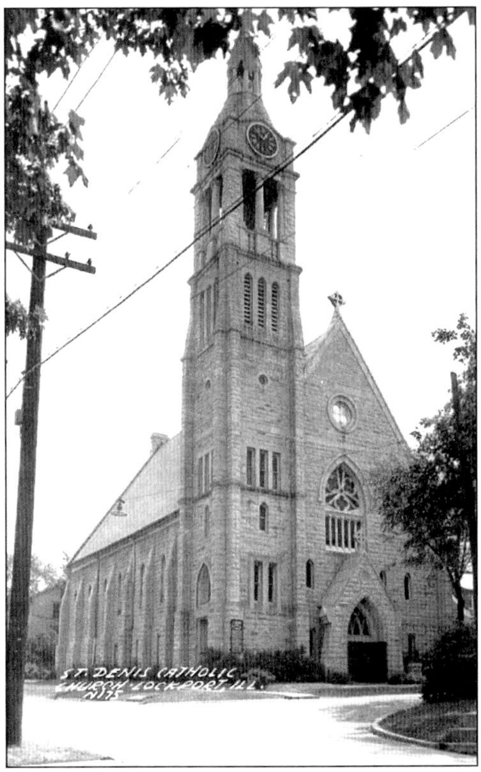

Located on the corner of Hamilton and Twelfth Streets, the impressive limestone church was designed by Egan and Hill, architects for the Archdiocese of Chicago, and constructed in 1877. Founded by Fr. Dennis Ryan, the parish originally served the Irish community that made up the first congregation. The large, 170-foot steeple of St. Dennis is a prominent architectural feature that is visible along the eastern bluff of the Des Plaines River.

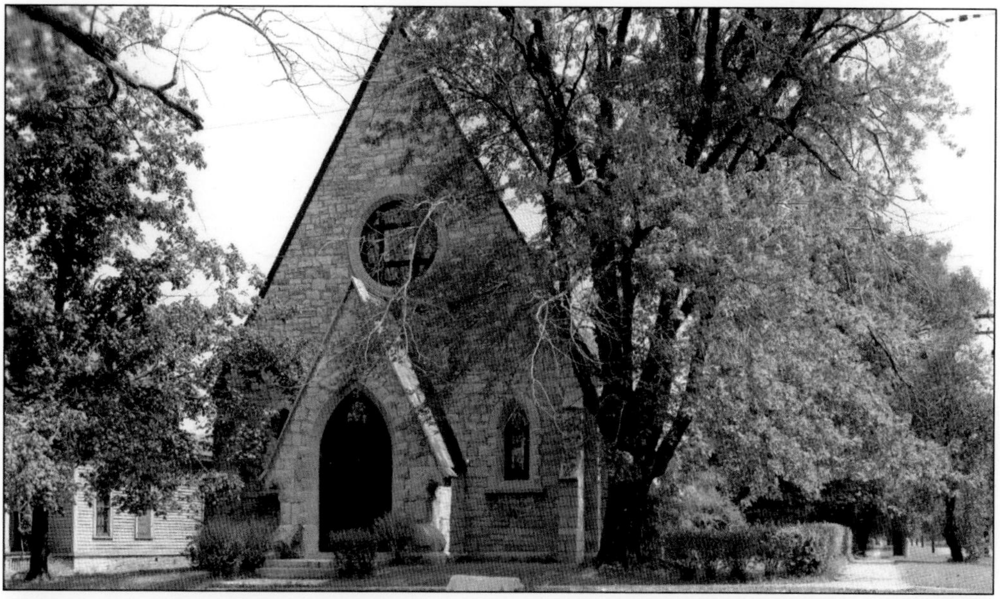

The history of St. John's Episcopal Church can be traced back to 1834, when the first religious services were held. In 1844, an oak-frame church was built several blocks east of the Illinois and Michigan Canal. This church was replaced in 1870 with a limestone building designed by local architect P. N. Hartwell in an English Gothic Revival style. Located on the southeast corner of Eleventh and Washington Streets, this picture postcard shows a view of the church looking east.

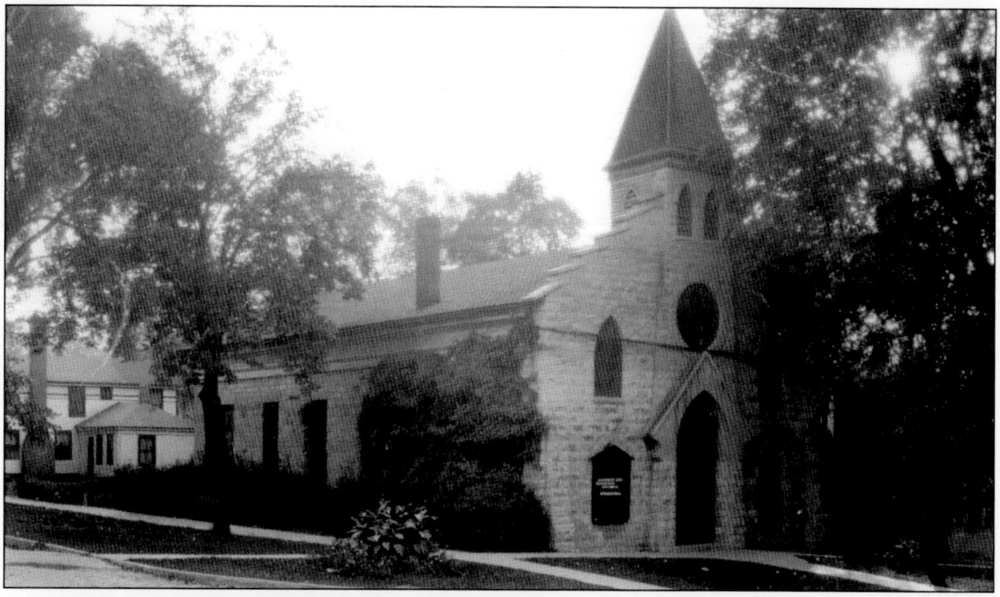

In 1837, the town square in Lockport was created as a way of re-creating the village green that early settlers left behind in New England. Erected in 1839 using local limestone, the old Congregational church was built facing the square on the southwest corner of Ninth and Washington Streets. The steeple and portico porch were removed during alterations in the late 19th century. Today the old Congregational church houses the Gladys Fox Museum and serves as a community center.

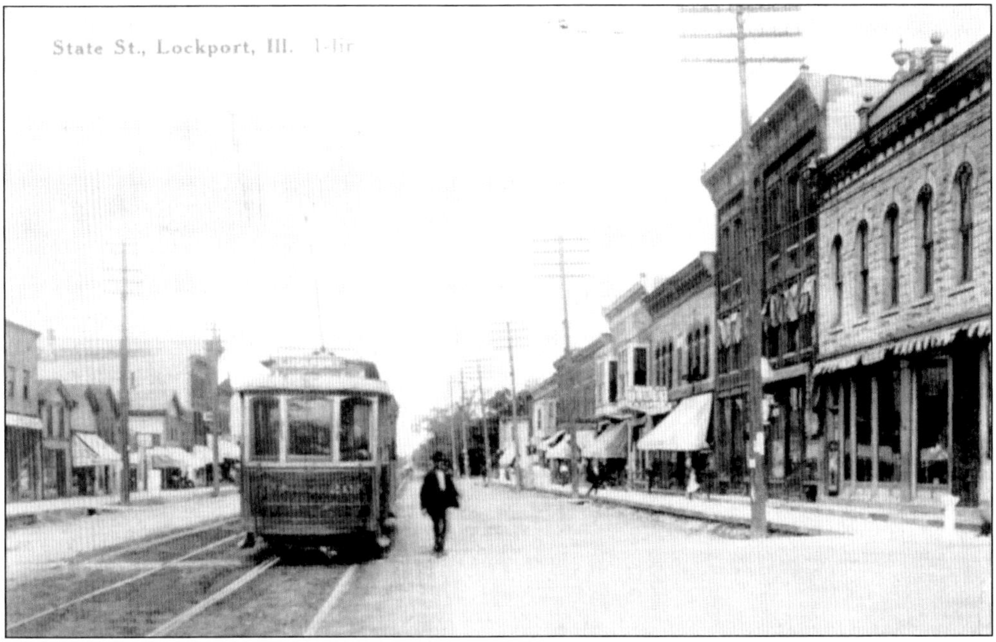

With a few exceptions, State Street today remains intact, and the streetscape is well preserved. State Street is also a major part of a national register historic district, which extends between Seventh and Eleventh Streets and from Canal Street to the public square. The east side of the block, with the exception of the Miller Hardware Store located in the old Norton store building, was burned in the 1895 fire and completely rebuilt within a few months. The postcard photograph above shows a view of State Street looking north from Tenth Street in the early 20th century. The streetcar in the middle of State Street was part of the Chicago and Joliet Railroad system that provided regular service to Lockport from downtown Joliet in the early 1900s. The postcard below shows a similar view of State Street in the 1940s.

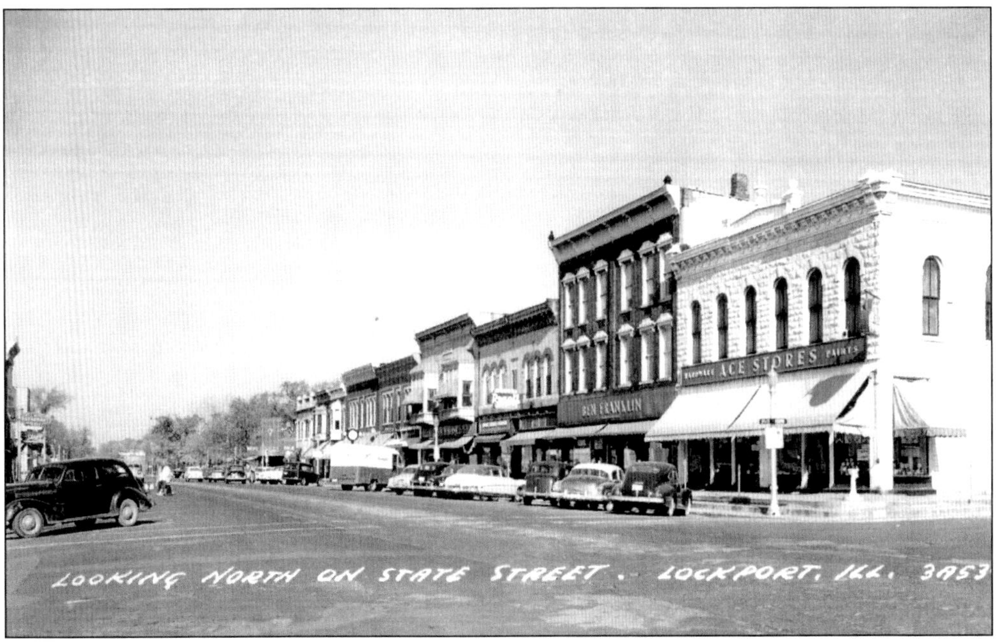

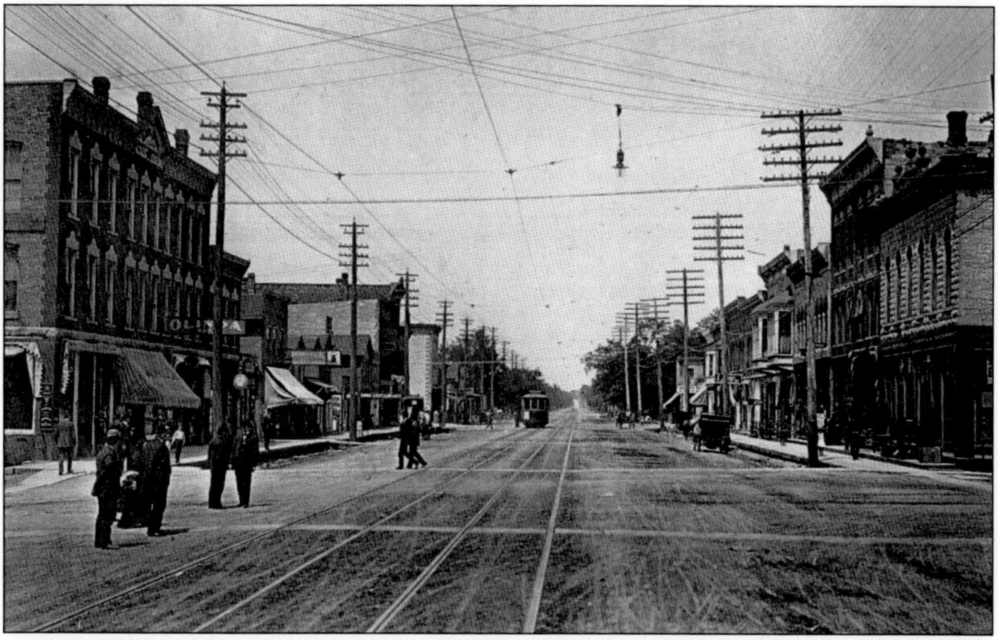

The postcard photograph above shows a view of State Street looking north from Tenth Street in 1907. The building to the right on the northeast corner of Tenth and State Streets is Norton's General Store, the only one on the east side of State Street that was saved from the August 1895 fire. Directly across the street on the northwest corner is the 1880 Ward Block building. It was initially a three-story structure (Olinda Hotel) with a commercial level along State Street that was divided into three separate spaces, a hotel lobby, a bank, and a dry goods store. Adjacent to the building on the north was a two-story brick structure, built in 1890, with similar architectural detailing. Many commercial businesses have used the storefront over the years, including R. J. Russell Billiards and Pool. The photograph below shows the same view around 1940.

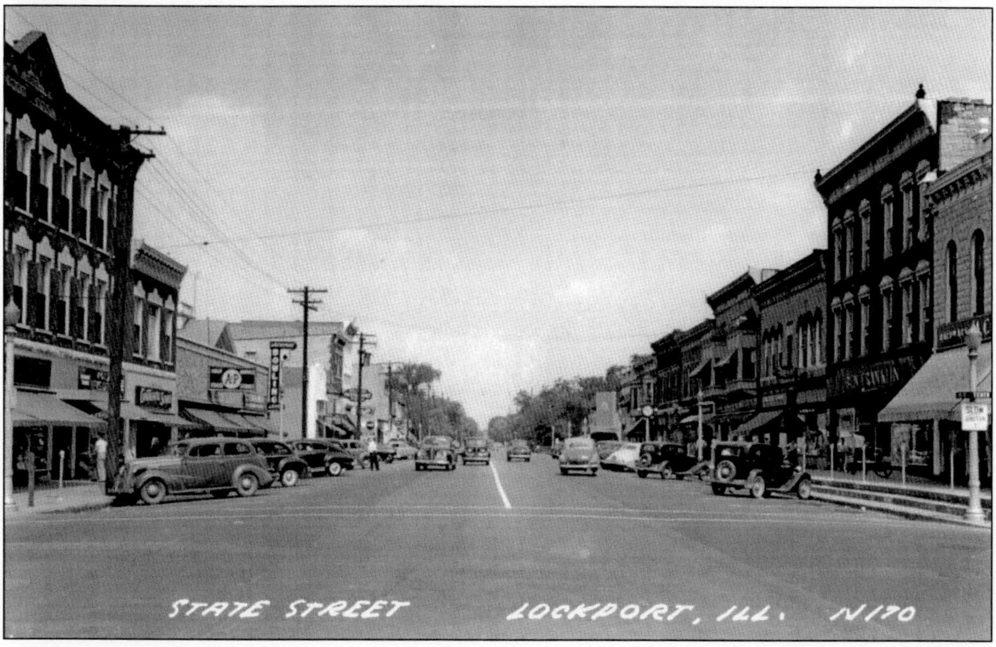

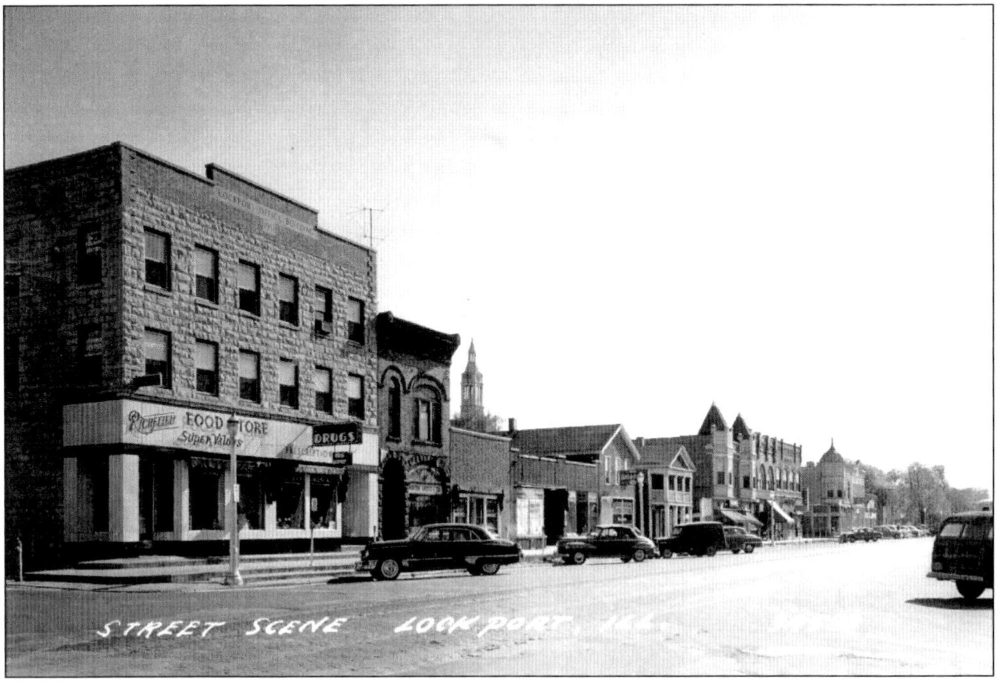

The downtown business district is one of Lockport's greatest commercial, historical, and architectural assets. The photograph above, taken around 1950, is a view of State Street looking south from Tenth Street and is part of the national register historic district. The building to the left on the southeast corner is the old Norton Opera House. The ground floor was a store, and the second story was a cultural center. Made of local limestone, the building was remodeled in 1951, and a third floor was added. Down the block on the southeast corner of Eleventh and State Streets is the Adelmann building, constructed between 1891 and 1894. The photograph below, looking north from the same corner, in the early 20th century, shows the two-story Norton Opera House on the right.

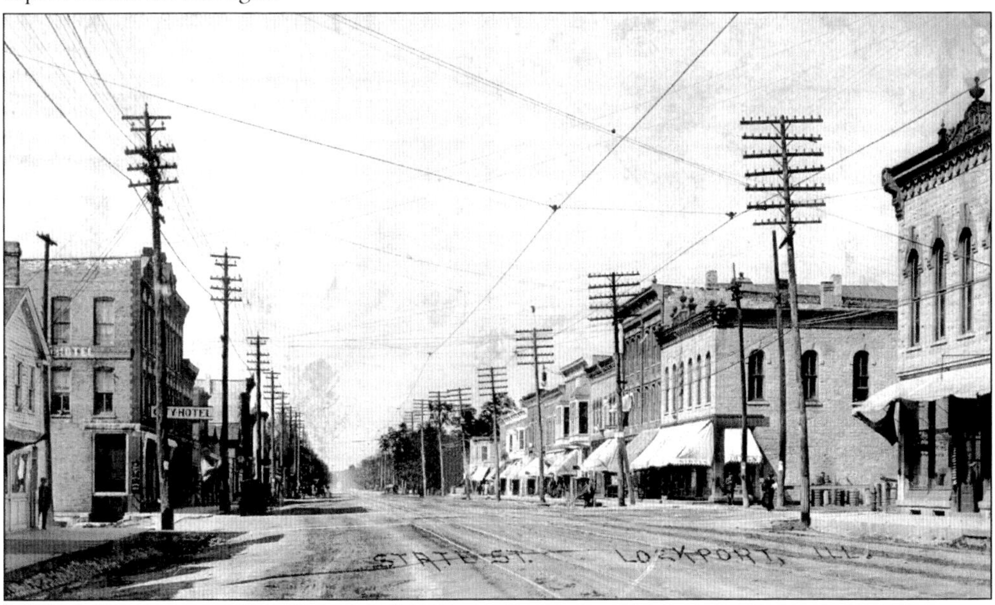

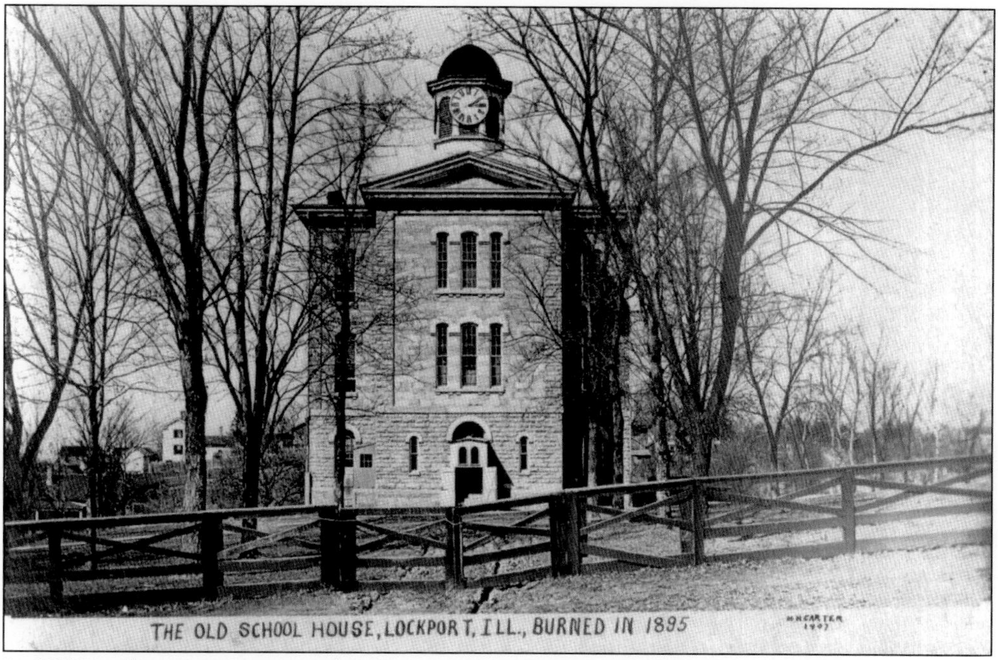

In 1857, a three-story stone schoolhouse, designed by architect Julius Scheibe, was erected on the public square in Lockport. The building burned in the 1895 fire and was replaced the following year with a handsome three-story Romanesque structure. The new school building was constructed from native limestone by architect John Barnes of Joliet. The school, which served the educational needs of the community for nearly 70 years, was considered highly innovative for the 1890s because the architectural plans placed such emphasis on large interior spaces with many big windows to let in light and air. Today the old school building serves as the Lockport Township government offices. The postcard photograph above shows a view of the 1857 school on the public square, and the postcard below shows the 1896 structure.

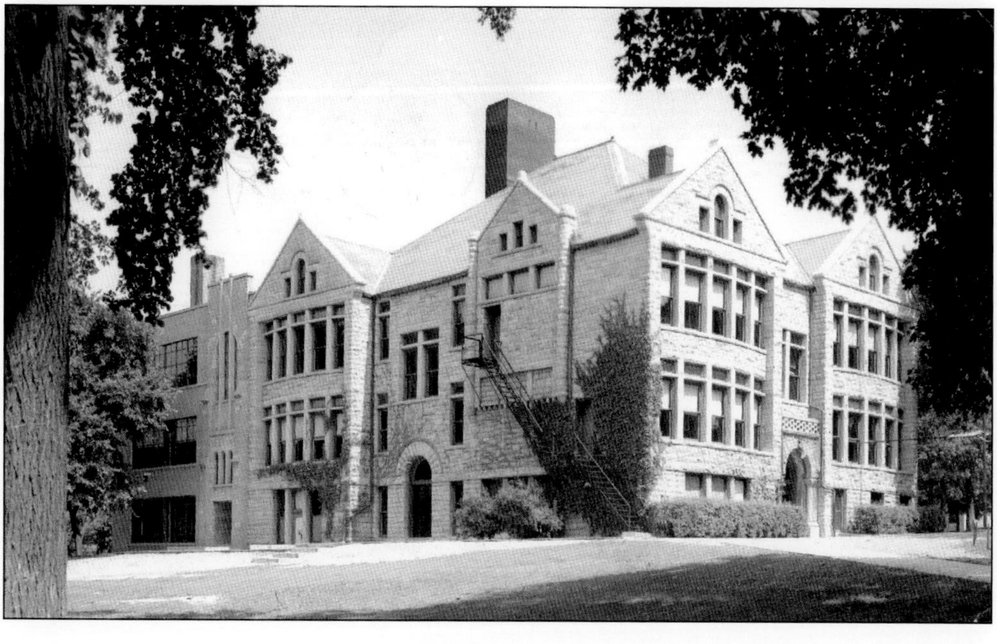

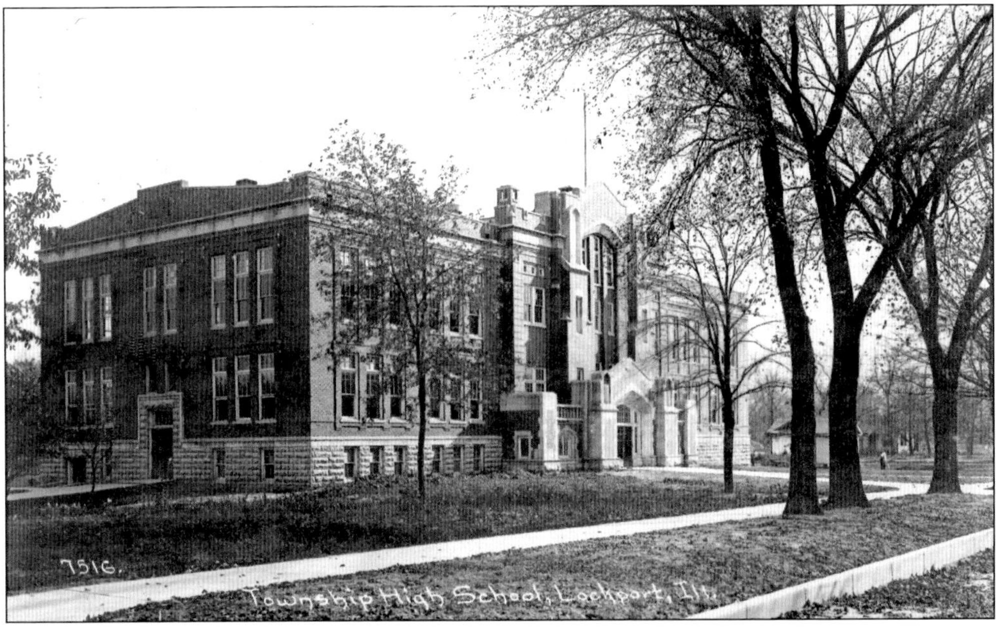

Soon after settlers arrived, school classes began in a log cabin on what is now Division Street. The first village school was built in 1857 and housed students of all ages. The three-story building was constructed from limestone quarried locally and featured a four-sided clock tower. Construction of a new high school on South Jefferson Street was started in 1909, and it opened a year later. This postcard shows the high school campus in 1910.

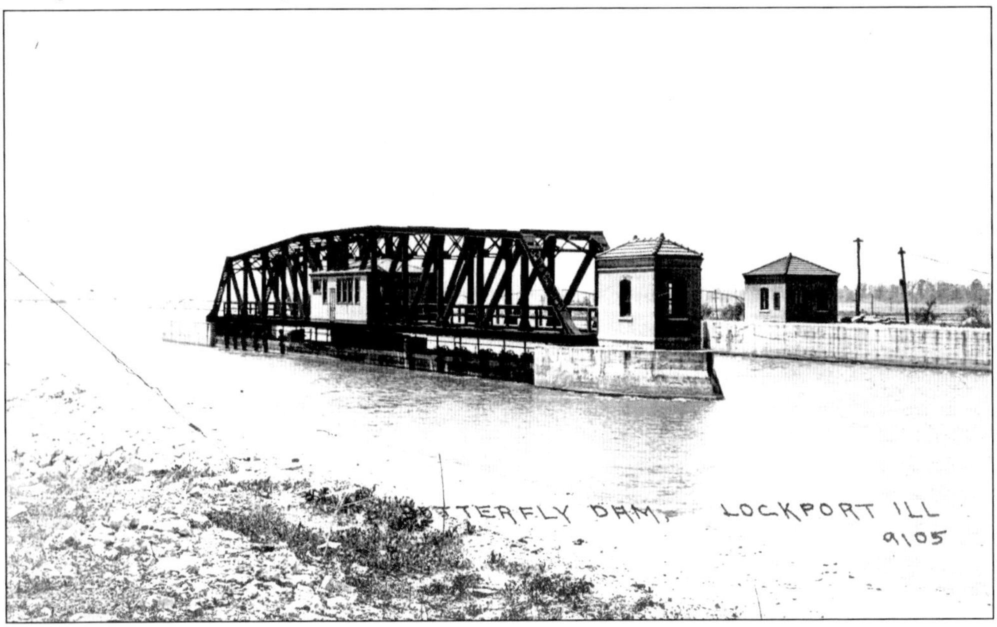

The Butterfly Dam at Lockport marked the end of the 28-mile Chicago Drainage Canal. The control of the water flow from the drainage canal into the Des Plaines River was not at the mouth of the Chicago River but at the terminus of the canal in Lockport. The postcard photograph shows the Butterfly Dam, which could be closed if there was a sudden rush of water from Chicago.

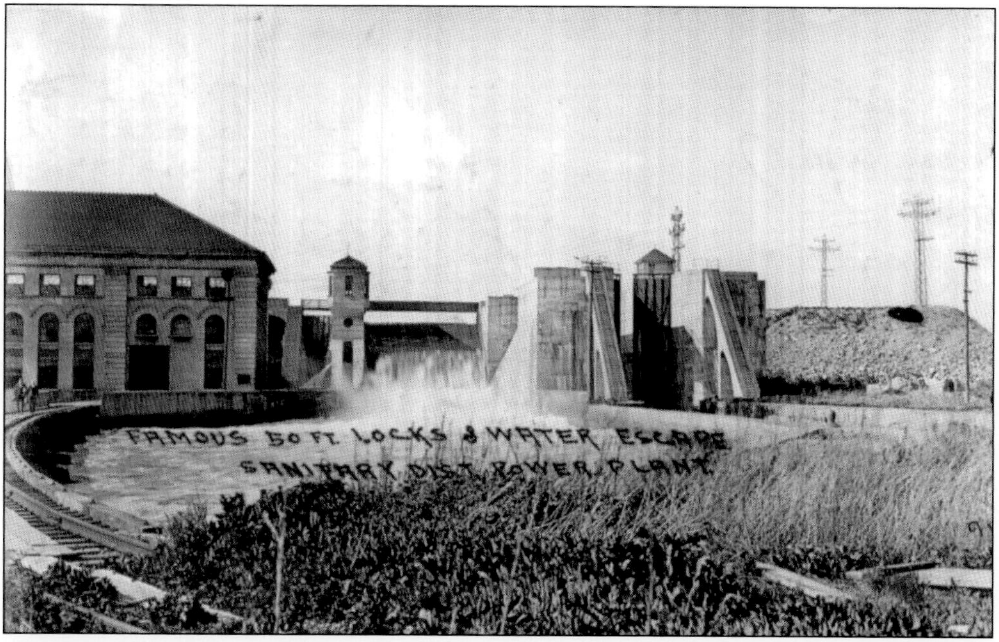

A major engineering achievement of the late 19th century was the construction of the Chicago Sanitary and Ship Canal. This canal was dug from Chicago to Lockport from 1890 to 1900 and extended to Joliet in 1902. It was 25 feet deep and 160 feet wide at its narrowest section. Taking advantage of the 40-foot drop in elevation from Lockport to Joliet, the power plant was able to develop 40,000 horsepower, which supplied Lockport with cheap power and made it a manufacturing rather than a commercial city. The postcard photograph above, looking north, shows the dam and lock, and part of the power plant is visible on the left. The postcard below shows a large power generation dynamo driven by a turbine that generated electricity in the plant.

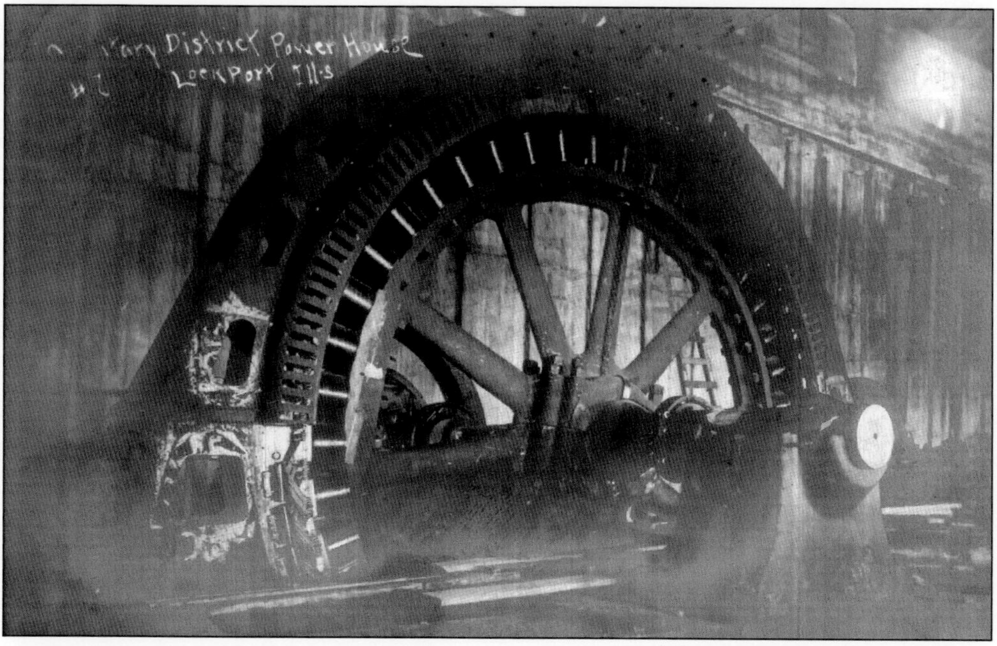

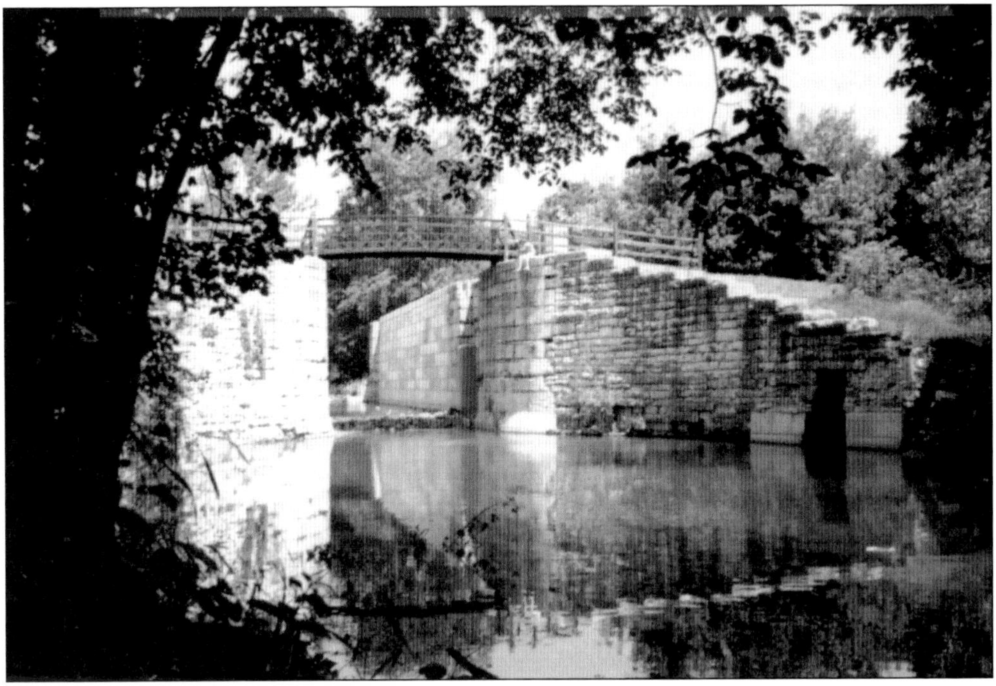

The Illinois and Michigan Canal changed the nation when it opened in 1848 and provided the last link in a chain of waterways that connected the eastern seaboard with the Mississippi River system. The Illinois and Michigan Canal was nearly 100 miles long and ran from Chicago to LaSalle. The 15 locks in the system created a water ladder that allowed boats to climb up or down the change in elevation between the Chicago and Illinois River. The creation of the Illinois Waterway in 1933 helped to create a modern, deep waterway link between the Great Lakes and the Gulf of Mexico. The postcard above shows lock No. 1 on the old Illinois and Michigan Canal in Lockport, and the postcard below shows a modern lock on the Illinois Waterway.

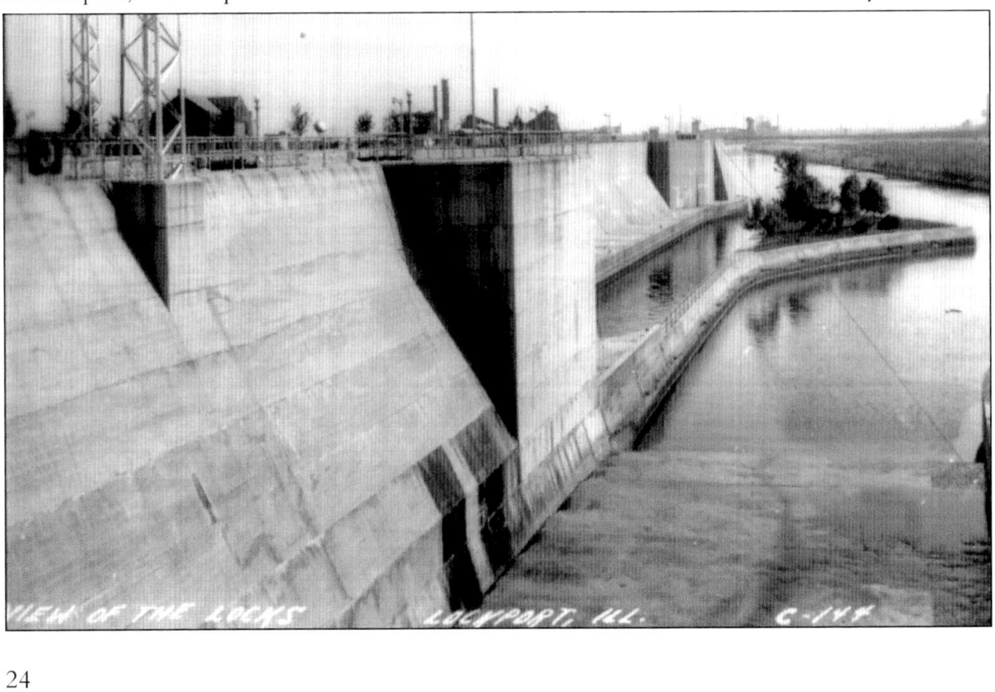

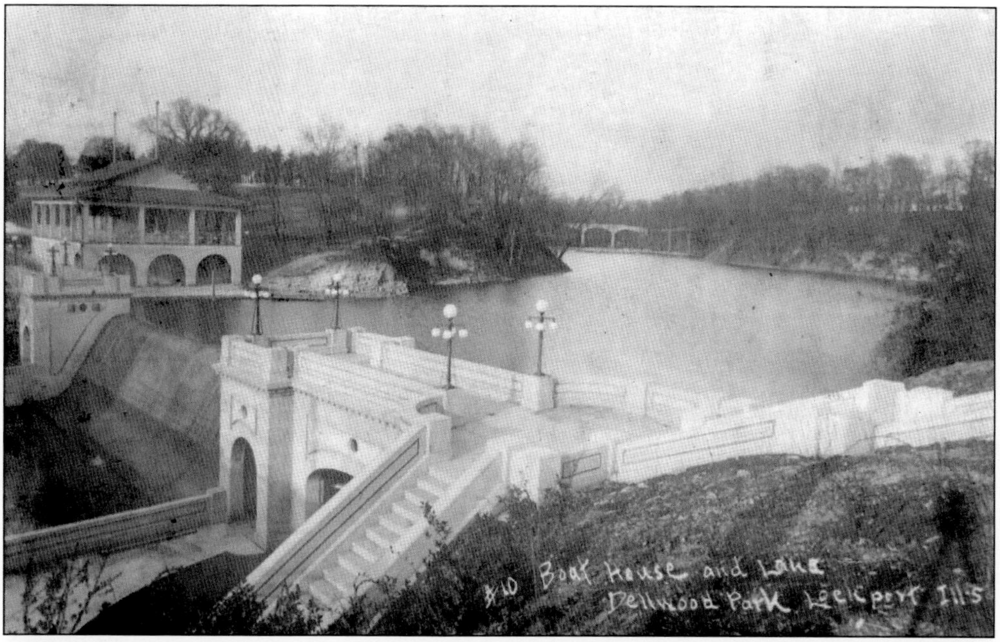

Dellwood Park was built in 1905 and 1906 by the Chicago and Joliet Electric Railway Company to help promote ridership on the line. For over 30 years, Dellwood Park, just north of Joliet in Lockport, was one of the finest amusement, recreational, and picnic areas in the region. Thousands of people came to the park each year by rail from Chicago and other surrounding communities. The postcard photograph above shows a view of the lake and dam at Dellwood Park. During the summer months, visitors used the lake to swim and boat. During the winter months, visitors enjoyed ice-skating on the frozen lake. The postcard below shows a view of the main entrance from the railroad tracks.

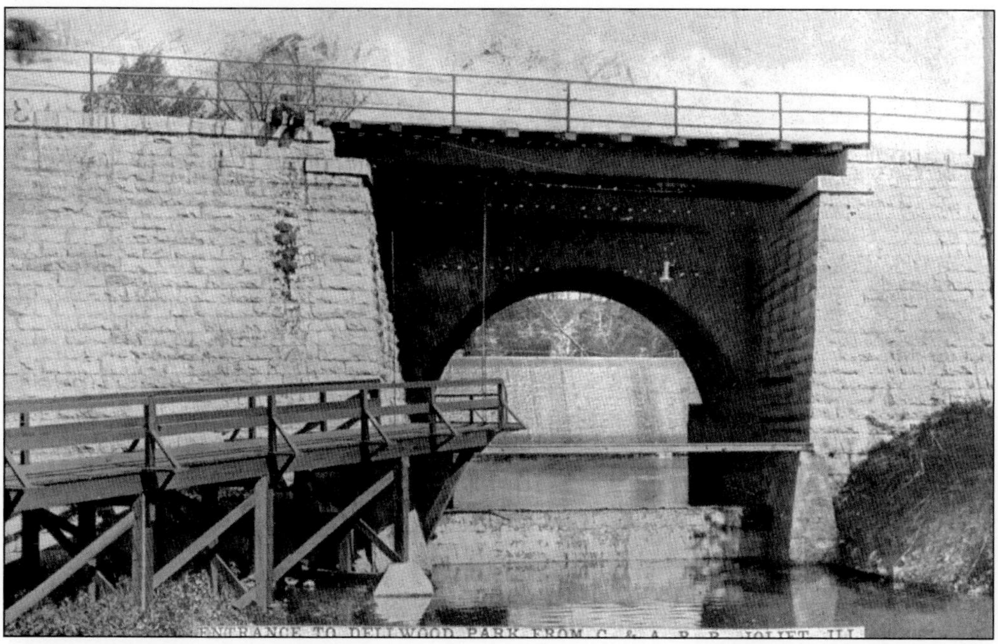

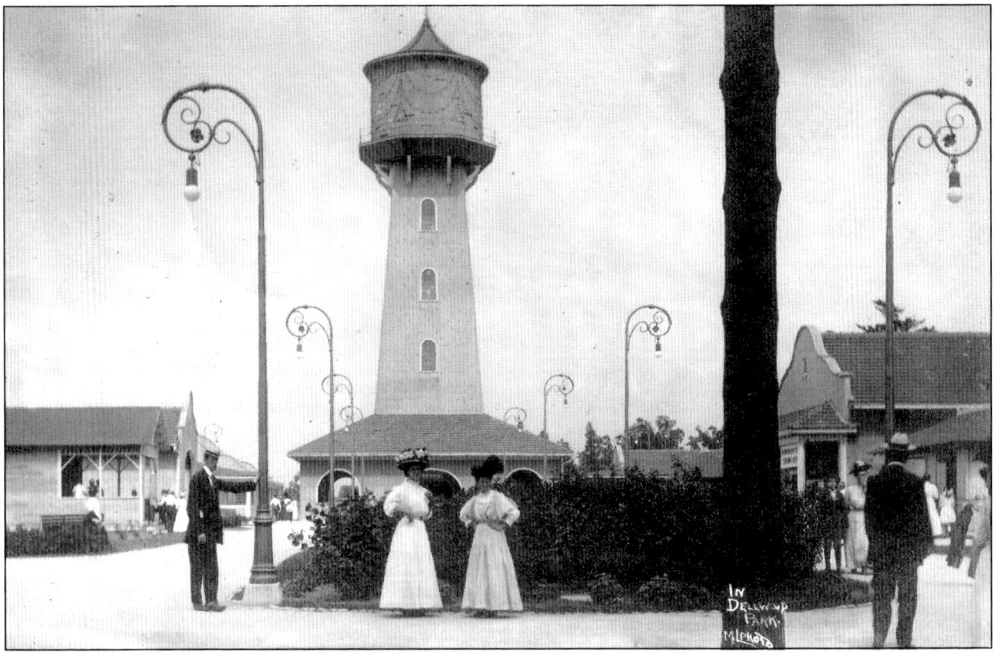

A boathouse, a boating course on the lake, a dance hall, a merry-go-round, an open-air theater, and a restaurant are just a few of the many attractions that made Dellwood Park a popular destination in the early 20th century for thousands of annual visitors from Chicago and the Joliet area. The postcard photograph above shows the water tower at the park. The water tower was illuminated at night, which created a perfect atmosphere for those who enjoyed a quiet stroll in the evening. The confectionery stand at the base of the tower was a popular place to get a drink or something to eat. The postcard below shows a view of the dance pavilion.

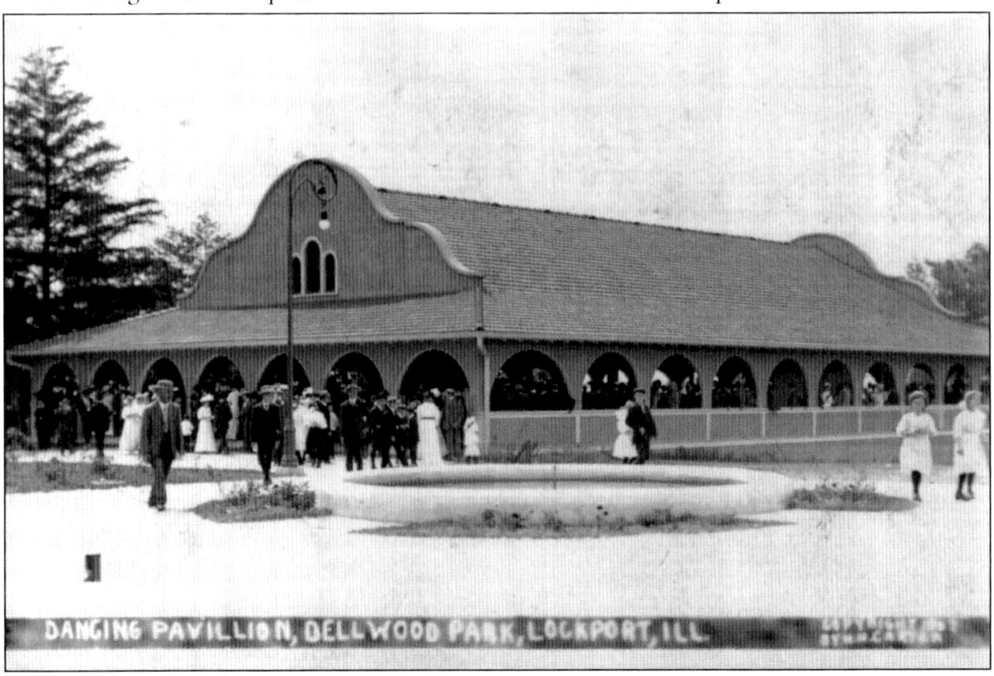

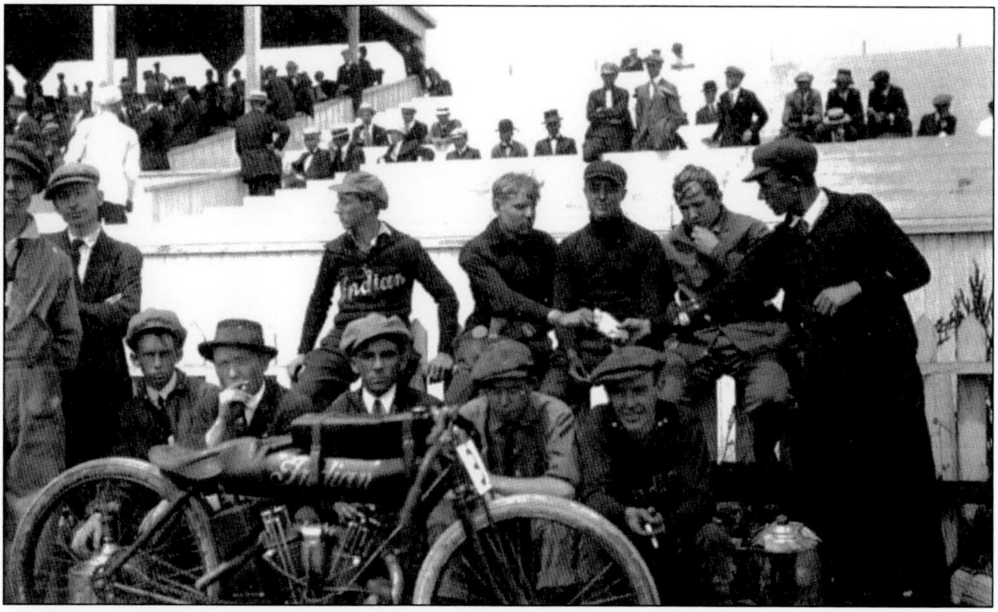

Costing nearly $300,000 to build, Dellwood Park officially opened on July 4, 1905, and quickly became one of the most outstanding and beautiful park sites in the state. During the peak years, as many as 15,000 persons visited the park on weekends during company picnics. A grandstand was built at a cost of $10,000, and as many as 5,000 spectators sat in the stands to watch many events, including baseball games and sulky races. The picture postcard above shows spectators in the grandstands watching a motorbike race. Notice the *c.* 1907 early model Indian motorcycle with its V-twin engine, which broke many records in motorcycle racing. The postcard below shows the Dellwood Park Band, which performed on many occasions during the summer months at the park's small bandstand.

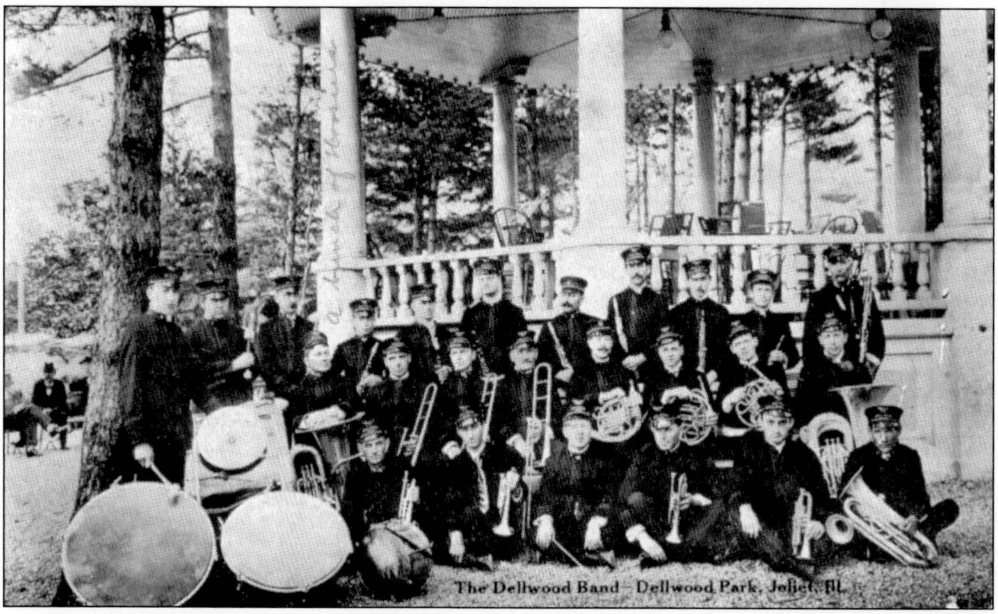

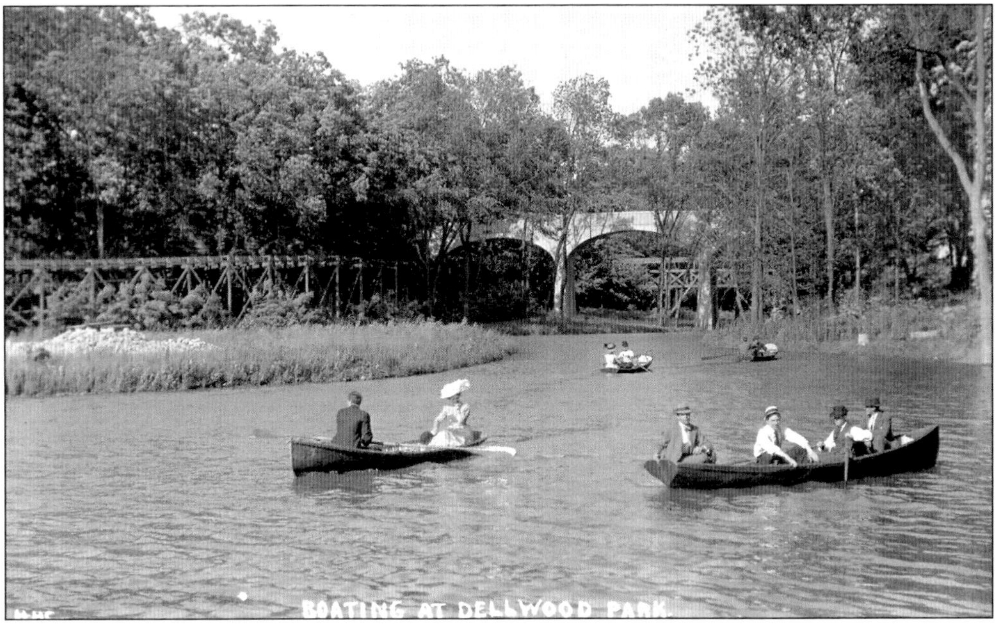

The natural beauty of Dellwood Park helped to make it a popular destination for summer outings and quiet picnics. One popular, natural attraction at the park was the picturesque lagoon, which drew its water supply from an artesian well 1,750 feet below the surface. The postcard above shows visitors boating on the lake in rented boats.

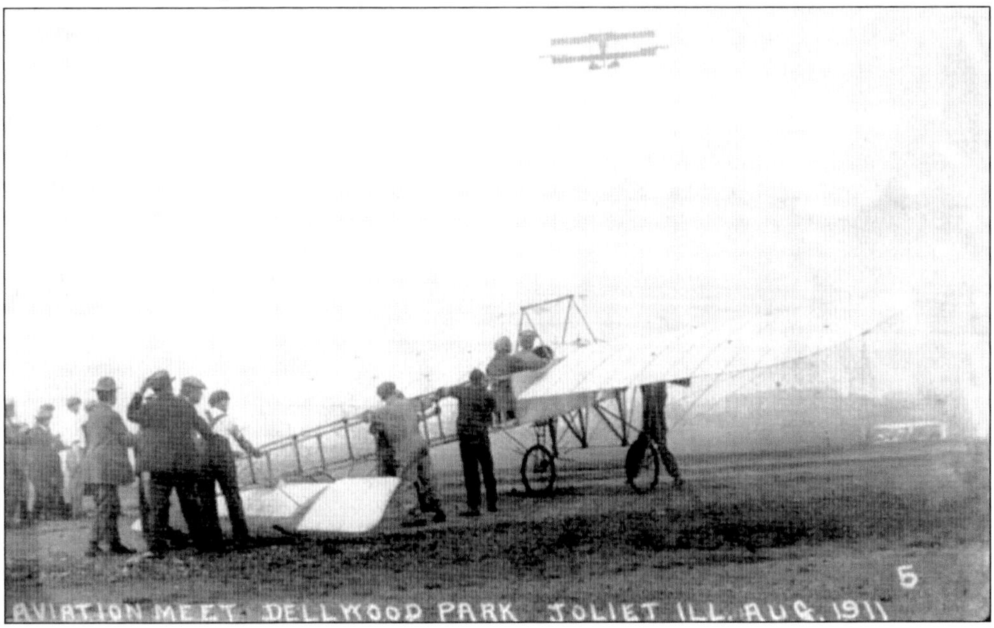

Joliet's Great Aviation Meet was held in Dellwood Park on August 25–27, 1911. Spectators who paid the 25¢ general admission fee were able to see Rene "Fool Flyer" Simon flying his Moisant monoplane. Pilot John Frisbie also entertained an estimated 10,000 spectators with his powerful Curtiss biplane. This picture postcard shows the biplane in the air and the monoplane on the ground. A week after the Joliet Aviation Meet, the daring Frisbie was killed performing in an air show in Norton, Kansas.

Three

Plainfield

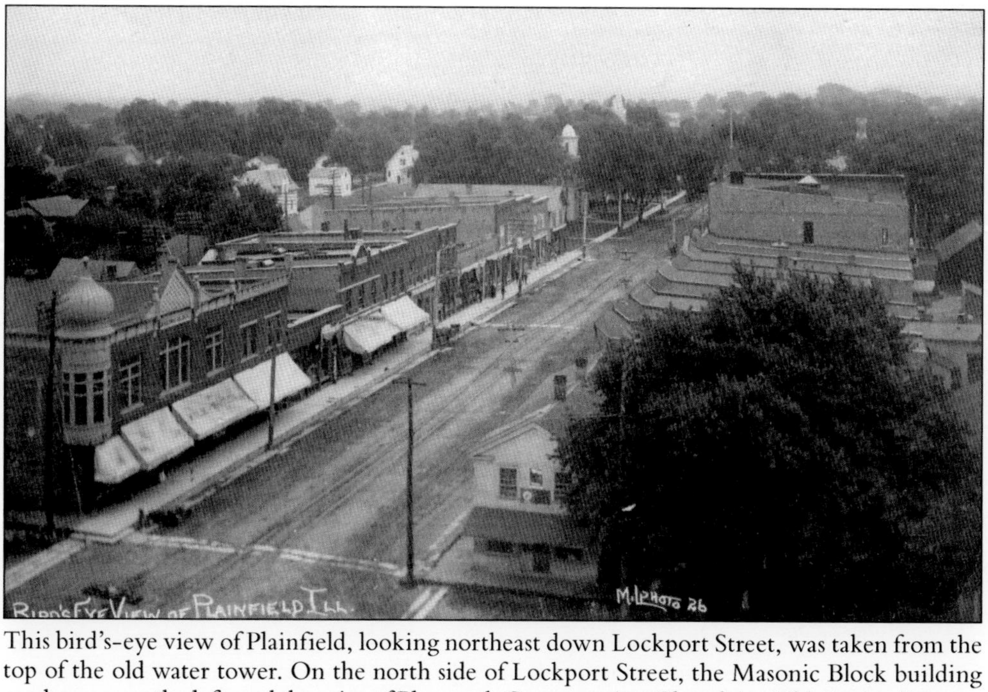

This bird's-eye view of Plainfield, looking northeast down Lockport Street, was taken from the top of the old water tower. On the north side of Lockport Street, the Masonic Block building can be seen on the left, and the spire of Plymouth Congregation Church is visible in the distance. On the south side of the block, the old Central Hotel can be seen on the southeast corner of Lockport and Des Plaines Streets.

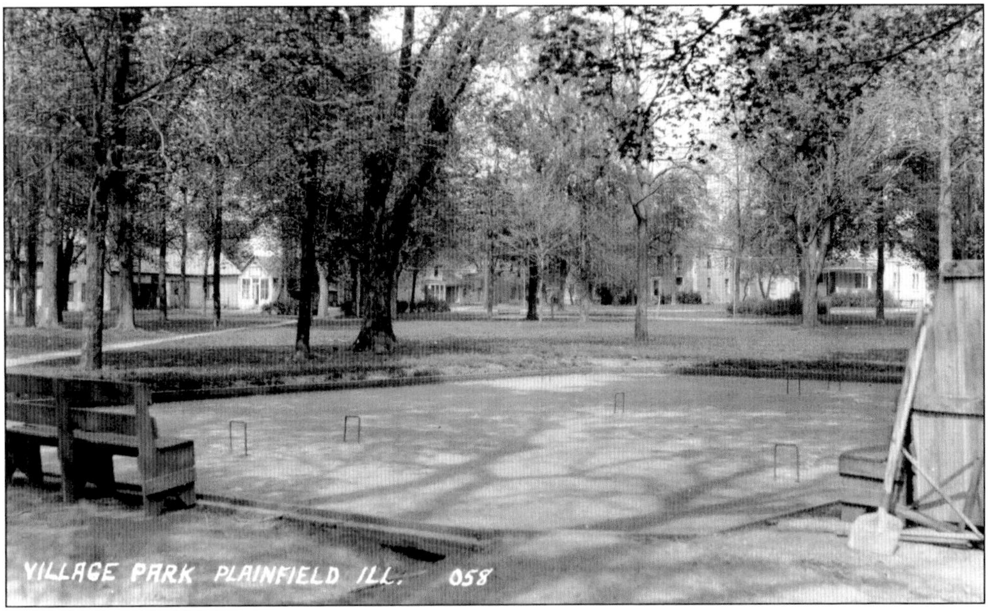

Long before Electric Park became the gathering place for summertime enjoyment, Village Green Park was a beautiful place to visit and relax. Located south of Lockport Street and bordered by Chicago, Des Plaines, Ottawa, and Fox River Streets, Village Green Park was part of the original 1834 plat of the village by Chester Ingersoll. This picture postcard shows a view of the croquet courts installed in the park in the early 1930s.

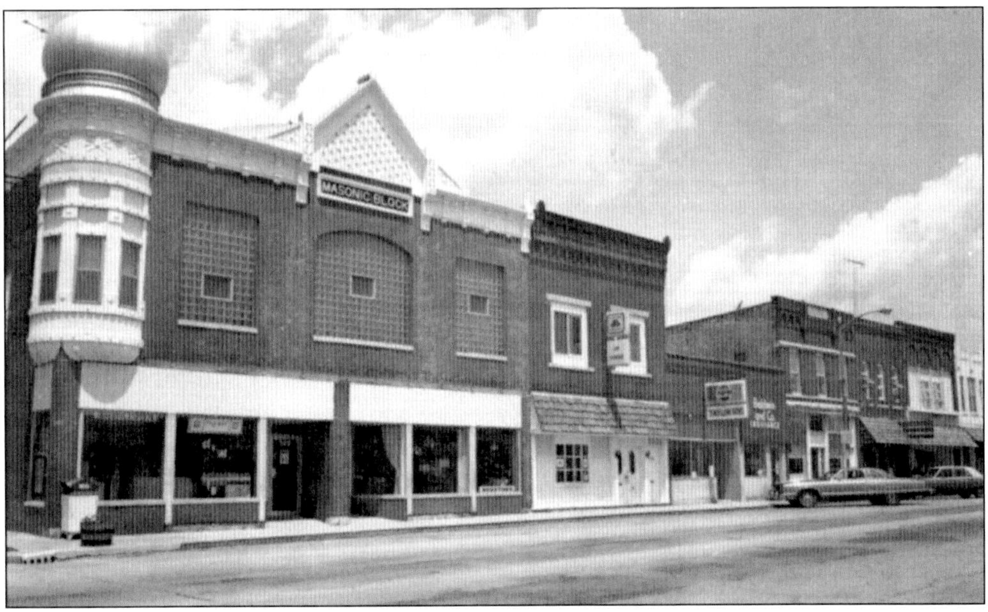

The Masonic fraternal lodge in Plainfield was chartered in October 1867. After the December 29, 1891, fire left the Masons without a meeting place, plans were made to construct a new building, and two lots were purchased on the northeast corner of Lockport and Des Plaines Streets. The new building, with its unique onion-shaped corner dome, was constructed in 1892 and officially dedicated in February 1896 and has been an important part of downtown Plainfield for over 100 years.

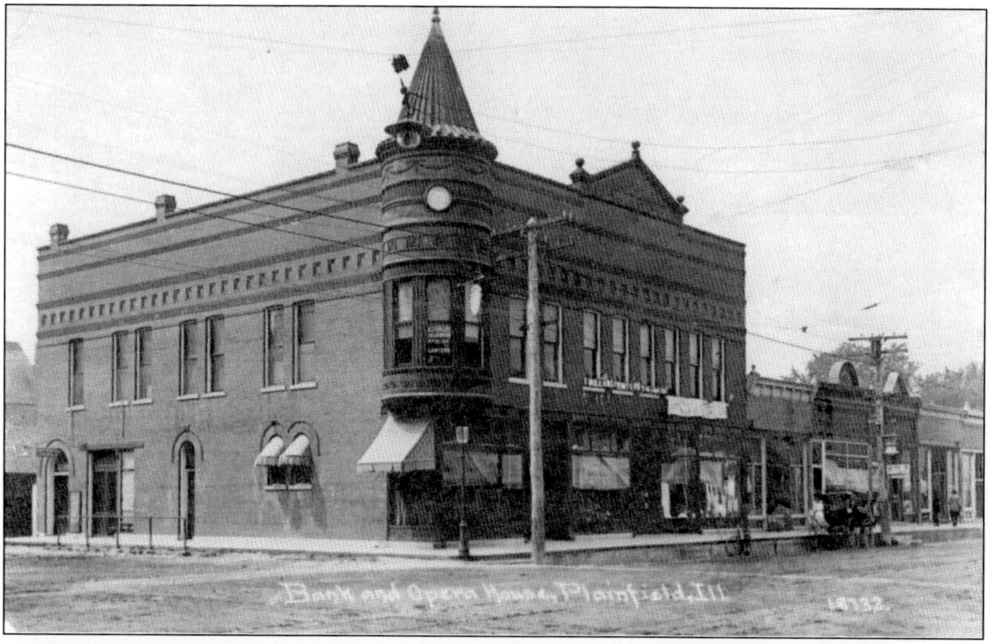

In 1889, the first opera house was built on the southwest corner of Lockport and Illinois Streets. The first floor housed a bank and a hardware store. The second floor had a theater and stage. In February 1898, a fire broke out on the south side of the block and destroyed a number of buildings, including the post office and opera house. Shortly after, a new redbrick opera house building was constructed on the old foundation. The picture postcard above shows the new building with a corner tower and clock mounted over the alcove windows. The *c.* 1930 postcard below shows a view of Lockport Street looking west and the opera house, without its corner cone-shaped tower, on the left.

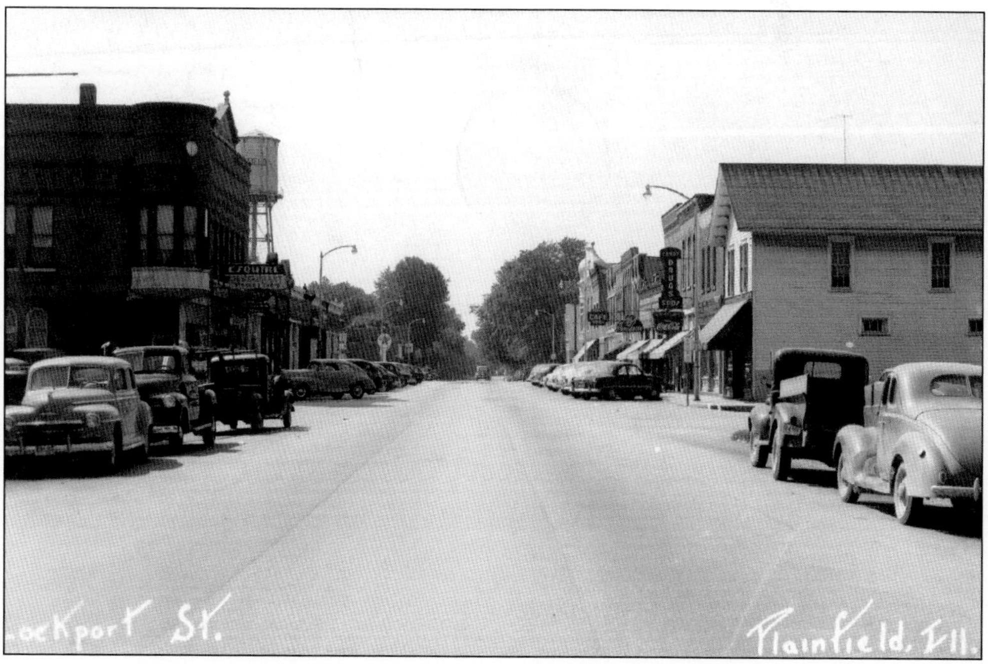

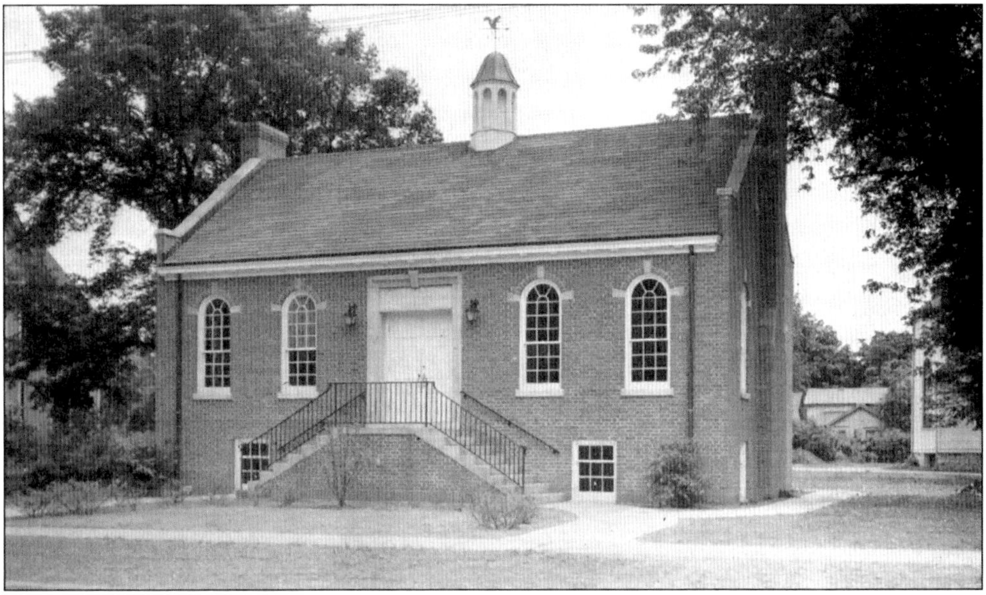

In 1925, Ebanezer and Celeste Nimmons left a $25,000 estate gift for the establishment of a public library. In April 1926, the first library, located in a small frame building on the south side of Lockport Street, opened its doors. In 1940, the library board decided to build a larger facility and purchased a lot from the Plainfield Congregational Church. On June 1, 1941, the new library was opened to the public, and the McClester and Nimmons names were carved in stone above the front entrance.

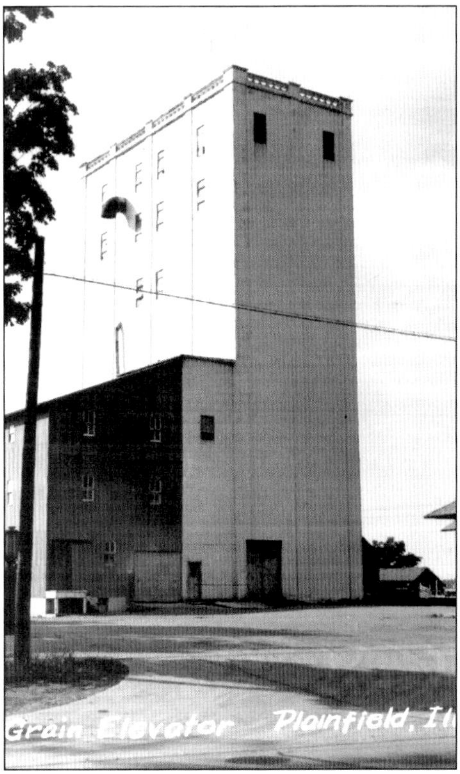

Incorporated in March 1911, the Plainfield Grain Company was an important business for the community. In the early years, the company purchased a number of area grain businesses and in 1921 built a large concrete grain elevator, nearly 100 feet tall. At the time of its construction, the elevator was one of the most modern grain elevators built.

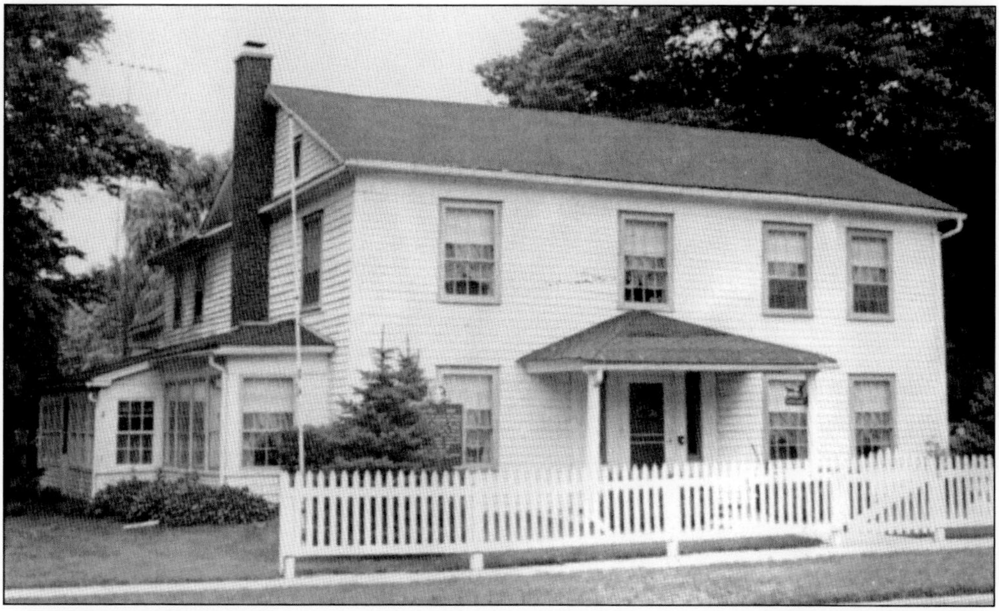

In 1834 and 1835, the southern, eastern, and northern portions of Plainfield were platted, and the new town was given its name. It was during this time that an inn and tavern was constructed on Main Street. Today it is the oldest documented building in town. Commonly called the Plainfield House, the building is otherwise known as the Halfway House and was added to the National Register of Historic Places in 1980.

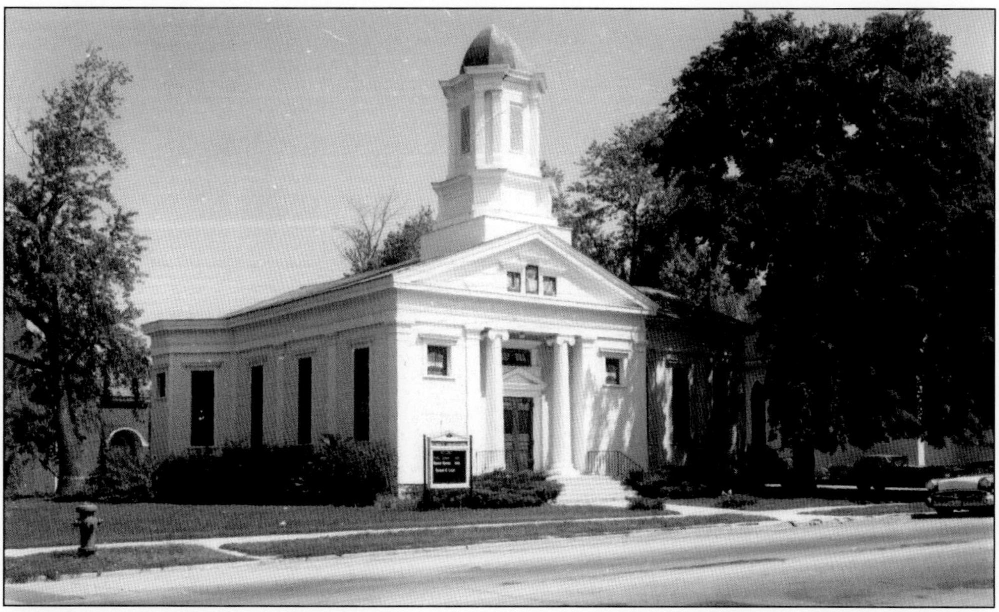

Plymouth Congregational Church can trace its beginnings to September 1834 when it was known as the Plainfield Congregational Church. Located on the northeast corner of Lockport and Illinois Streets, the church was constructed as a Greek Revival frame building in 1850 and dedicated in June 1851. The building was remodeled in the early 1900s, and memorial stained-glass windows were installed in the 1930s.

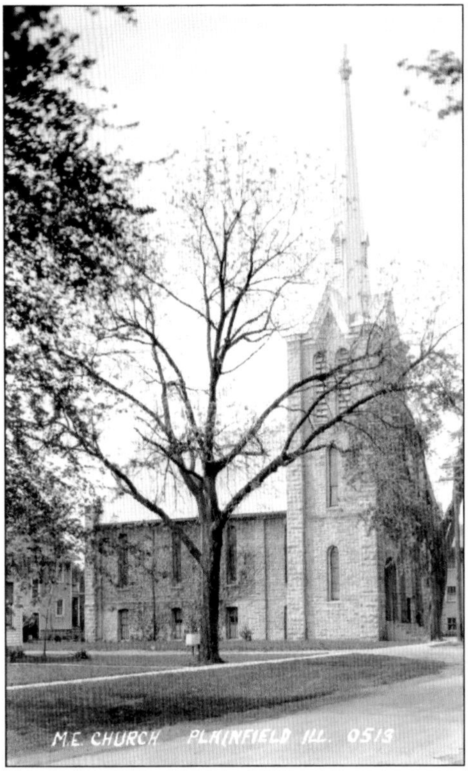

In 1829, Rev. Jesse Walker and 10 other settlers met together in Walker's Grove and formed the first Methodist church in the area. The first meetings were held in a log cabin near the intersection of Joliet Road and Route 59. In 1866, a stone church was constructed on the northwest corner of Illinois and Chicago Streets. Built using local quarried limestone, the construction cost was nearly $20,000. This postcard shows a view of the church looking northwest from Illinois Street.

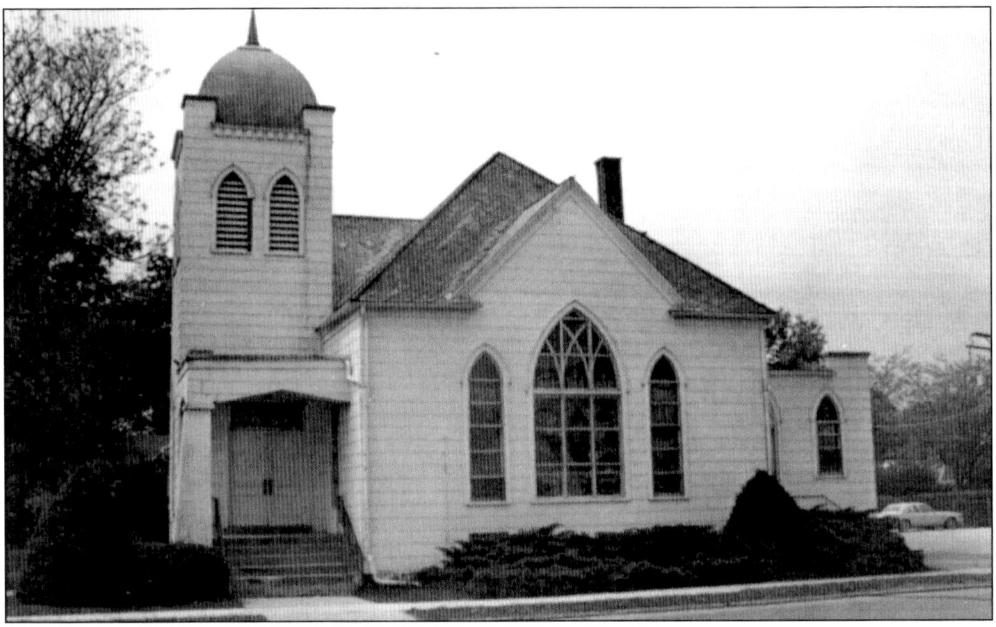

In August 1834, Rev. J. E. Ambrose arrived in Plainfield and helped arrange for the formation of the First Baptist Church. The first meetinghouse was occupied until 1857, when a new and larger house was built on the same site. In December 1914, a fire destroyed the old church. A new church was constructed and dedicated in November 1915. On September 4, 2004, the historic landmark church, located on the corner of Route 59 and Lockport Street, was razed.

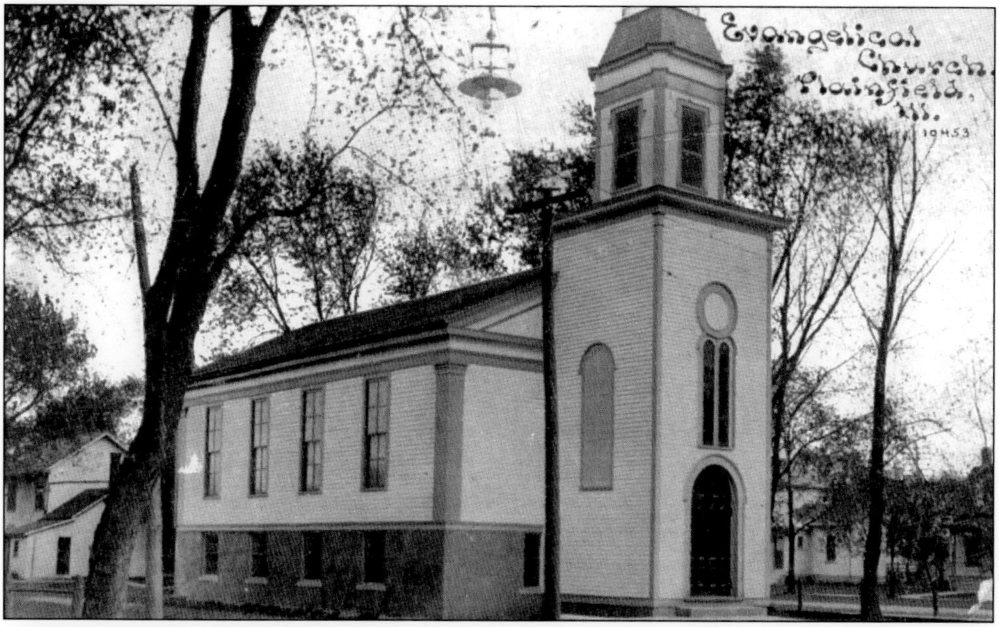

In 1847, Daniel Shreffler and his family migrated to the area from Pennsylvania. About the same time, Rev. George Mottinger arrived from Ohio, and together both men were responsible for the beginning of the Evangelical class. The Rose of Sharon Church was constructed in 1855 on the southeast corner of Dillman and Lockport Streets. After the Civil War, the front facade of the Greek Revival church was modified with the addition of the present bell tower.

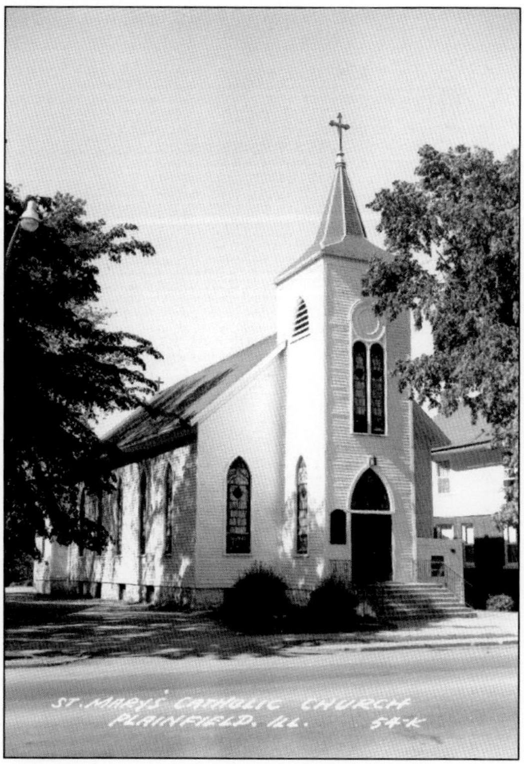

Located on the north side of Lockport Street between Illinois and Division Streets, the old Universalist church was built in 1868. In August 1907, Fr. William McNamee, pastor of St. Mary's Church in Joliet, purchased the old frame church. This postcard shows a view looking north from Lockport Street of the old Universalist (St. Mary's) Church. Today Baci Italian Ristorante operates in the old parish building.

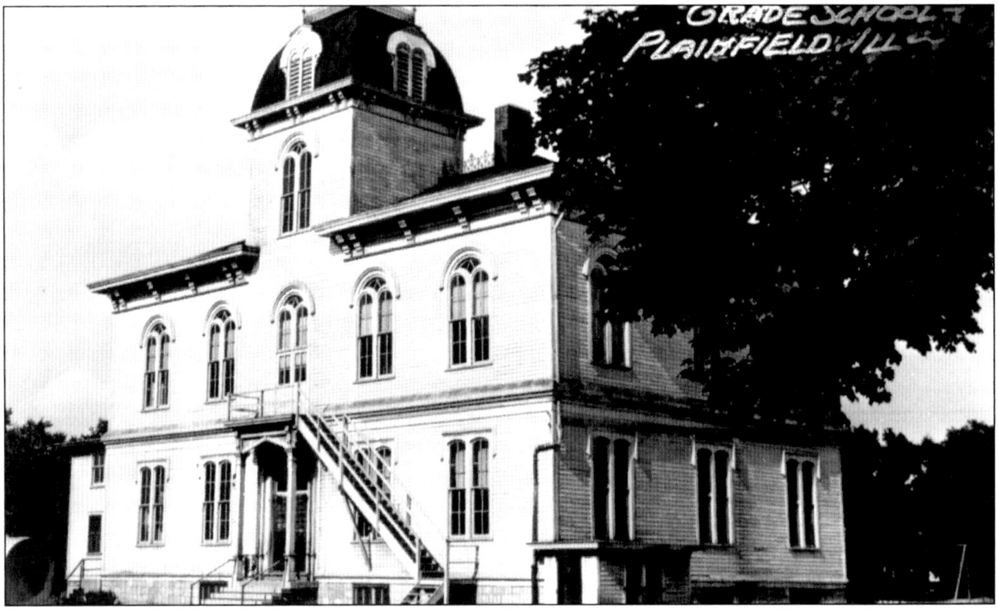

In 1861, a three-story wood-frame building was erected on the corner of Division and Lockport Streets to be used for a high school. In 1872, the building became the Plainfield Academy, and within a year, a mysterious fire broke out and the school burned to the ground. In 1882, a new school building was completed on the old stone foundation of the college and looked similar in design. Over the years, it was known as the White School and housed elementary and secondary schoolchildren. As the population in the village increased, new buildings were erected on the same corner, including the 1915 redbrick Plainfield High School and the 1951 elementary school. The postcard above shows the old White School building, and the postcard below shows a view of the 1951 elementary school. After nearly 80 years of service, the White School was razed in 1960.

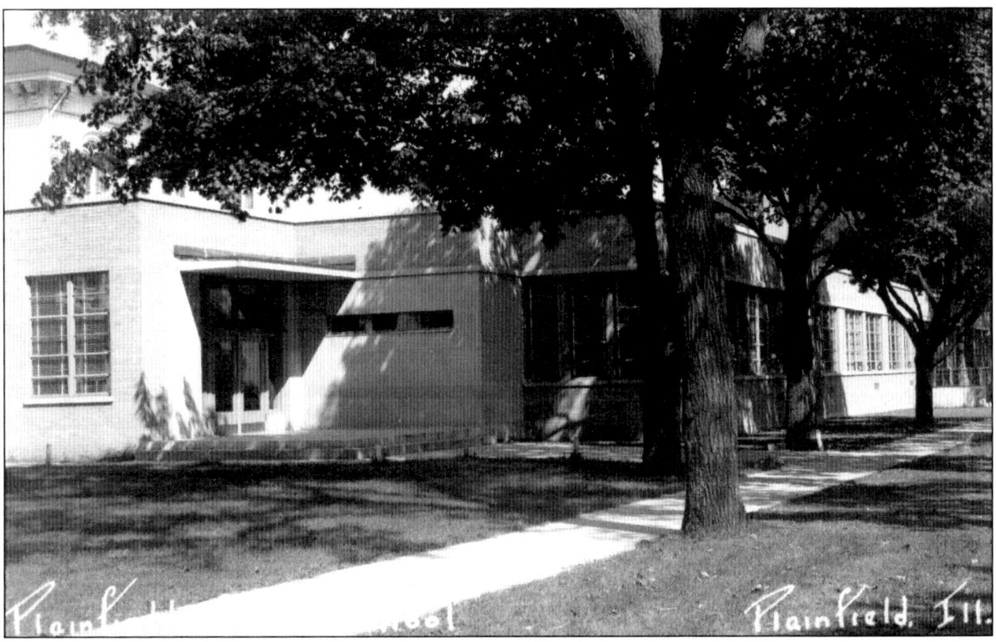

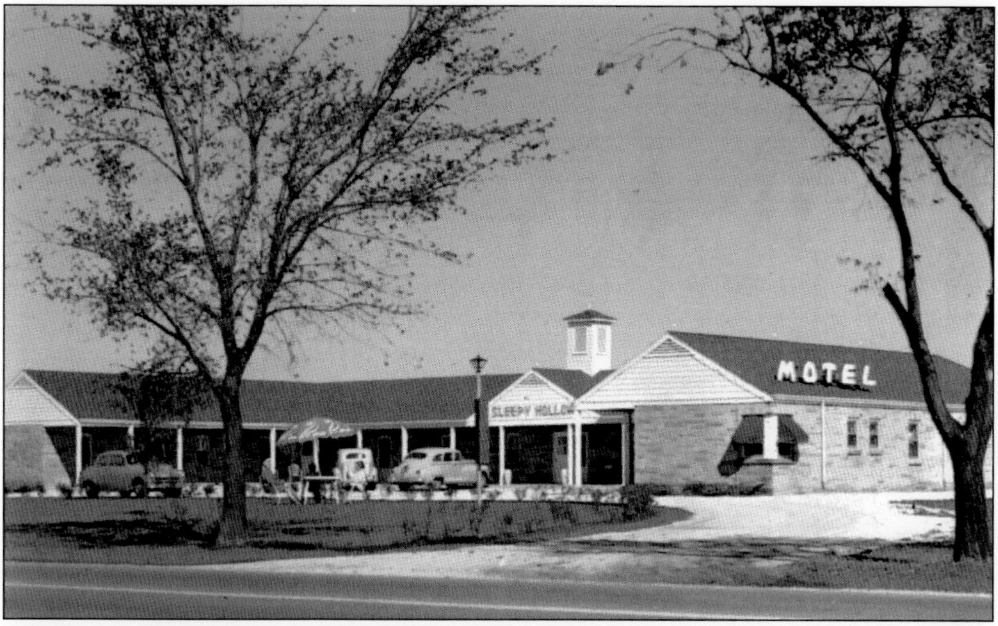

Stretching nearly 3,400 miles from New York to California, for the first time, the Lincoln Highway helped to connect small-town America with larger urban areas via a hard-service road. As the American public took to the road, motor courts, inns, and highway motels appeared and catered to the traveling public. In 1921, Plainfield built its portion of the highway through its main street (Lockport Street) and collected neighboring towns on what is now Route 30. Southeast of Plainfield, two motels catered to the traveling public as they traversed the transcontinental highway. One was the Sleepy Hollow Motel, located for years near today's Louis Joliet Mall. The other was the Lakeview Motel across from Lake Renwick. The latter motel still operates today.

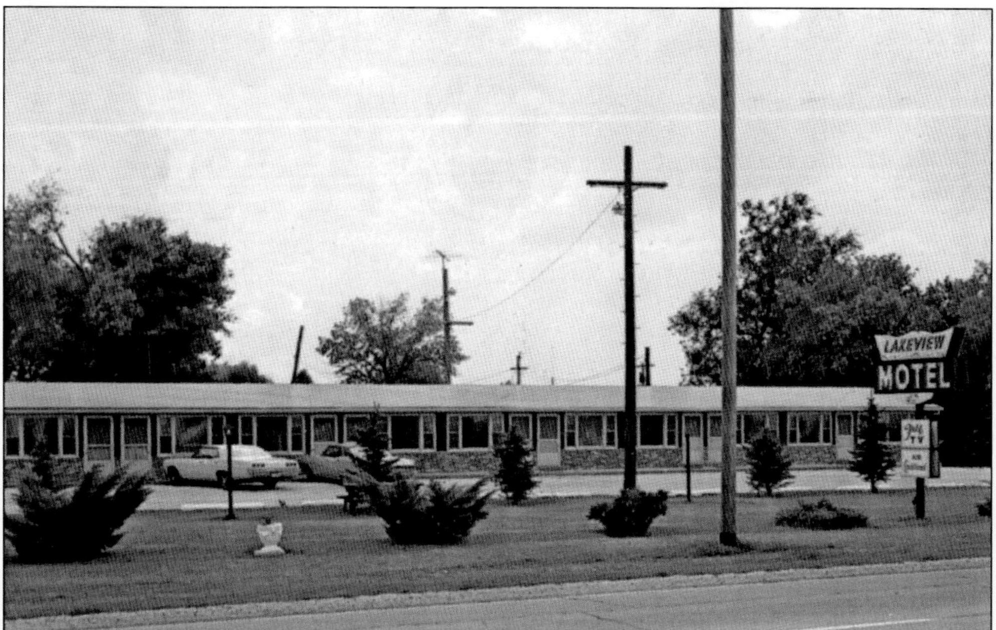

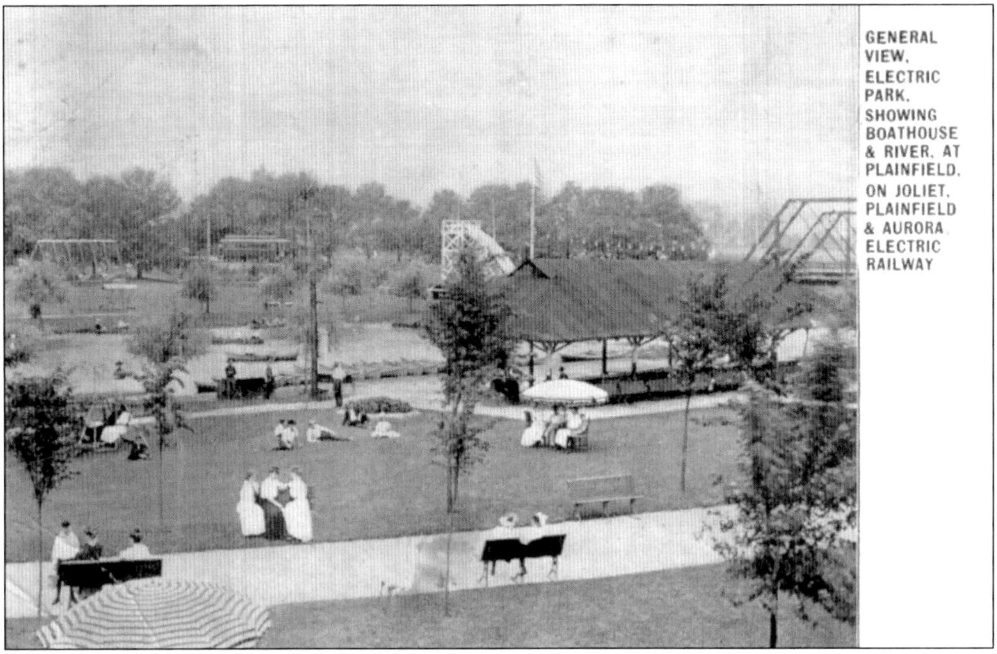

In 1904, the Aurora, Plainfield, and Joliet Railway established a streetcar line with a popular 20-acre camping resort in Plainfield. Known as Electric Park, the attraction included camping cabins, a large auditorium, a dance pavilion, a restaurant, a bowling alley, a swimming pool, and boating along the banks of the DuPage River. A baseball diamond with an enclosed grandstand and horse-driving track were also included. The park closed in 1923 when the streetcars were replaced by buses. The postcard photograph above shows an overview of the park, including the boathouse, river, and toboggan slide. The postcard below shows the main entrance of the park at the corner of James and Lockport Streets.

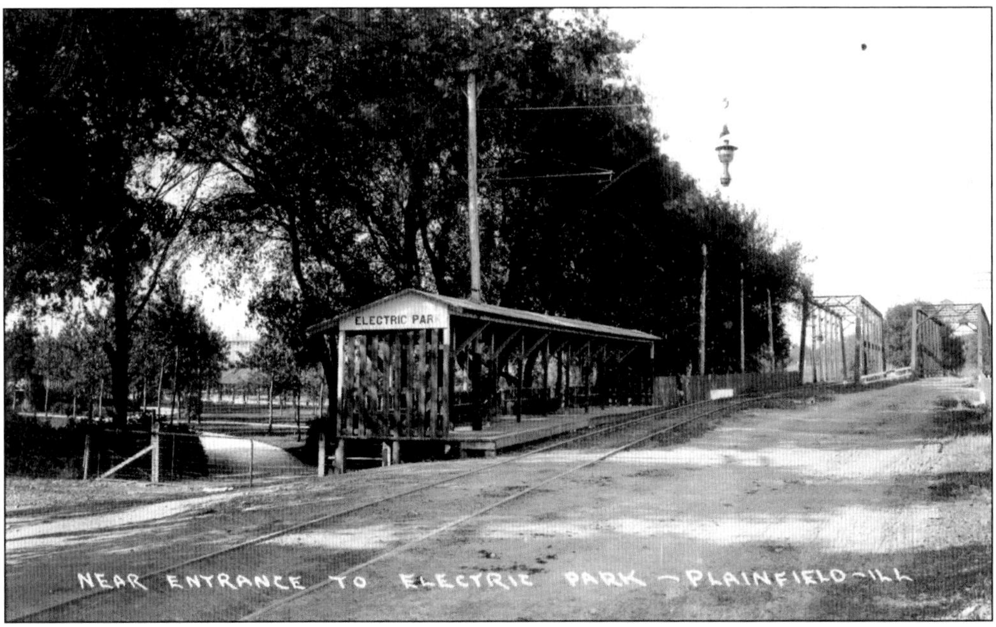

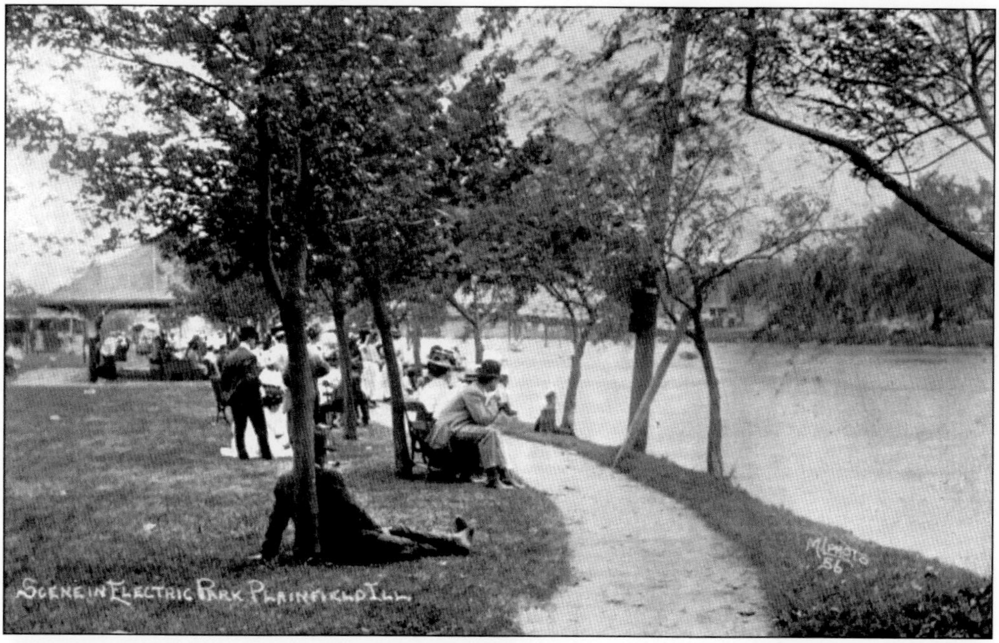

When constructed in 1904, Electric Park was intended to provide the trolley line excursionist an ideal summer resort spot. Built along the banks of the DuPage River, the attractions at the park drew thousands every summer to enjoy camping, paddleboat rides, dancing, baseball, bowling, and balloon rides. This postcard photograph shows park visitors relaxing along the banks of the DuPage River.

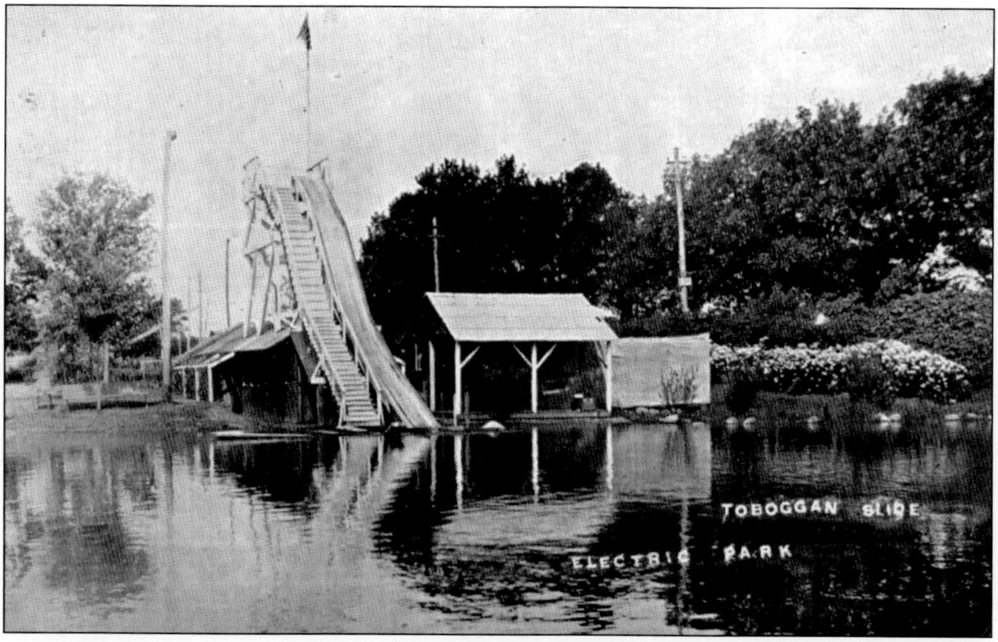

For many visitors at Electric Park, swimming in the DuPage River was a thrilling adventure. As the park straddled both sides of the river, it was a popular attraction on a hot summer day. Located on the west side of the DuPage River, the ever-popular toboggan slide had a bathhouse at the base and 150 steps to the top, and many young visitors enjoyed a steep slide into the water.

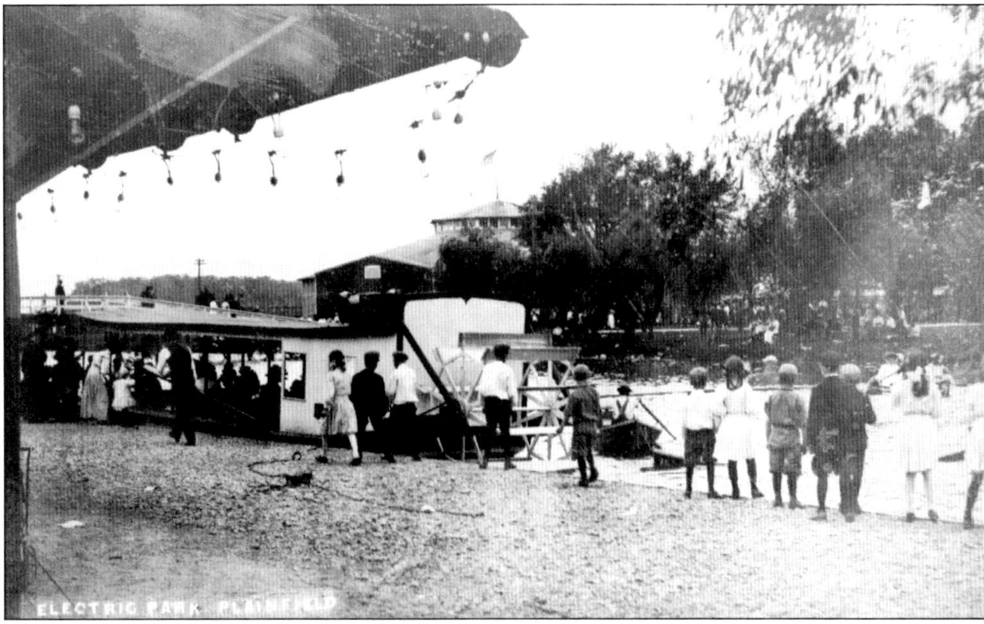

Another popular water activity at Electric Park was boating on the DuPage River. Not only could adventurous patrons rent rowboats for a nominal fee, but also large groups could climb aboard the *Mary Lee* for a paddle wheel boat pleasure ride up and down the river. This picture postcard shows the east bank of the DuPage River with the boat pavilion to the left and patrons preparing to depart on the *Mary Lee*.

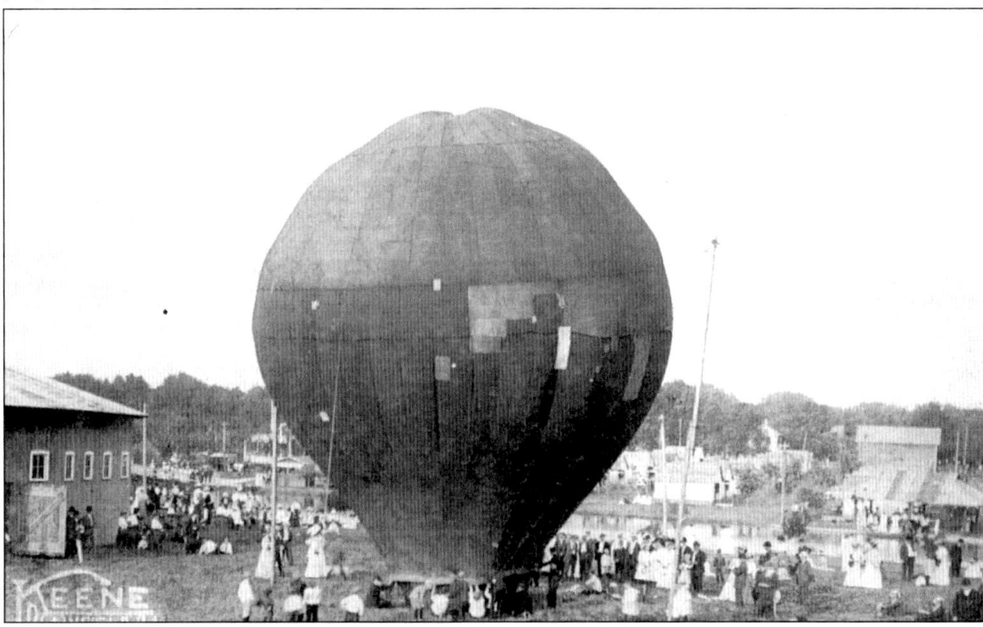

Prof. Harry Darnell of Chicago was performing his trapeze act on a hot-air balloon at Electric Park on July 26, 1911, when he fell 700 feet to his death. Nearly 2,000 persons watched as he attempted his "great swing" from the trapeze bar and lost his grip before falling into the DuPage River. Efforts to revive him were unsuccessful, and he was buried in Plainfield Cemetery. This postcard photograph shows one of the balloons used by Darnell at Electric Park.

Four

New Lenox and Marley

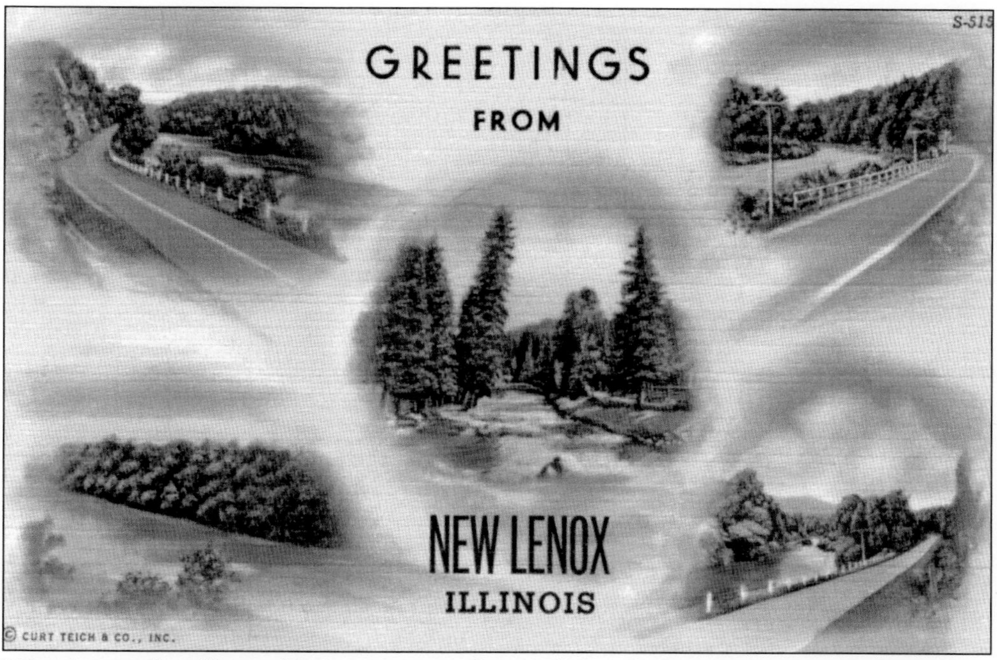

What is now the village of New Lenox was first settled in the late 1820s in the area known as Gouger crossing (Route 30 and Gouger Road), and it was called Van Horne Point. New Lenox Township was established in 1852. Originally the town was named Tracy in honor of the general superintendent of the Rock Island Railroad.

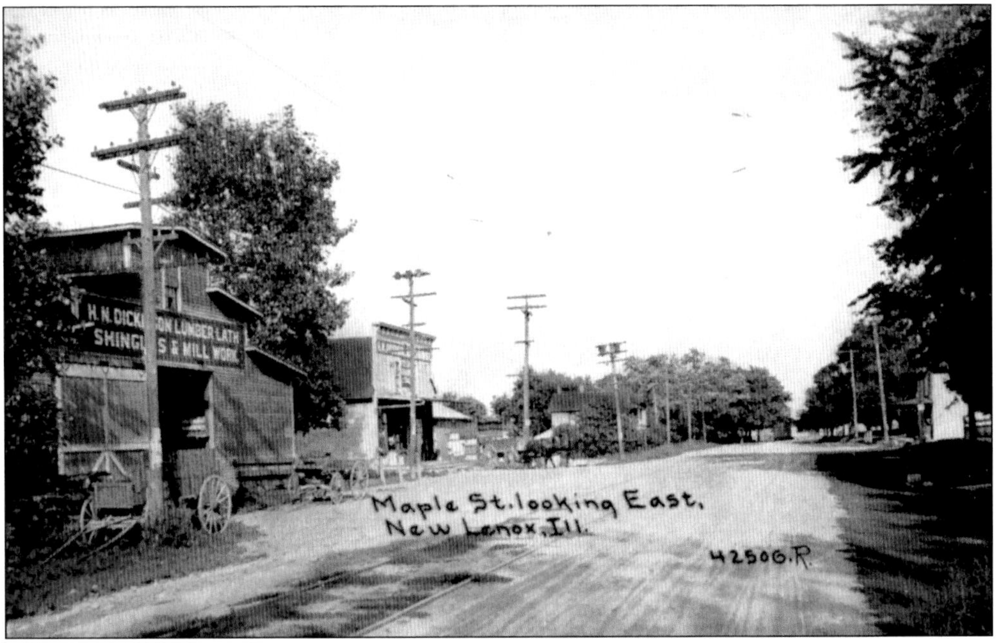

This *c.* 1909 postcard photograph shows a view of Maple Street looking east toward Cedar Road. The buildings to the left are the H. N. Dickinson Lumber Yard and Mill Work and the H. N. Dickinson General Store. The Joliet and Southern Traction streetcar tracks in the middle of the road connect New Lenox with Joliet to the east and Frankfort to the west.

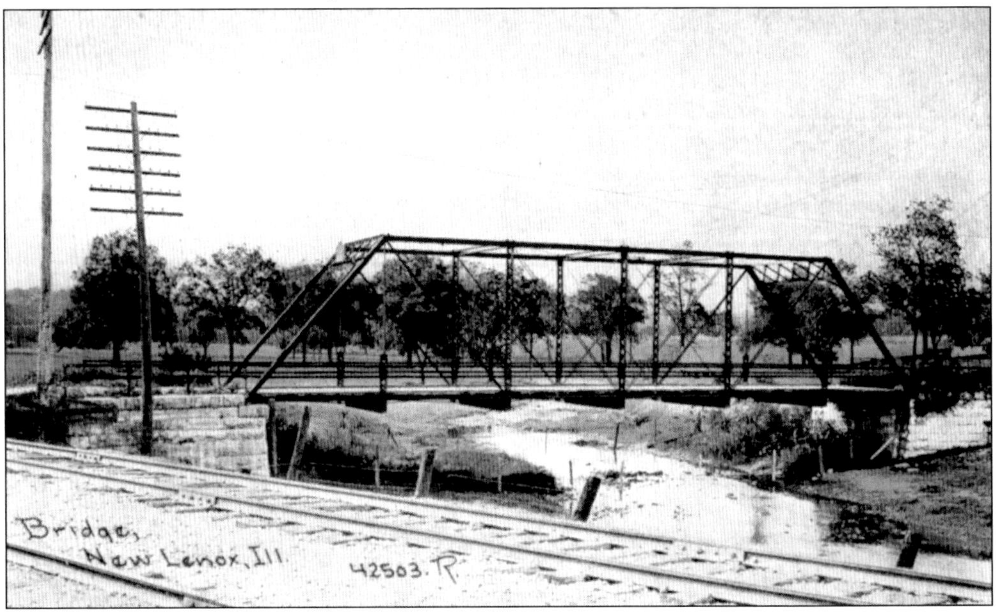

Hickory Creek flows southwestward through the heart of New Lenox Township, feeding into the Des Plaines River at Joliet. Following Route 30 much of the way through its 21-mile journey, the creek flows through many southern communities, including Mokena, Frankfort, New Lenox, and Joliet. This postcard photograph, looking west from the Rock Island Railroad tracks, shows a view of the old steel bridge at Cedar Road, which crosses Hickory Creek just west of the Rock Island depot.

The first schoolhouse in New Lenox Township dates from 1832, when a log structure located along Hickory Creek was built. By 1860, there were seven wood-frame schoolhouses located across the township. In 1869, a large, two story, wood-frame schoolhouse was constructed in Maplewood Cemetery. When the Haven Avenue School was built in the late 1920s, this two-story structure, which housed all eight grades, was closed.

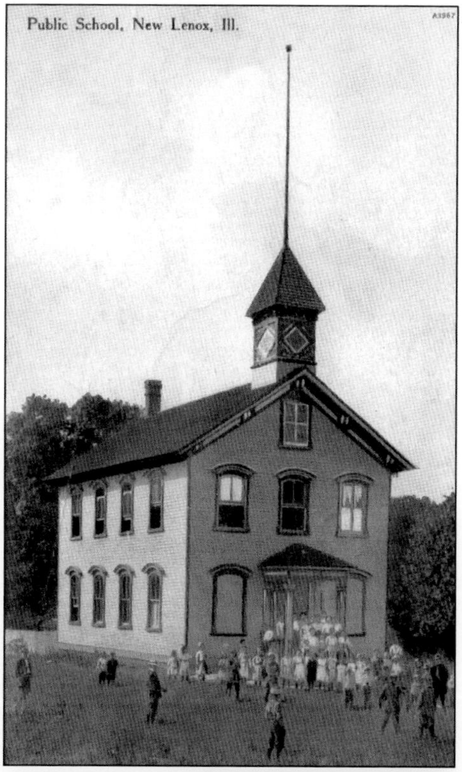

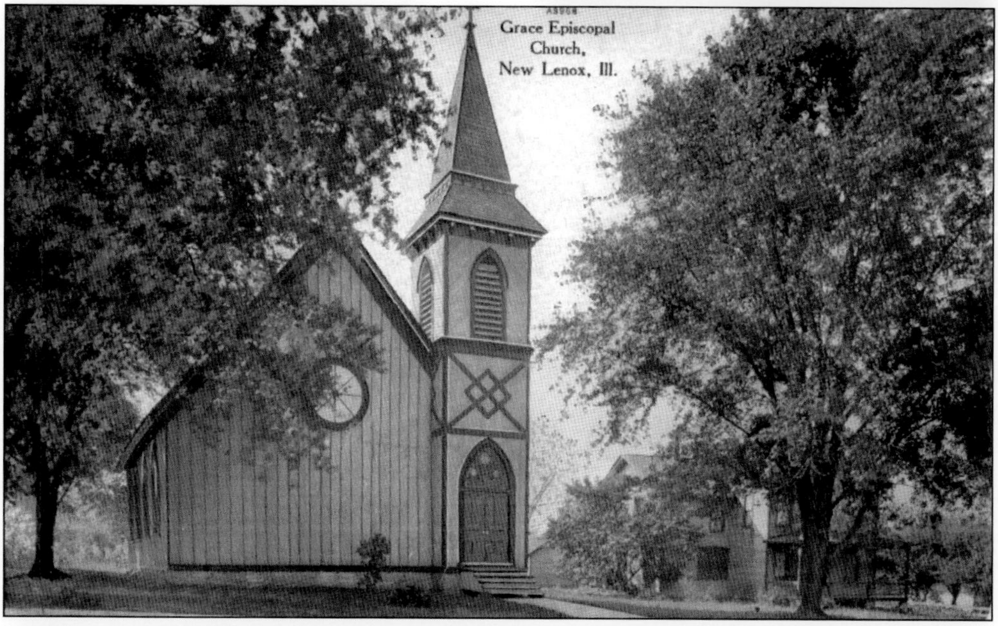

In 1868, several families in the New Lenox area met in the Methodist meetinghouse until they could find property to build their own church. Within a year, a lot south of Hickory Creek was purchased, and a Prairie Gothic church was constructed. The "little white church with red doors" has been a part of New Lenox for over 125 years. This postcard photograph shows Grace Episcopal Church looking west from the northwest corner of Pine and Hickory Streets.

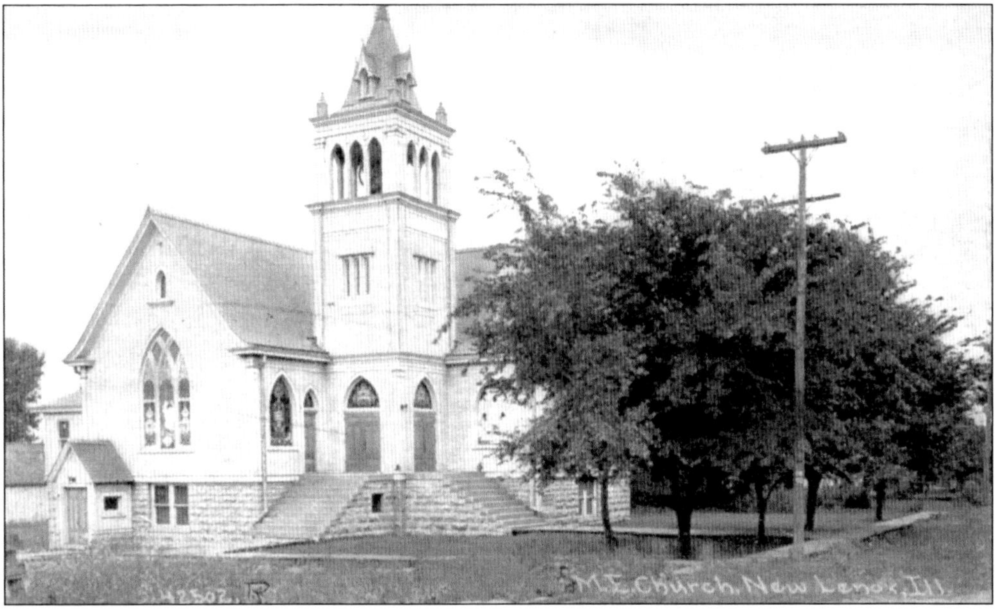

As the population of New Lenox Township grew, a new Methodist church was built in 1863 on Hickory Street, just east of Pine Street. By the 1890s, a new church was needed and was constructed on the northeast corner of Church Street and Haven Avenue. The impressive building, with its many large and beautiful stained-glass windows, opened in 1899. The church served the congregation for nearly 80 years and was sold when a new church was constructed west of town in 1977 on the old campground property.

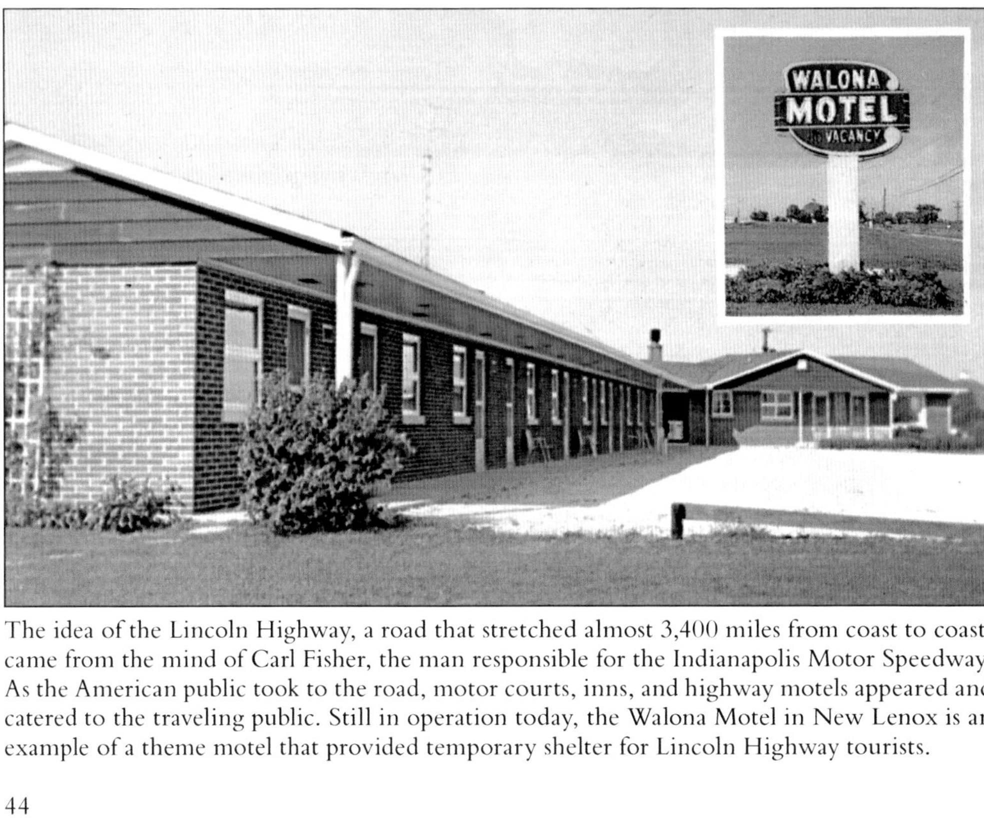

The idea of the Lincoln Highway, a road that stretched almost 3,400 miles from coast to coast, came from the mind of Carl Fisher, the man responsible for the Indianapolis Motor Speedway. As the American public took to the road, motor courts, inns, and highway motels appeared and catered to the traveling public. Still in operation today, the Walona Motel in New Lenox is an example of a theme motel that provided temporary shelter for Lincoln Highway tourists.

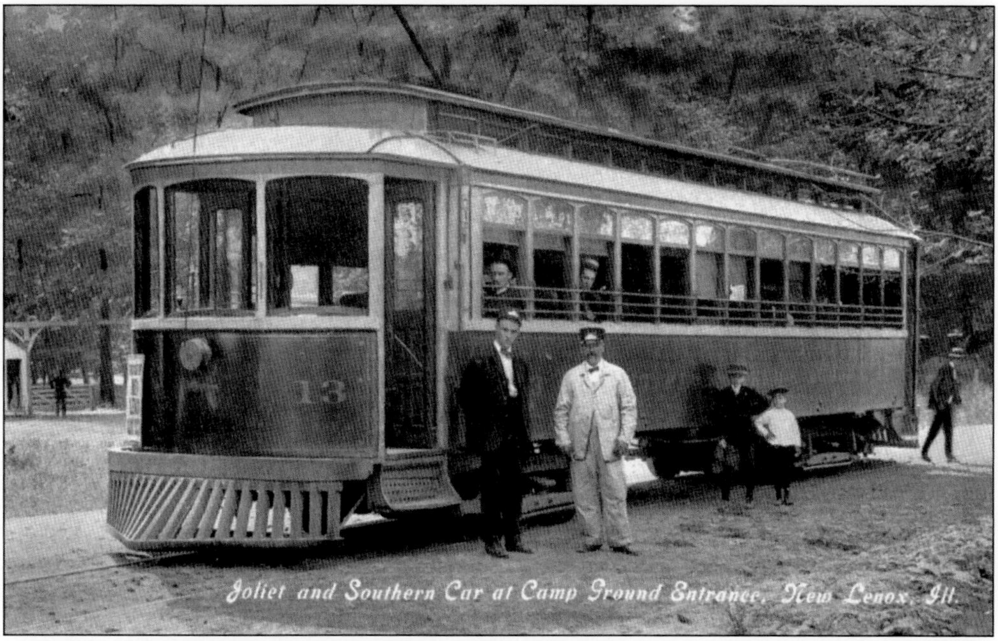

The Joliet and Southern Traction Company operated rail service east from Joliet to Chicago Heights beginning in 1905. The line ran east, parallel to the Michigan Central Railroad tracks, and connected the southern communities of Joliet, New Lenox, Frankfort, and Matteson before ending in Chicago Heights. The first interurban cars to run on these tracks were architecturally little more than long streetcars, but in later years, the streetcars look more like small trolleys. The picture postcard above shows the interurban trolley stopping at the entrance to the campground in New Lenox. The postcard below shows a group of area residents standing on Maple Street near the Cedar Road intersection with the first streetcar to arrive in New Lenox from Joliet on a cold winter day in December 1907. The building on the left is the H. N. Dickinson Lumber and Mill Work Shop.

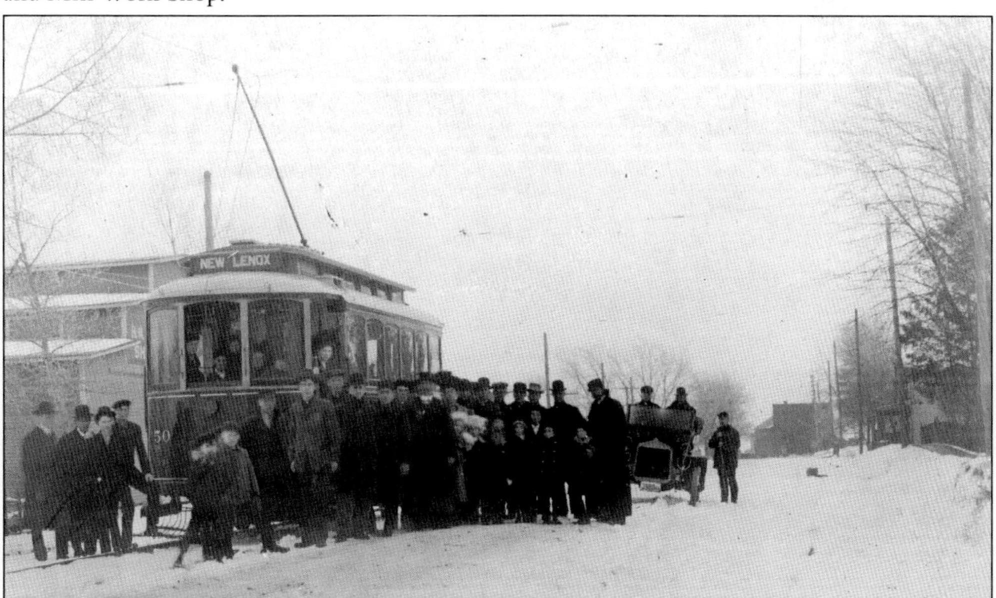

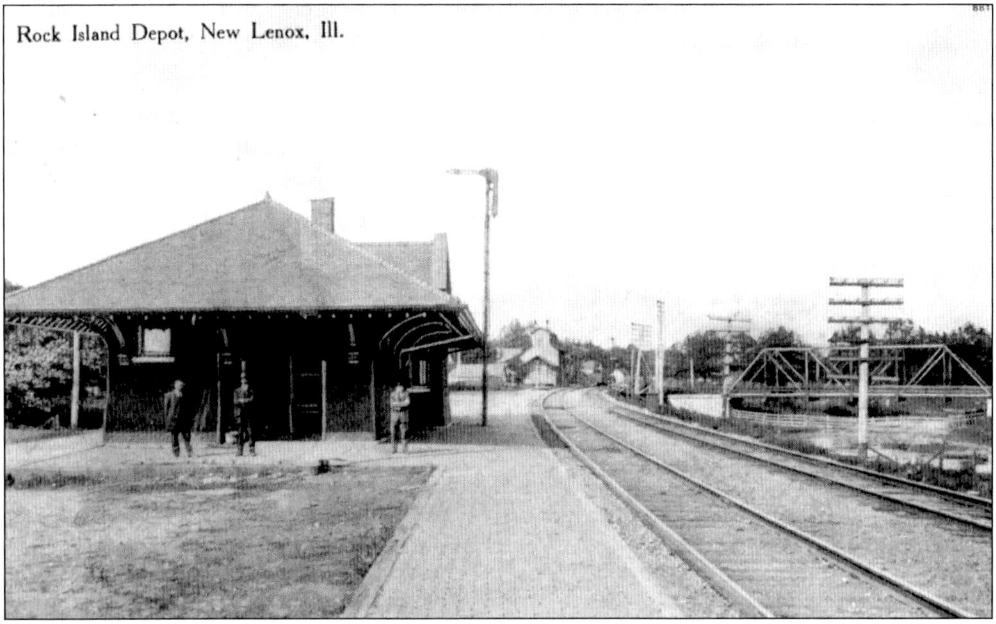

New Lenox Township was established when Will County was created in 1852, with the building of the Rock Island Railroad between Chicago and Rock Island. With the railroad as the conduit, New Lenox developed a strong economy based on agricultural production. Early businesses, like a grain elevator, wagon shops, mills, lumber shops, and blacksmiths, highlight early New Lenox as an agricultural settlement. Located just east of Cedar Road, the Rock Island depot is visible in both postcard photographs. The postcard above shows a view looking west from the Rock Island tracks in the early 20th century. In the distance, the old steel bridge at Cedar Road crossing Hickory Creek can be seen. The postcard below shows the depot looking east near Cedar Road.

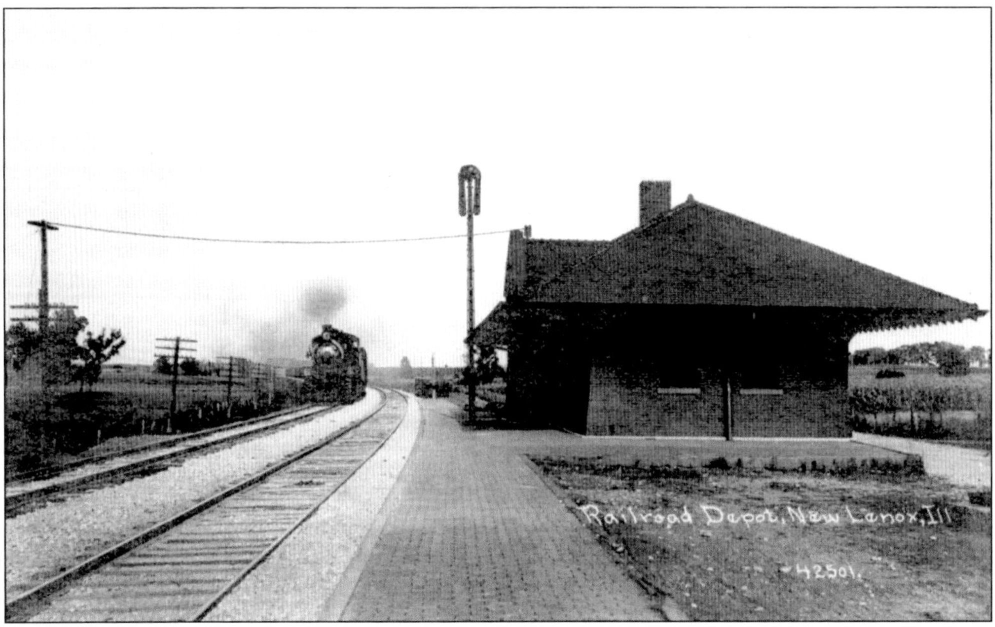

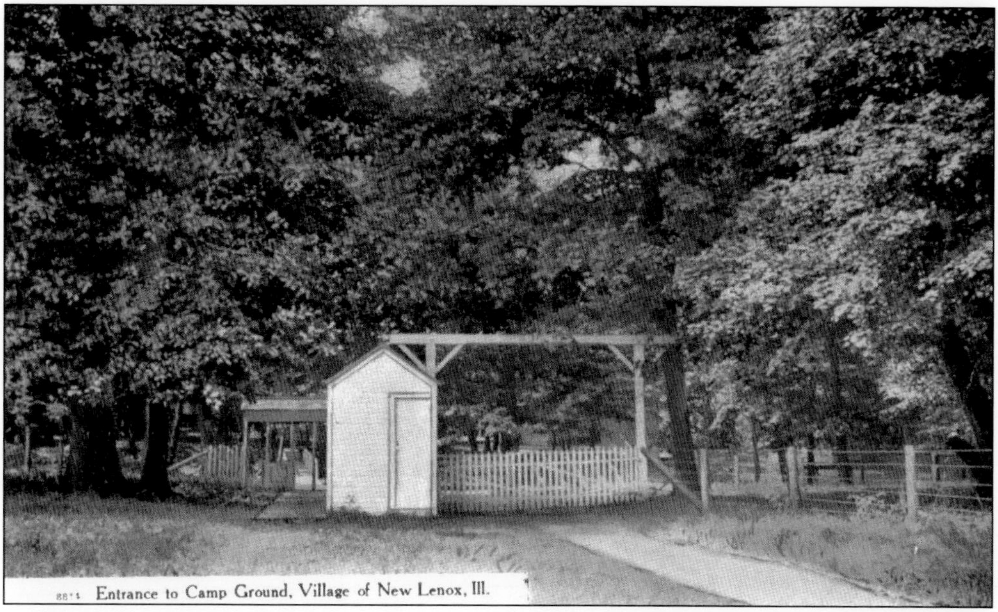

In 1867, the 21-acre campground on the west edge of the village was purchased by the Centenary Campground Association of the Methodist Conference for annual summer camp meetings of the church. Organized by four Methodist church leaders, George Barr, Charles Francis, Fred Haven, and Cal Nicholas, the first meeting was held in 1868. This picture postcard shows a view of the campground entrance just off Maple Street in New Lenox.

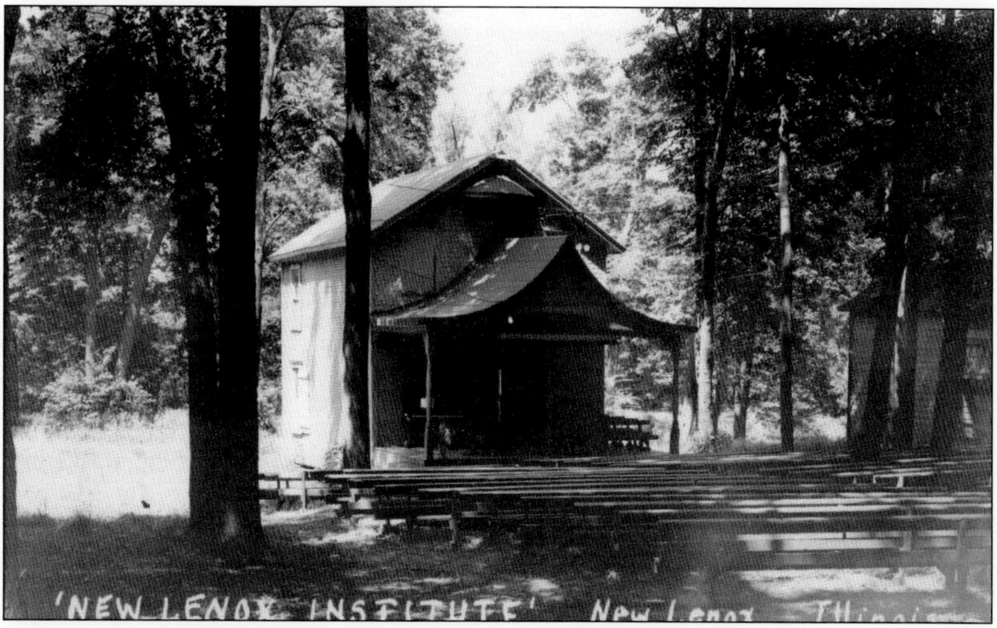

The chapel at the Methodist campground was a small building with a unique, curved canopy roof in the front that allowed speakers to address the congregation seated outdoors on wood benches. This *c.* 1905 postcard photograph shows the chapel in the woods at the Methodist Centenary Campgrounds. Notice the rows of wooden benches, shaded by tall trees, placed in front of the chapel building.

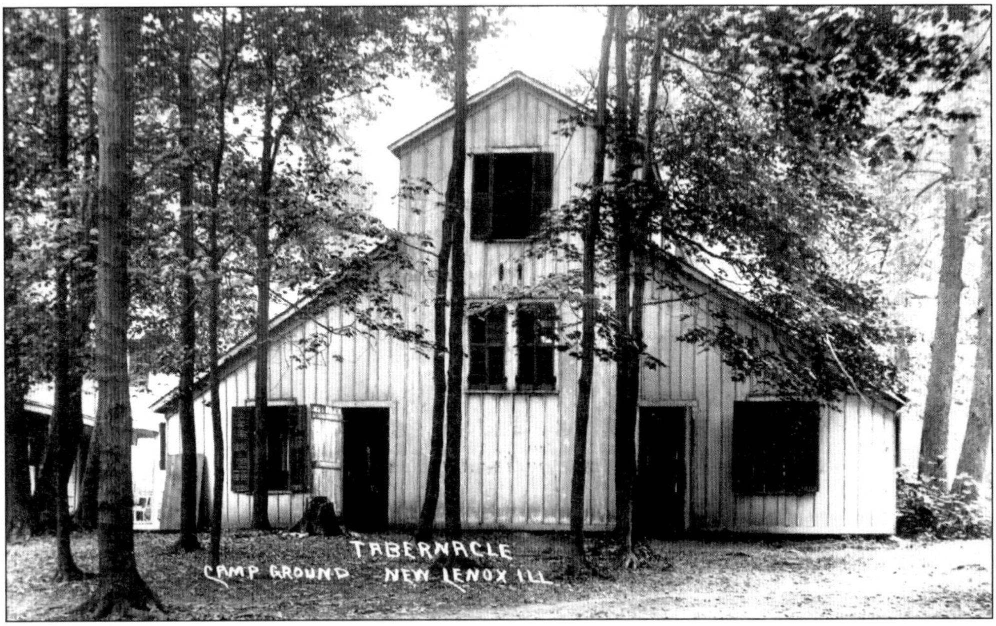

Over the years, many permanent structures were constructed at the Methodist Centenary Campgrounds, including an entrance gatehouse, a tabernacle, a bathhouse, and a dining hall. As more visitors attended the summer meetings, tents were replaced by wood-framed cottages constructed in rows facing each other, which was a common arrangement at camp meeting sites. Eventually a hotel was built on site to cater to camp visitors, who sometimes numbered in the thousands. The picture postcard above shows a view of the tabernacle building, and the postcard below shows the hotel. Notice the young children seated on the front porch for the picture.

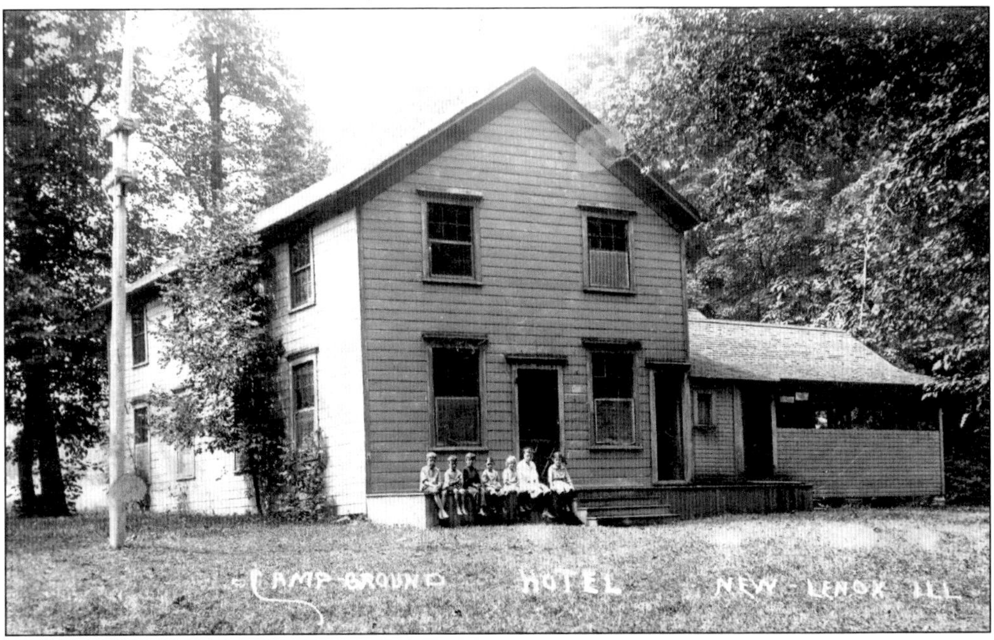

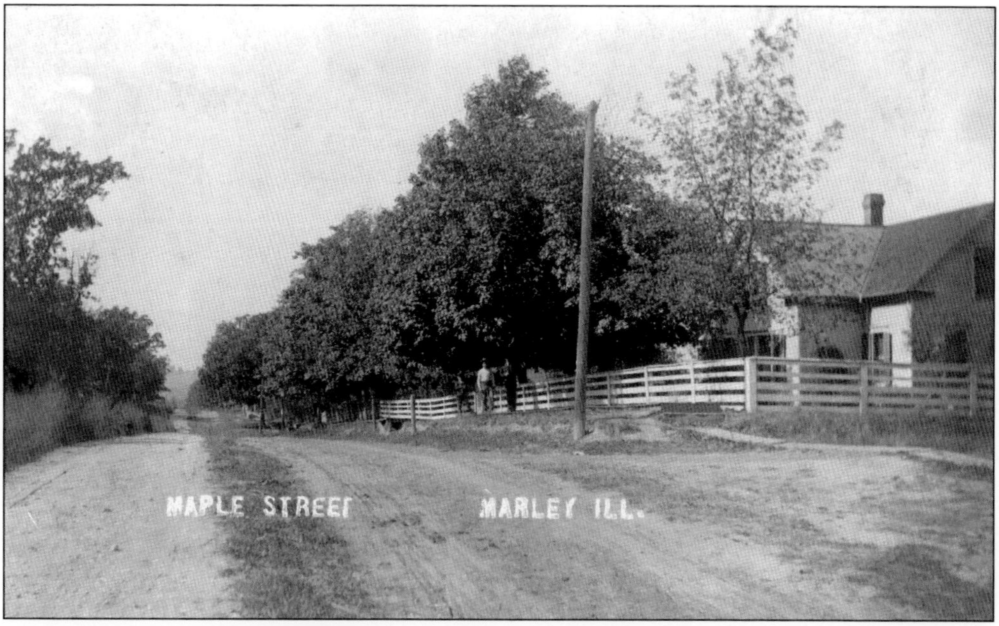

In the 1860s, the dirt road that led from Joliet eastward through New Lenox Township was given the name Maple Street because of the maple trees that once lined the old road. The maple trees were part of the vision of Charles Snoad, who owned several hundred acres of land near the road and planted the trees in a straight line on what soon was known as Maple Street (187th Street). Over the years, many of the original trees planted by Snoad died and were replaced. In the 1930s, a good portion of the trees were uprooted to make way for Southwest Highway (Route 6). The postcard above shows Maple Street, and the postcard below shows the old iron bridge on Maple Street with wide plank boards, which spanned the creek just west of the Wabash Railroad tracks.

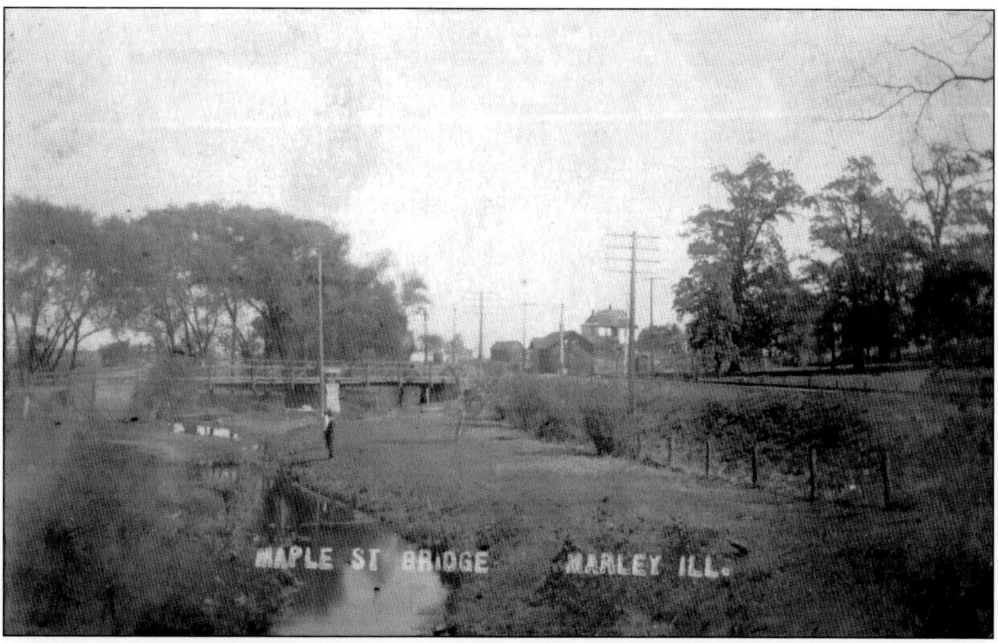

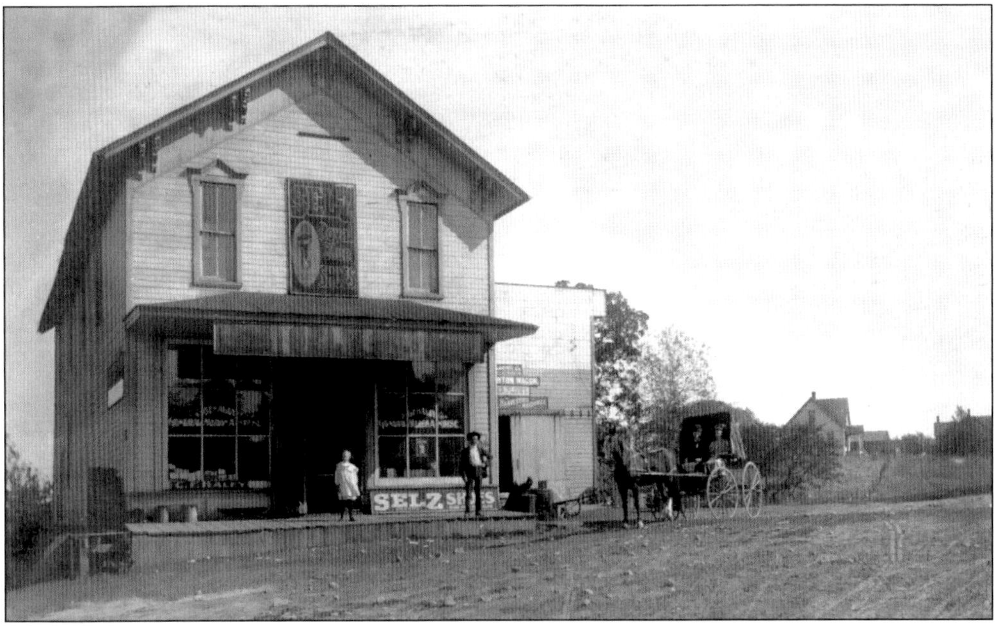

In 1880, George Haley helped to layout and survey the triangular 16-acre tract of land that was soon known as Marley. The growth of Marley can be traced to the construction of a railroad right-of-way in 1881, which became an extension of the Wabash, St. Louis, and Pacific Railway from Forrest to Chicago. A depot was constructed on the east side of the tracks near Maple Street, and soon other businesses followed, including a granary, a stockyard, a blacksmith shop, and a general store. In 1893, C. F. Haley constructed a new general store at the corner of Main and Valley Streets. This larger store included a hall above for community activities. The postcard above shows the Haley family general store. The postcard below shows the old store building that was moved to Maple Street by Haley and converted into a nine-room residence.

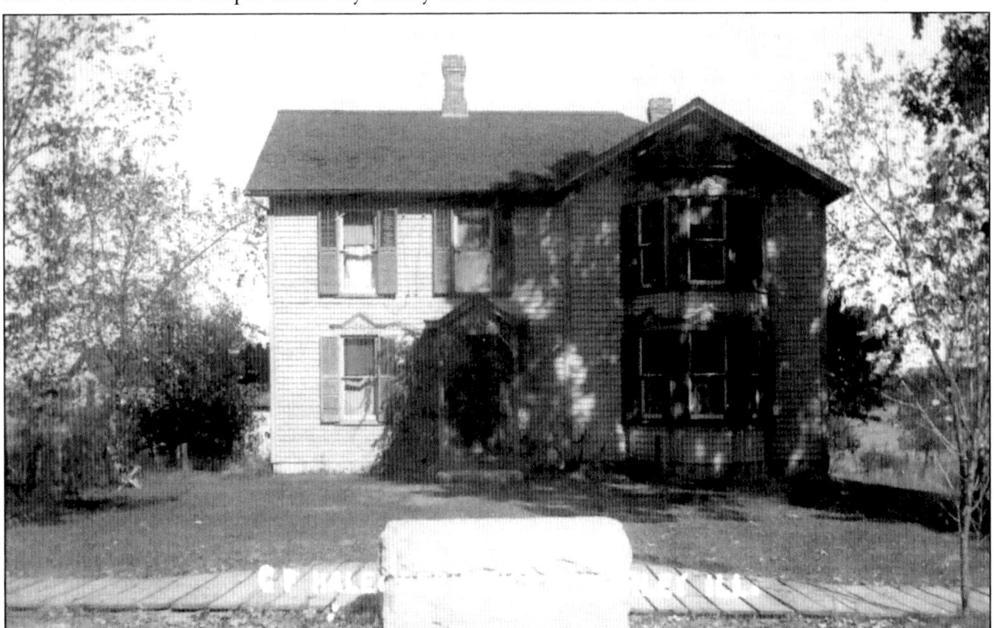

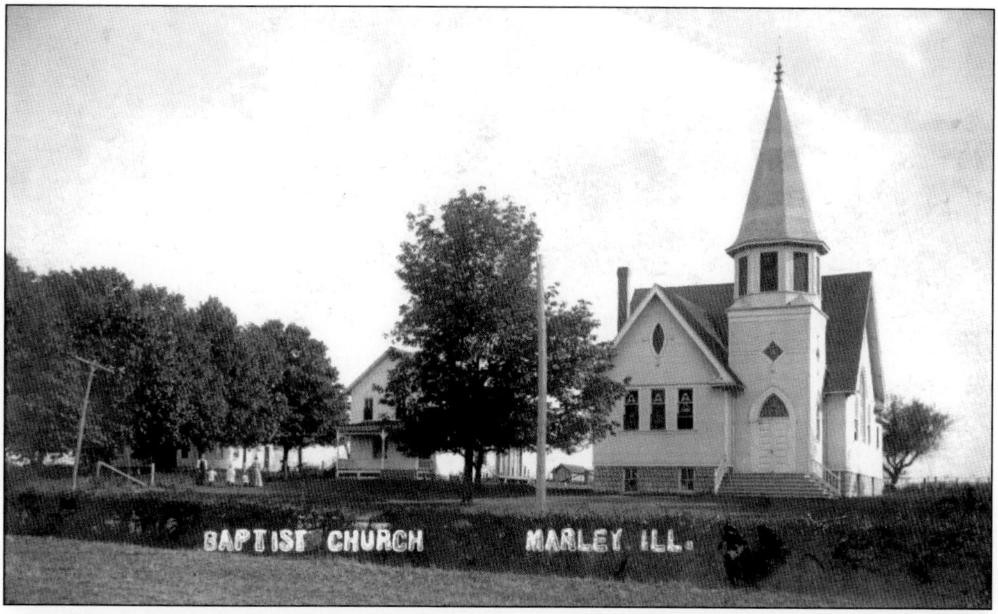

The origins of the Baptist church in Marley can be traced to a Baptist missionary named Allen B. Freeman, who helped organize the O'Plain Baptist Church in 1833. In 1850, a small, white frame church was built at the village of Hadley, and it was renamed the Hadley Baptist Church. As the thriving village of Marley began to grow, ground was broken in 1899 for a new church east of town on Maple Street. Dedicated on January 6, 1901, the church soon became the center of community life. In 1914, the name was changed to the Marley Baptist Community Church. Known as the Marley Community Church today, it continues to serve the area and its residents. In the postcard below, the Marley Baptist Community Church can be seen in the distance to the left of Hadley's store, the long, white building in the center.

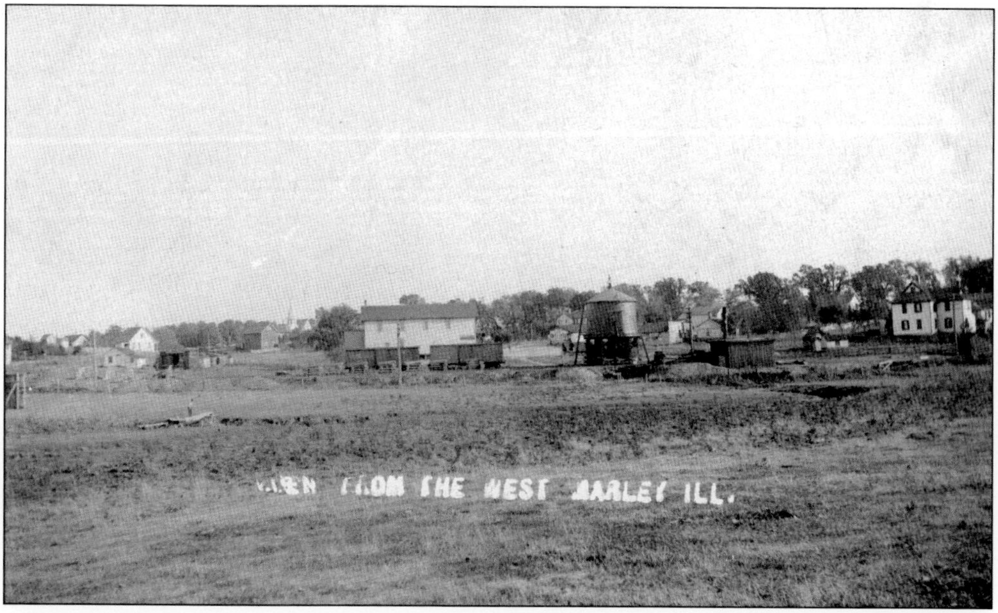

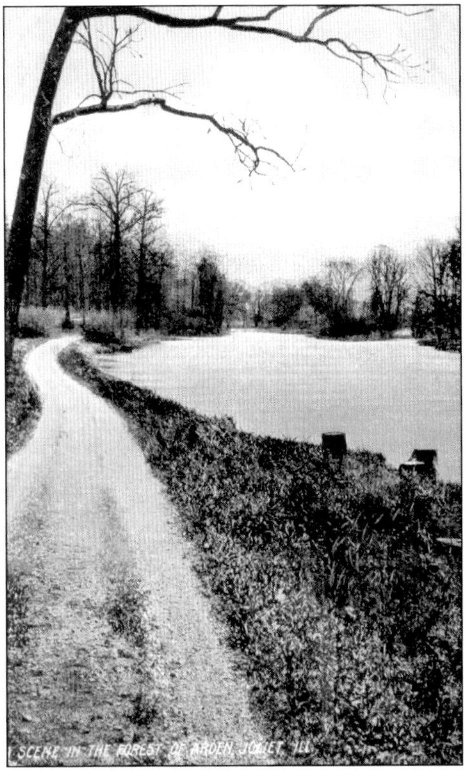

Pilcher Park was started by Harlow N. Higginbotham, who made an effort to have many trees and shrubs native to Will County transplanted to a private arboretum on his property, which he named the Forrest of Arden. As president of Chicago's World's Columbian Exposition Corporation and the Council of Administration, Higginbotham used many of the trees that were part of the exhibits to help create the arboretum. In 1920, Robert Pilcher, a self-taught naturalist and businessman, purchased the land from Higginbotham and donated the original 327 acres to the City of Joliet. Today Pilcher Park is perhaps the most popular local park in Will County for nature lovers. Located in the northwest portion of New Lenox Township on Gougar Road, the park offers over 300 acres of rare trees and other interesting specimens of nature, both flora and fauna.

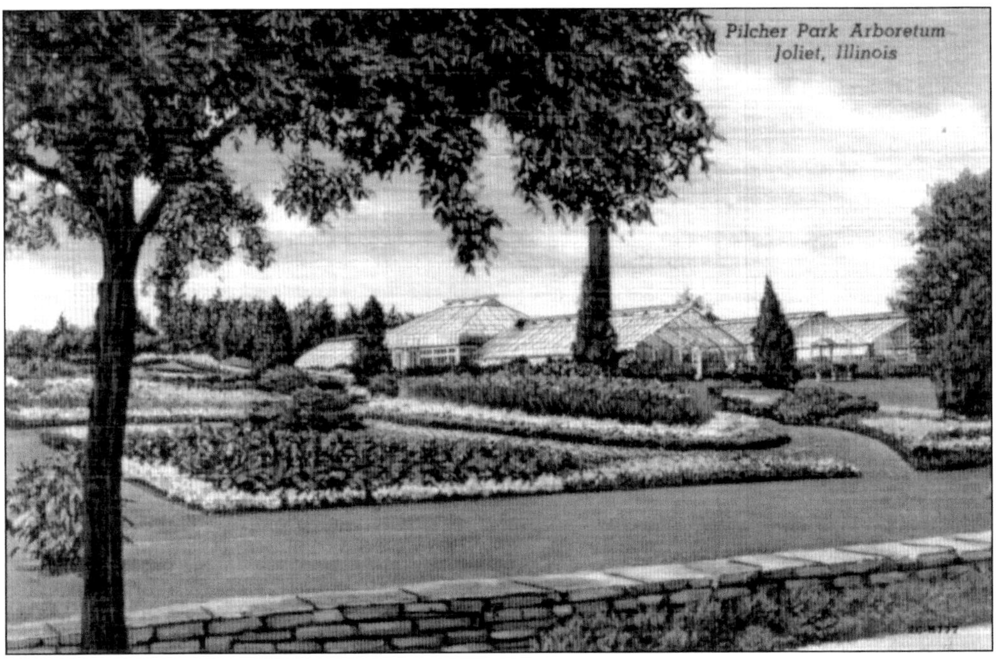

Five

Frankfort

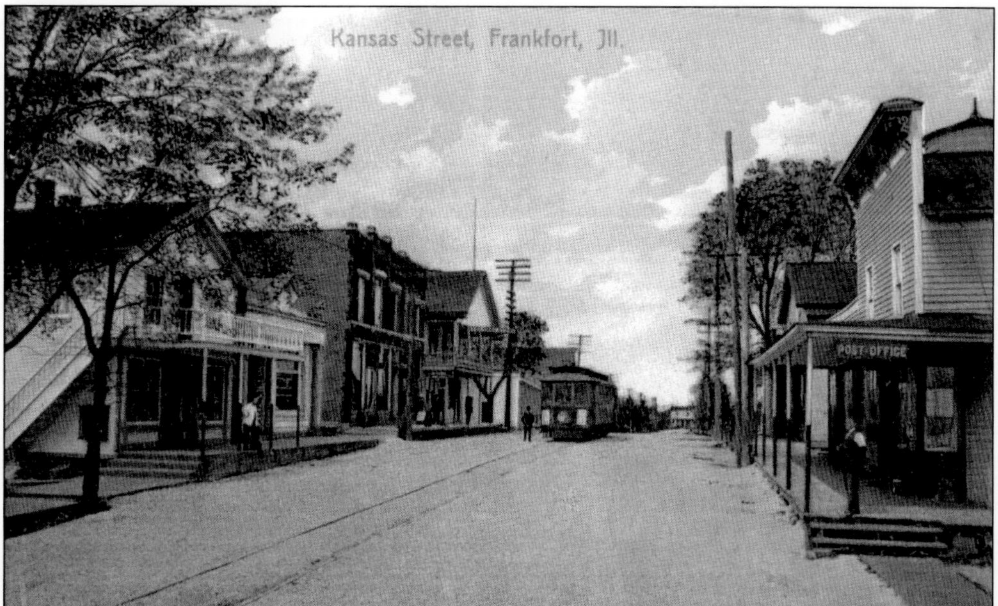

This early-20th-century photograph postcard shows a view of Kansas Street looking west. The white building on the near left was a barbershop and harness shop. The trolley car is stopped in front of Folkers Hotel, located on the southeast corner of Kansas and Hickory Streets. On the north side of the street, the post office, drugstore, and Johnny Feil's Grocery Store are visible.

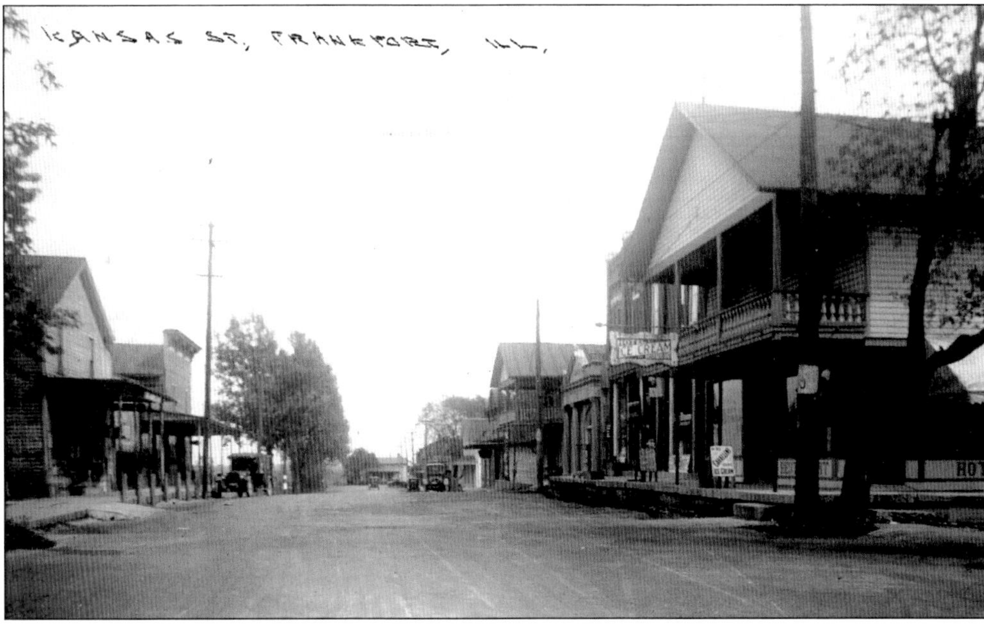

Located on the southeast corner of Kansas and Hickory Streets, the Folkers Hotel was owned and operated for many years by Johnson Folkers and eventually his three sons, William, Frank, and Peter. The partnership formed by these three brothers carried on numerous businesses begun by Johnson that were important to the growth of the community of Frankfort, including a livery stable, a slaughterhouse, contracting the construction for the Elgin, Joliet and Eastern Railway tracks, and locating the first telephone exchange on the second floor of the hotel. These picture postcards show Kansas Street looking east from Hickory Street. Folkers Hotel is the two-story building on the right in both photographs.

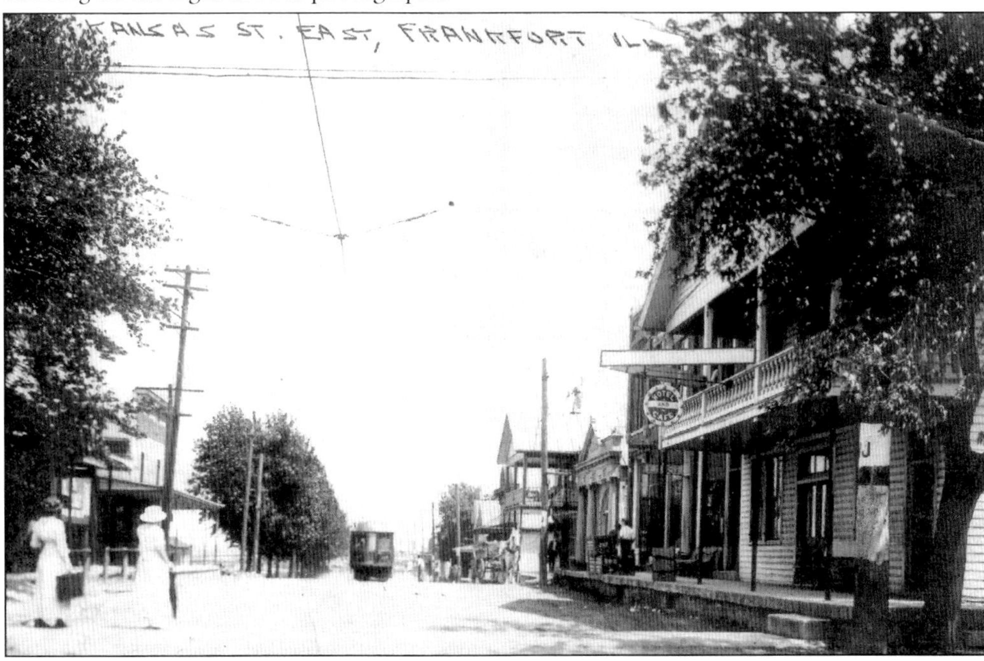

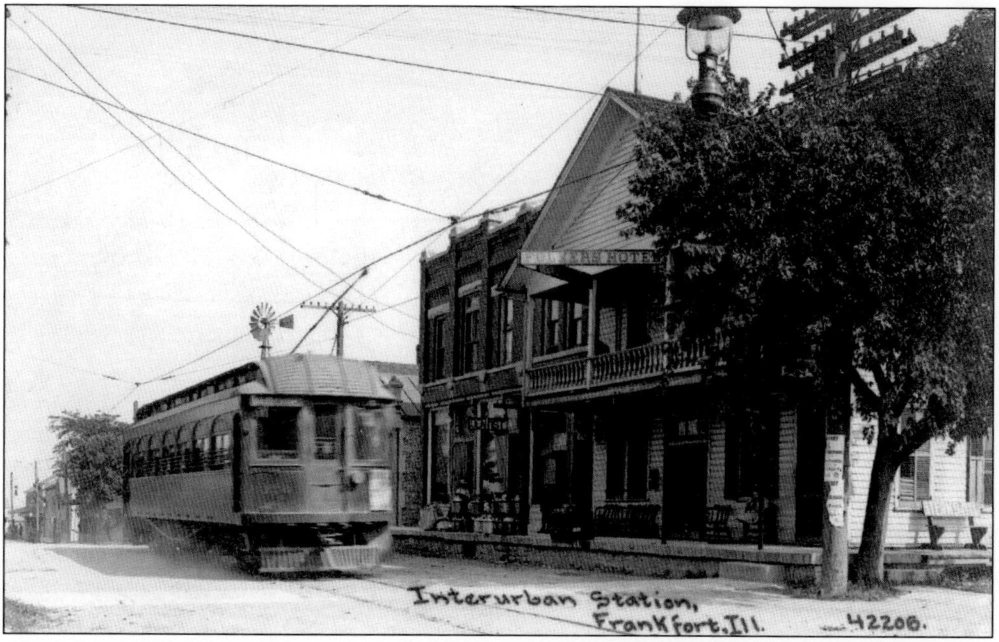

The Joliet and Southern Traction Company, a sister company to the Aurora, Plainfield and Joliet Railway Company, operated rail service east from Joliet beginning in 1905. The line ran east, parallel to the Michigan Central Railroad tracks, and connected the southern communities of Joliet, New Lenox, Frankfort, and Matteson before ending in Chicago Heights. The first interurban cars to run on these tracks were architecturally little more than long streetcars but in later years had a unique arch-shaped roof and windows, which became a traditional interurban styling. These picture postcards show the interurban trolley running past the Folkers Hotel, an interurban station in Frankfort. Notice the conductor helping travelers load their luggage in the photograph below. By the early 1920s, automobiles and the paving of the Lincoln Highway made the Aurora-Joliet-Chicago Heights interurban service unnecessary.

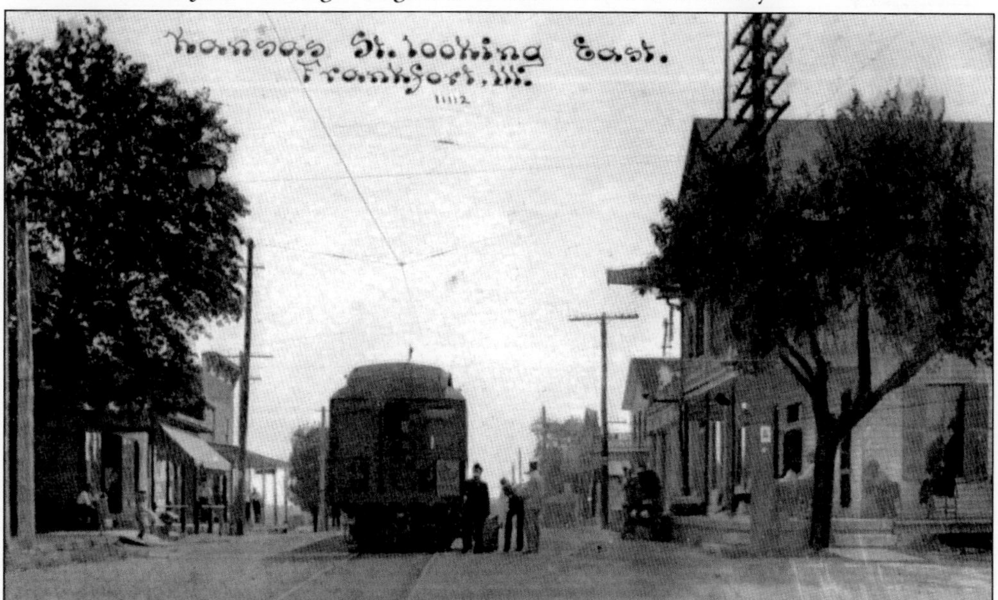

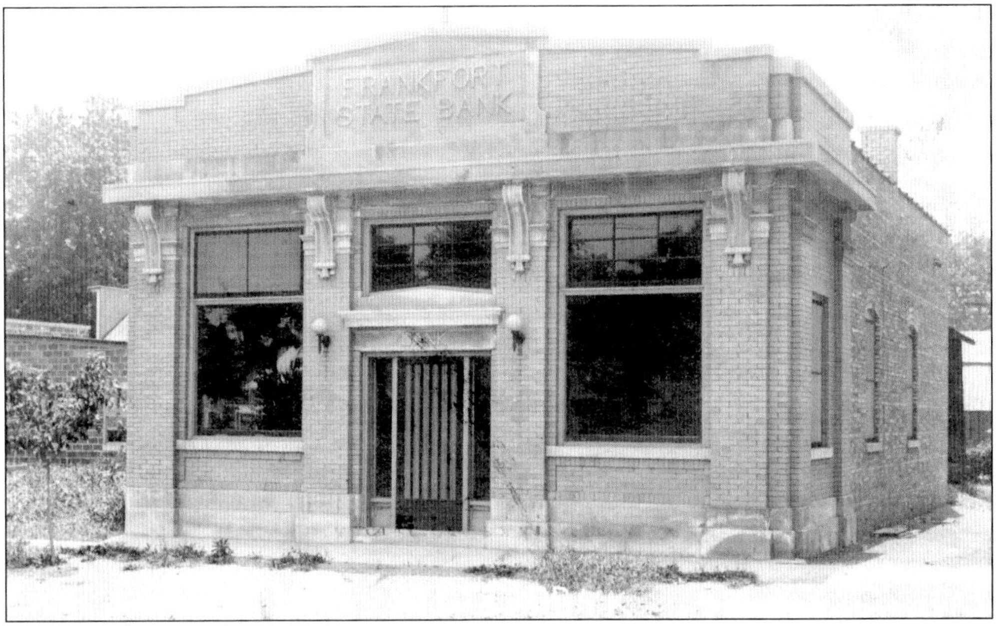

The history of the Frankfort State Bank can be traced back to June 1913, when a group of citizens saw the need for a state bank in the community. The bank began with $25,000 in paid capital and started its operation on August 27 of the same year. The following January, a new building, shown in this postcard photograph, was completed.

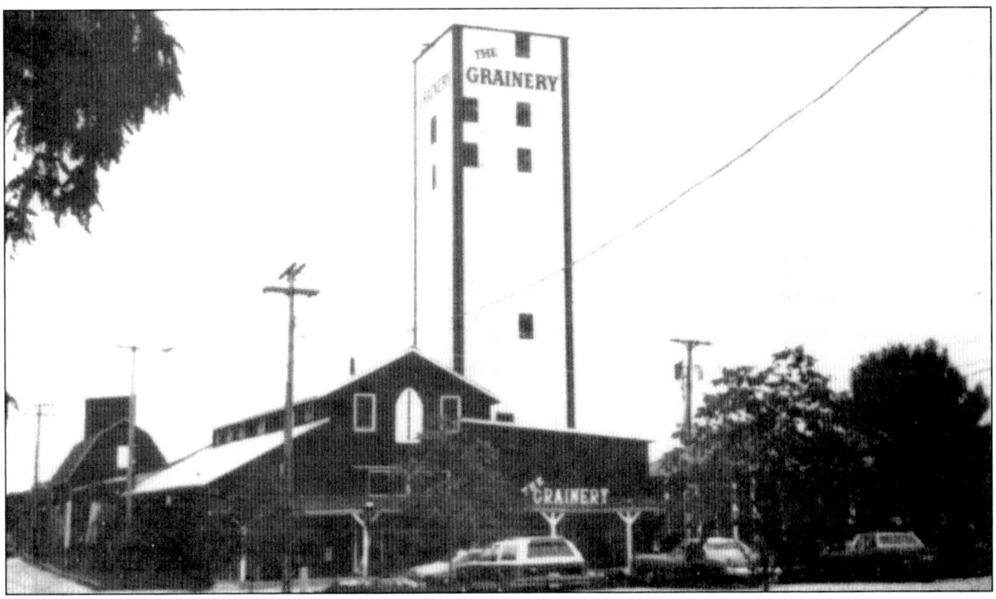

The first grain bought in the Frankfort area was done so by Norman A. Carpenter, who bought for J. L. Hurd and Company of Detroit. Together they built the first grain elevator in 1856 near the Michigan Central Railroad tracks (known as the Old Plank Road Trail today). Numerous times over the years, the wooden grain elevator caught fire, and in the 1940s, the entire structure was rebuilt using concrete. Today the grain elevator stands 132 feet high and can be seen from miles around. This postcard photograph shows the area around the old granary and the scale house.

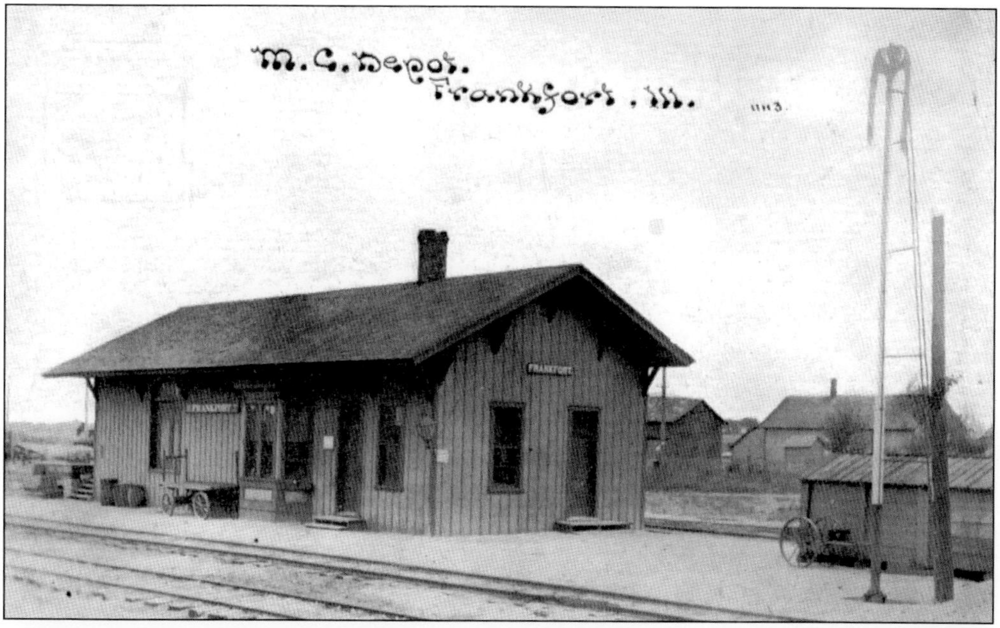

In 1855, the Joliet and Northern Indiana Railroad built a line through Frankfort, connecting it with Joliet to the west and the railroad's main line in Indiana. In the same year, Sherman W. Bowmen laid out plans for a village along the tracks, and the area became known as Frankfort Station. The Joliet and Northern Indiana Railroad was leased to the Michigan Central Railroad and thrived in the early years.

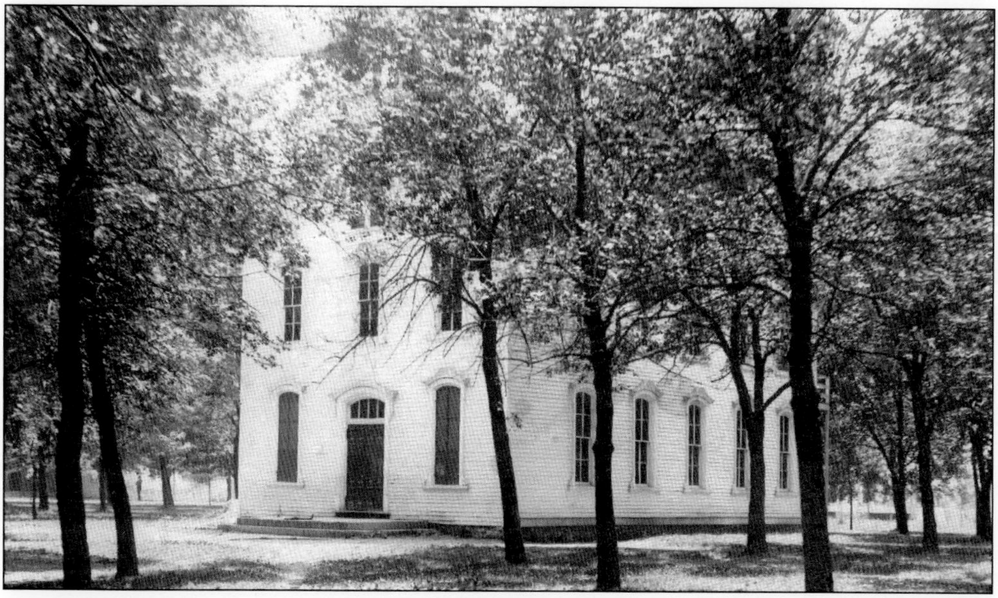

The first schoolhouse in the village was a small, one-room-long cabin built in 1856 and taught by a young woman named Lizzie Kent. As the school became overcrowded, a two-story frame structure that contained three classrooms was built in 1870 at a cost of nearly $5,000. The old schoolhouse was located near the southwest corner of Oak and Oregon Streets. In 1925, this building was replaced by the Frankfort School. This picture postcard shows a view of the old 1870 school.

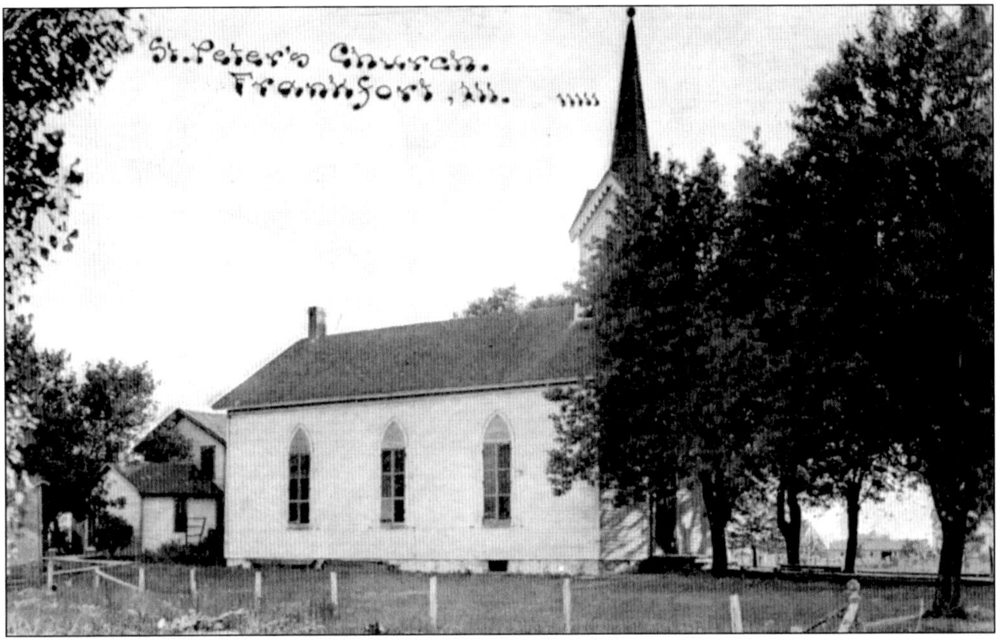

St. Peter's German Evangelical Church was organized on October 28, 1867. Thirteen German and Swiss families sought to begin a congregation where they could practice their Evangelical faith and worship in their native tongue. By 1910, the original white frame church, shown in the postcard above, proved to be too small for the growing congregation. On February 6, 1916, a new church, located on Sauk Trail just east of Ash Street, was dedicated. Educational wings were added to the church building in 1953 and 1967. The sanctuary is known for its traditional architecture, beautiful stained-glass windows, rich wood furnishings and carvings, an organ, a carillon, and a large steeple. The photograph below shows a view of the 1916 church.

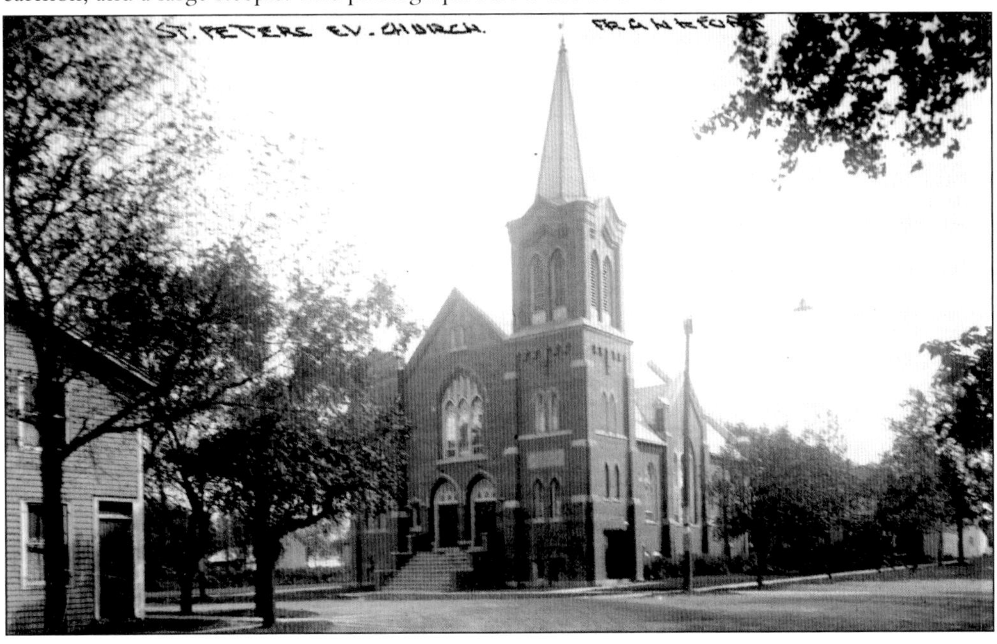

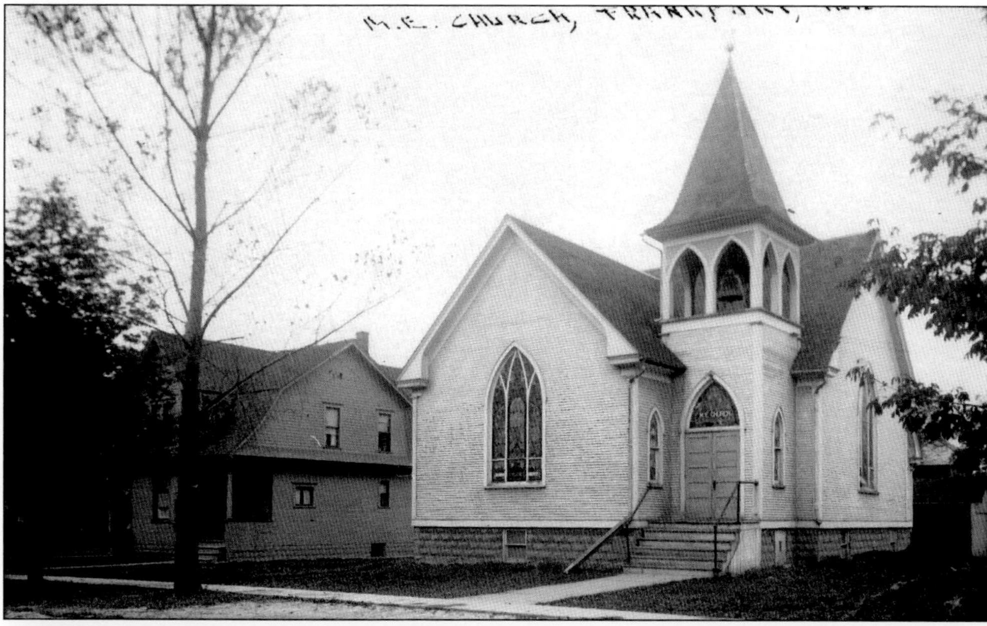

In 1856, a year after the village of Frankfort was founded, the Methodist congregation erected the first church building in the village on Hickory Street. With the growth of the village, the congregation saw a need for a new building, and in 1908, one was erected at a cost of $3,500 and dedicated in February 1909. In 1933, the First Methodist Church at Green Garden joined with the Frankfort church, and in 1937, an extensive program of remodeling took place. In 1955, the two congregations separated, and two years later, the Frankfort United Methodist Church congregation built a new parish on the corner of Linden Drive and Sauk Trail. The old Hickory Street church was sold in 1956 to the Good Shepherd Lutheran congregation, which used the structure until it built a new one in 1988.

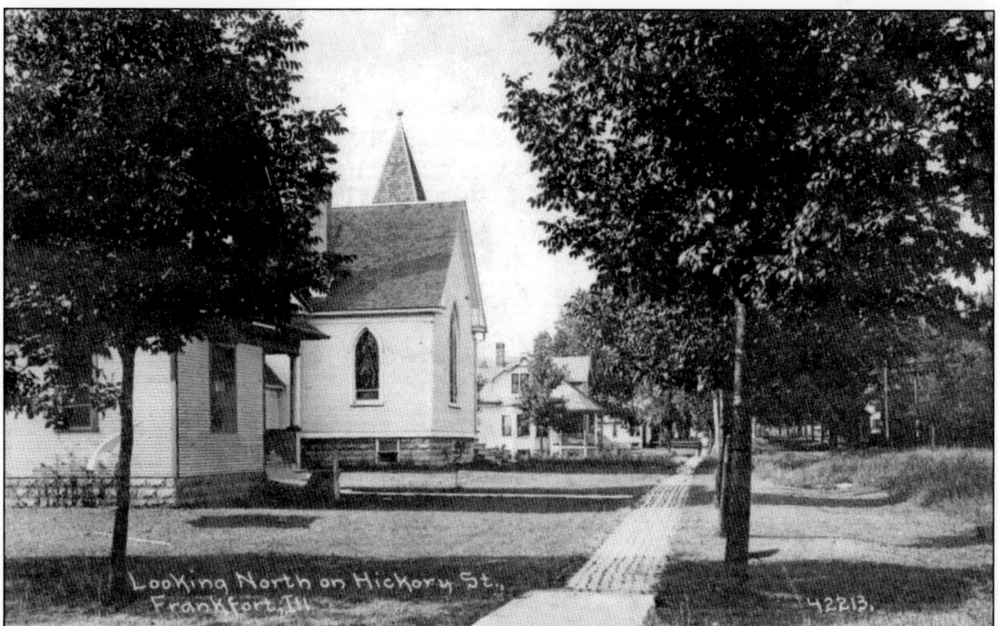

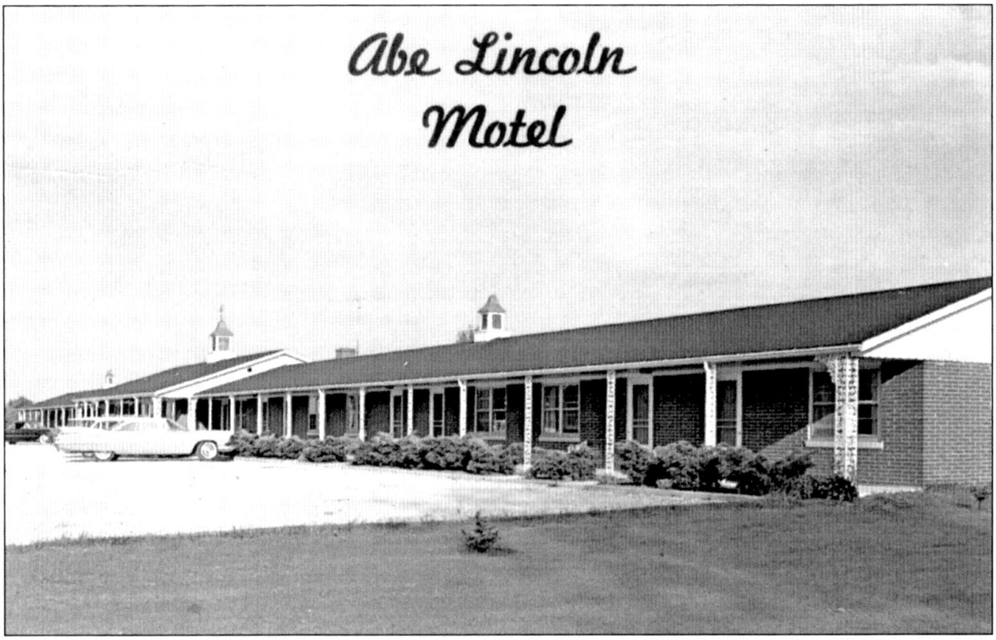

The Lincoln Highway was once the most famous road in America. Stretching almost 3,400 miles between New York City and San Francisco, the old highway connected small-town America with larger, urban areas. The Abe Lincoln Motel in Frankfort, built in the late 1950s and still in operation today, is an example of a theme motel that provided temporary shelter for Lincoln Highway tourists.

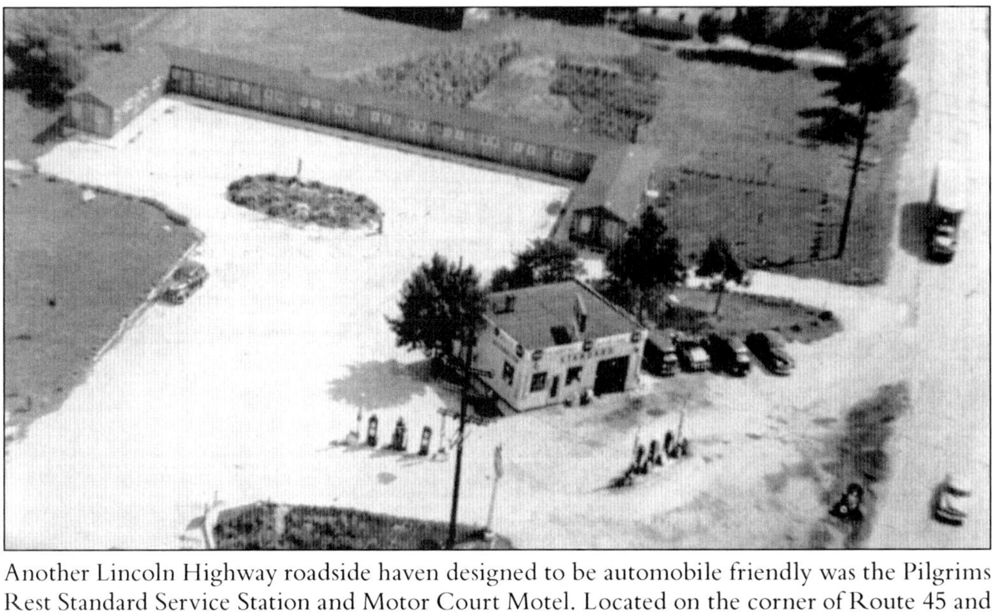

Another Lincoln Highway roadside haven designed to be automobile friendly was the Pilgrims Rest Standard Service Station and Motor Court Motel. Located on the corner of Route 45 and the Lincoln Highway (Route 30) in Frankfort, it offered the travel-weary motorist a fine roadside motel and filling station that offered 24-hour service daily. This aerial postcard photograph shows the standard station in the foreground and the U-shaped motor court in the background.

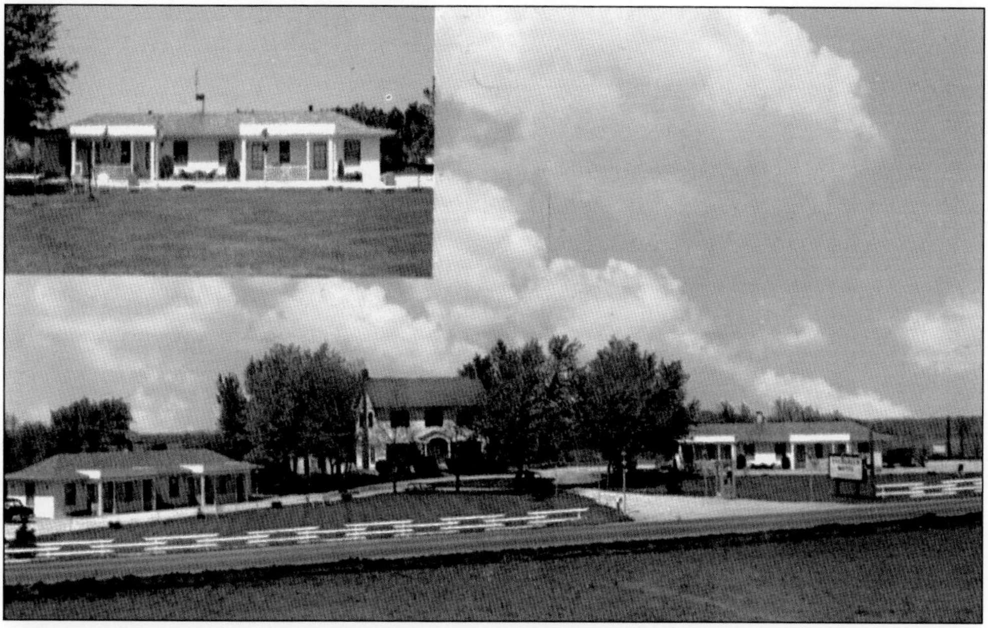

It was not until the 1920s that cheap, basic accommodations for road travelers appeared in the form of motor camps, open-air camping grounds with communal laundries and washrooms. These facilities were gradually superseded by sites providing individual huts containing beds, and thousands were built across the country between 1929 and 1933. These establishments were the forerunners of the typical tourist court, a semicircular layout of cabins around a manager's office. Soon most courts had running water in their rooms, and over the following years, air-conditioning, radio, and eventually television were introduced. These picture postcards show two such establishments in Frankfort on the old Lincoln Highway. The postcard above shows the Evergreen Motel, which included 10 acres of rolling country with an orchard and shade trees, playground equipment, and picnic tables. The postcard below shows the Valley View Motel, which included 14 modern units, a restaurant, a cocktail lounge, and a swimming pool.

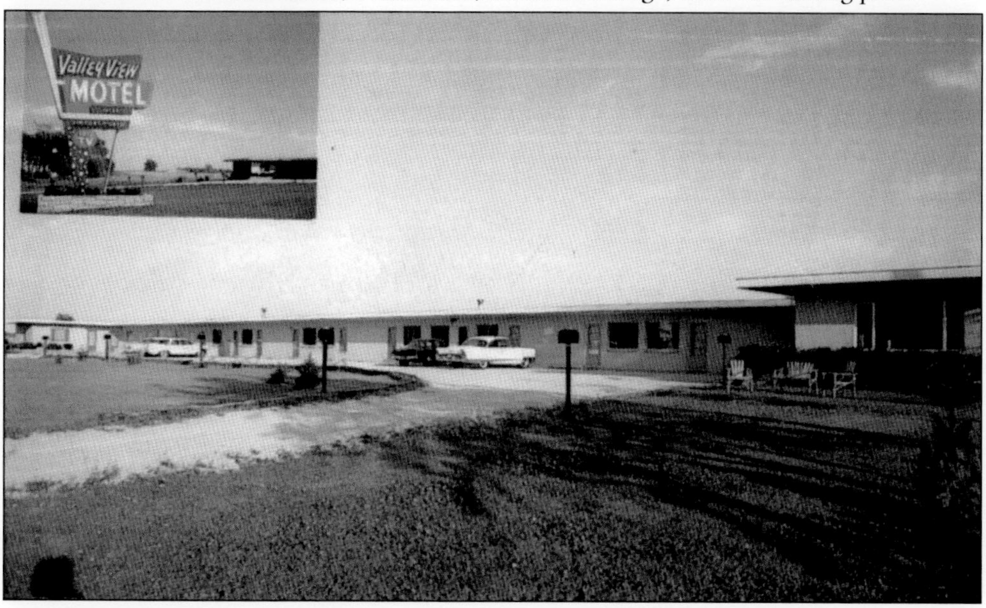

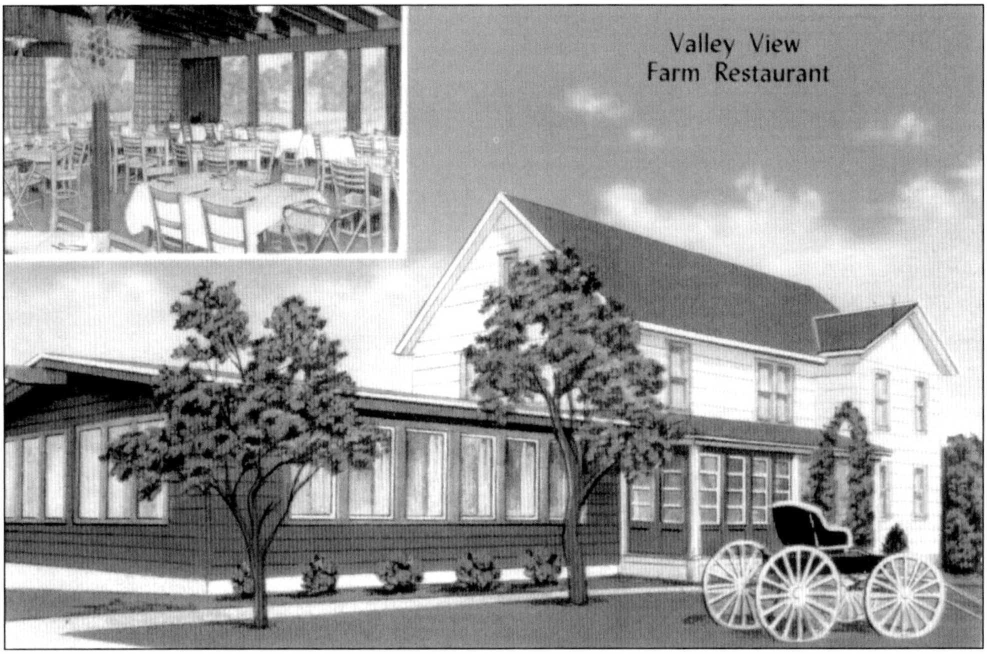

Located just east of Wolf Road on Route 30, the Valley View Farm and Restaurant in Frankfort was a favorite spot for locals or Lincoln Highway tourists who wanted good food and a relaxing environment. Although the majority of food served in the restaurant was raised on the farm, Valley View Farm was best remembered for its numerous dining rooms, including the Sun-Air Room and the Lean-To Lounge, with its piano bar. Tourists who needed to stay the evening could find accommodations in the vacation center, which included a motel and swimming pool. The postcard below shows a view of the motel swimming pool around 1960. Today the Frankfort Township offices are located on the old farm complex. The swimming pool, which for many years offered area residents a place to cool off in the summertime, was closed in 2005, and a new township building was built in its place.

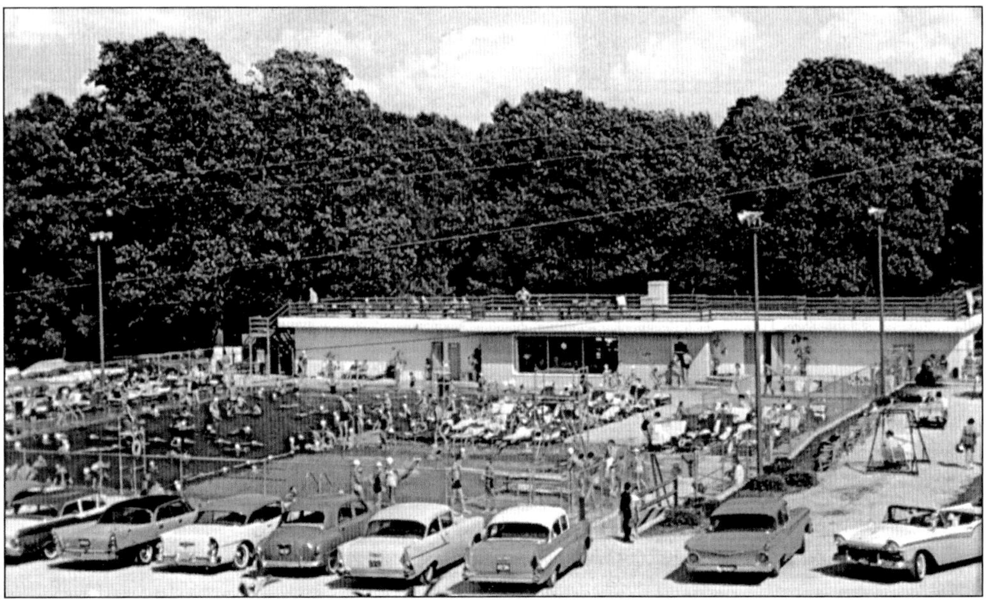

Six

MOKENA

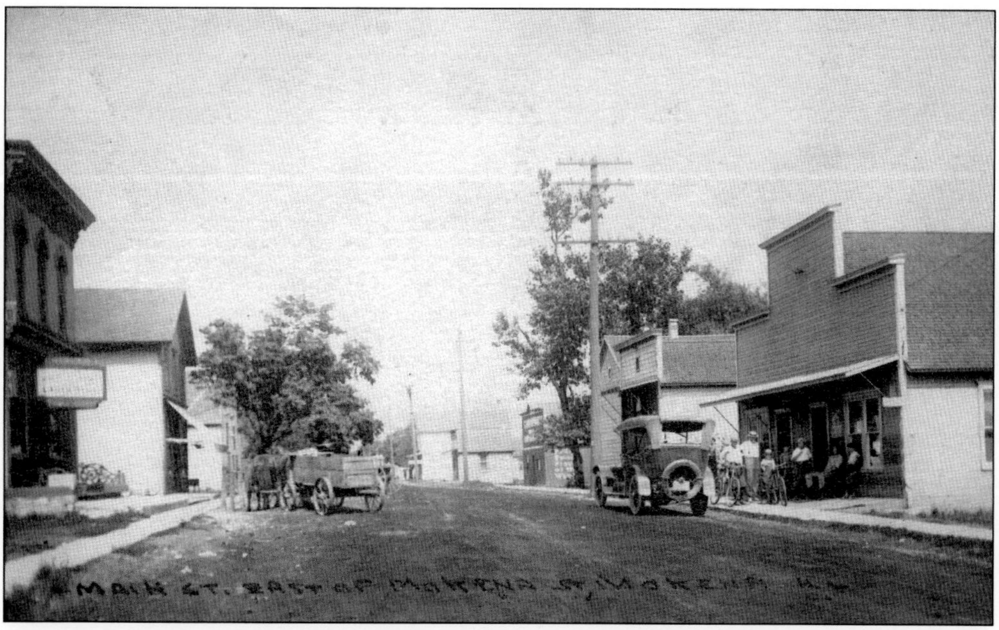

Front Street (Main Street) runs parallel to the Rock Island Railroad tracks in Mokena and has always been an important part of village growth and commerce. This picture postcard shows Main Street, still a dirt road, looking east from Mokena Street.

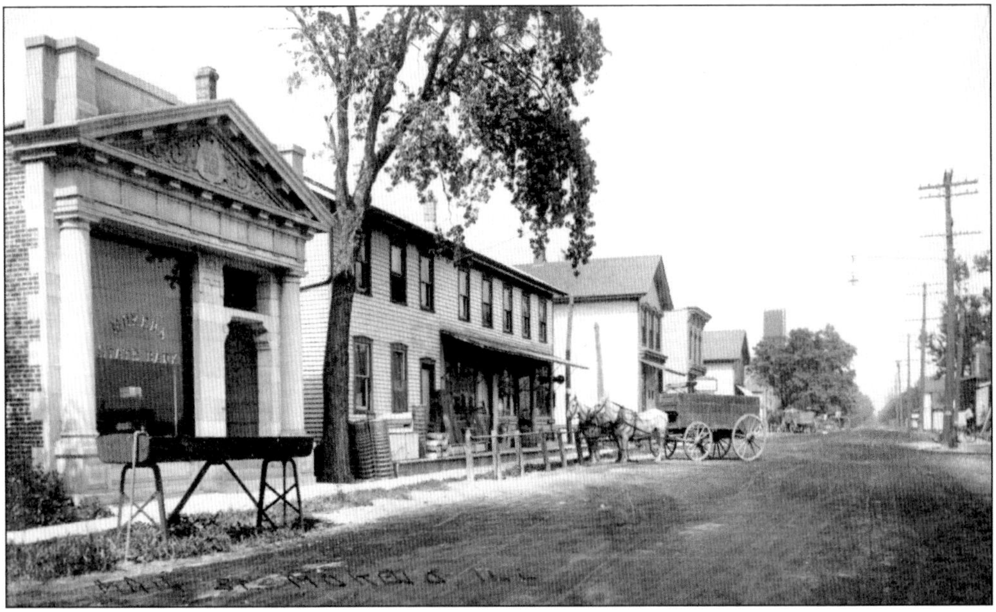

The arrival of the Rock Island Railroad in 1852 led to the plotting of the village of Mokena that year by Allen Denny. The original plot included 13 lots on what is now Front Street from present-day Wolf Road to Mokena Street and 6 lots from Mokena Street to Division Street. The postcard photograph above shows Front Street looking northeast. The two prominent buildings located on the left are the Mokena State Bank and the Old Exchange Hotel, which later became home to the Kolber Hardware Store. The electric lines and overhead streetlights running down the south side of the street were added in 1913. Notice the water trough that was set up in front of the bank for horses along Front Street. The postcard below shows a similar view of Front Street. Notice the train depot just to the right of the photograph.

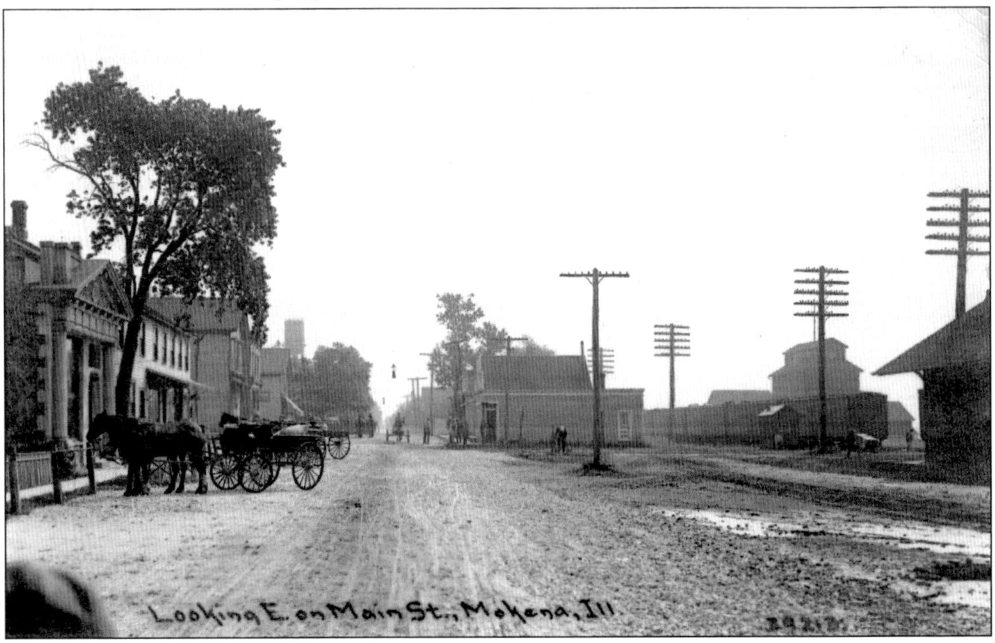

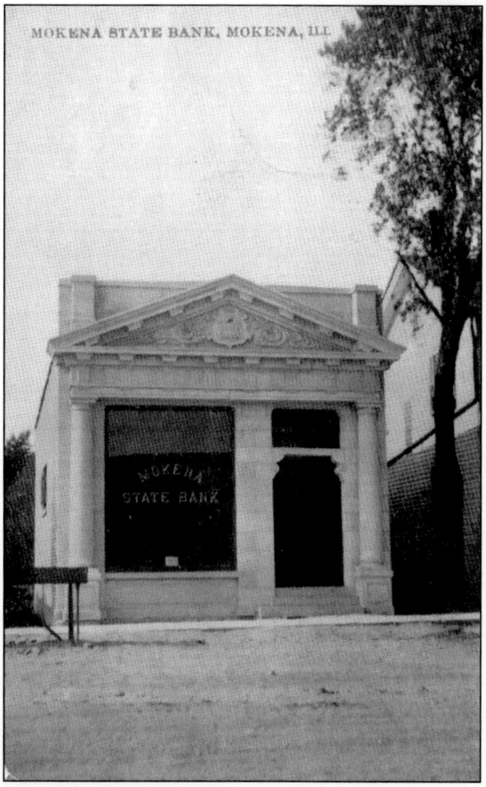

The Mokena State Bank, located on Front Street, was organized in 1909 with a capital stock of $25,000. Before the state bank was organized, a few local merchants served the community as bankers. Four robberies, in 1912, 1924, 1934 and 1956, are part of the bank's history. It continues to operate in the community today as the State Bank of Illinois. The postcard photograph to the right, showing the white Bedford stone facade, was taken shortly after the bank's construction. Notice on the left the water trough that was set up in front of the bank for horses along Front Street. The photograph below, taken in the 1920s, shows a view of Front Street looking east, and an old car is parked in front of the bank.

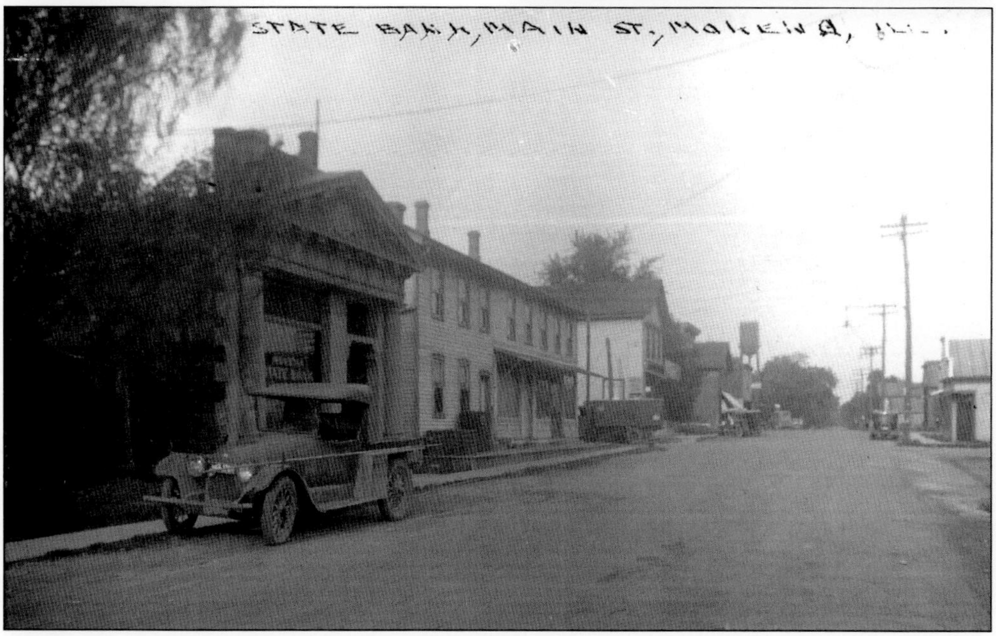

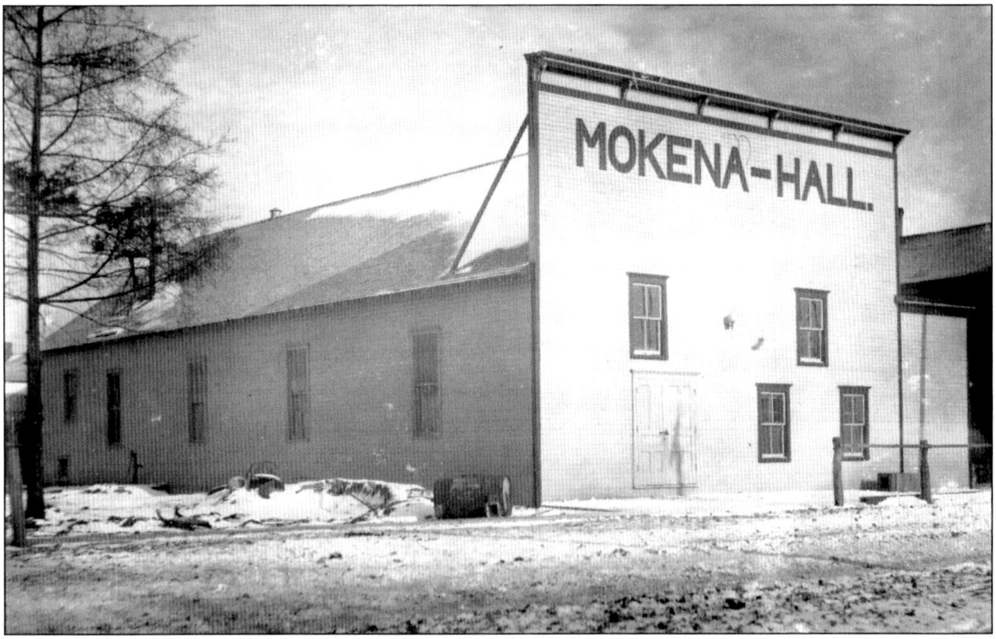

Constructed in the early 20th century, the Mokena Hall was a building that was used by residents as a meeting hall for church gatherings, dinners, banquets, and early Hollywood movies. Located on the north side of Front Street just east of Mokena Street, the building and land eventually became home to the Cooper and Hostert Ford dealership from 1920 until the late 1970s.

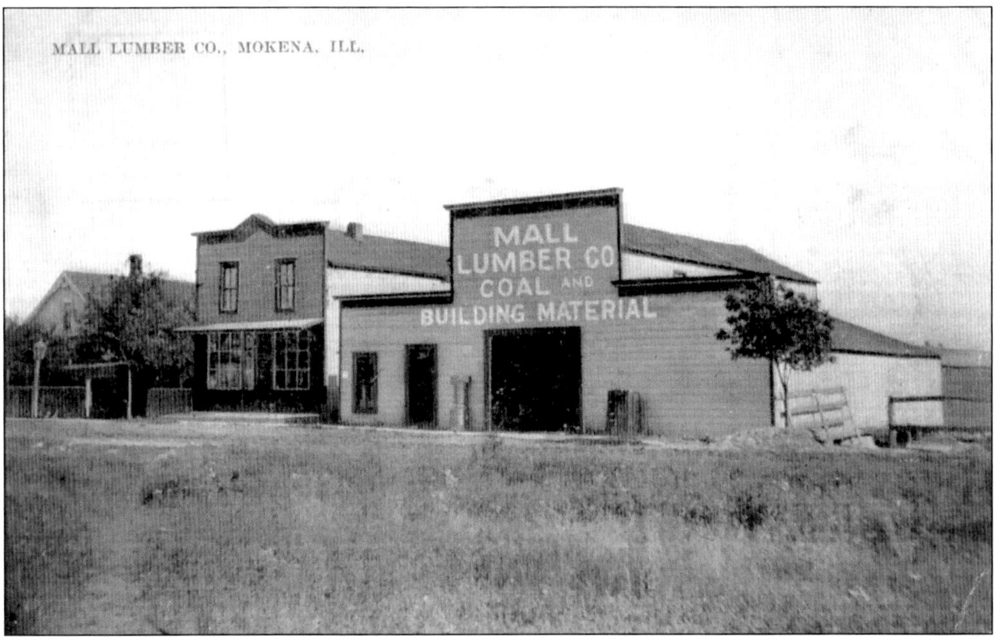

Located south of the Rock Island Railroad tracks on McGovney Street between Wolf Road and Hacker Street, Mall Lumber Company was an important material supply company in the village. Originally known as Hacker Lumber, the company changed hands in the early 1920s, and Harry Mall became the owner. Mall was the mayor of Mokena from 1929 to 1931 and again from 1937 to 1945. Mall Lumber continued to operate until around 1950.

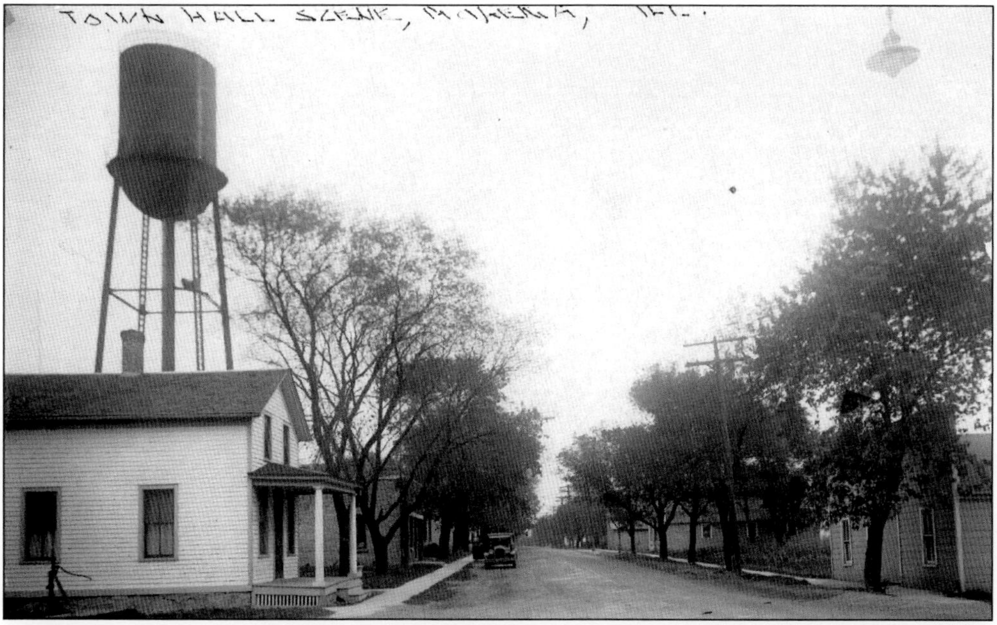

In 1898, the village fathers of Mokena hired the Chicago Bridge and Iron Company to construct a modern, iron water tower at a cost of $3,100. The tank had a capacity of 60,000 gallons. It served as the village's only source of water until a 500,000-gallon tank was completed in 1980. This picture postcard looking east on Front Street from Division Street shows the old water tower just east of the town hall building.

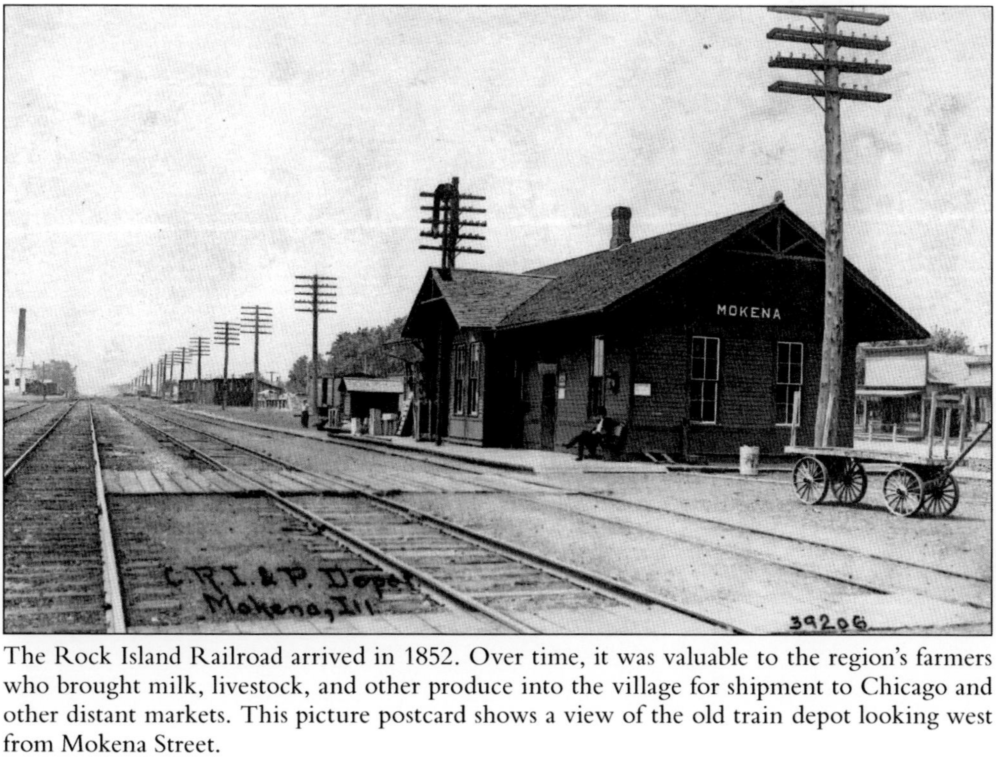

The Rock Island Railroad arrived in 1852. Over time, it was valuable to the region's farmers who brought milk, livestock, and other produce into the village for shipment to Chicago and other distant markets. This picture postcard shows a view of the old train depot looking west from Mokena Street.

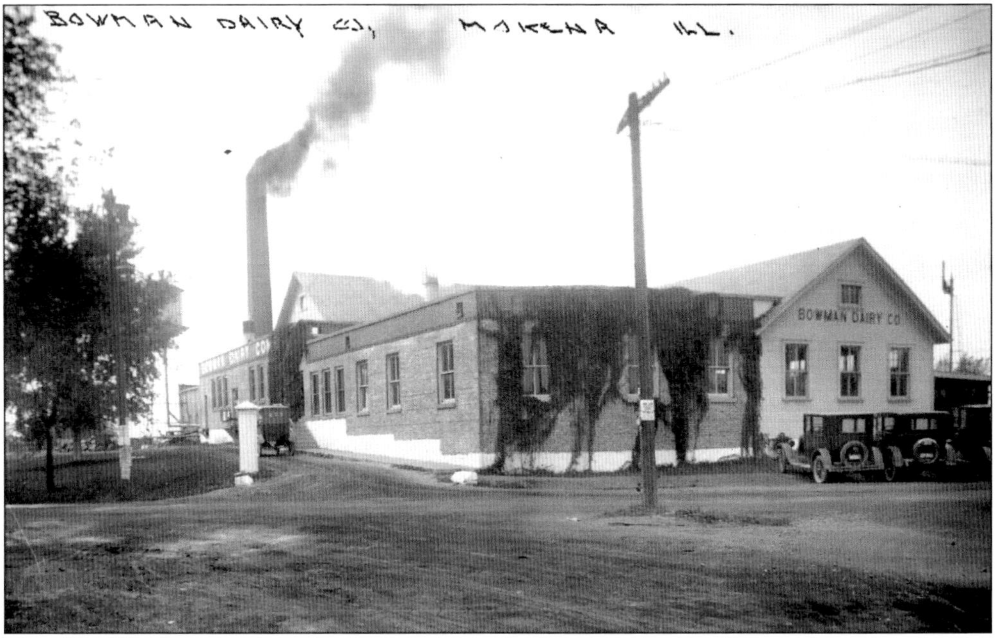

In 1885, J. R. Bowman entered the Chicago dairy market by purchasing the milk business of M. A. Devine. Six years later, he sold his St. Louis operation and moved to Chicago, where he formed the Bowman Dairy Company. Over the years, the Bowman company expanded its markets outside Chicago and built large bottling plants on the south side of the city. One such plant was built on Wolf Road adjacent to the Rock Island Railroad tracks in Mokena. The plant existed for a number of years and was eventually converted into a brewery and wallpaper mill. In February 2004, the old factory building was razed, clearing the way for a retail and residential center. Bowman continued to flourish as a large business until 1966, when it was purchased by a local rival, the Dean Foods Company.

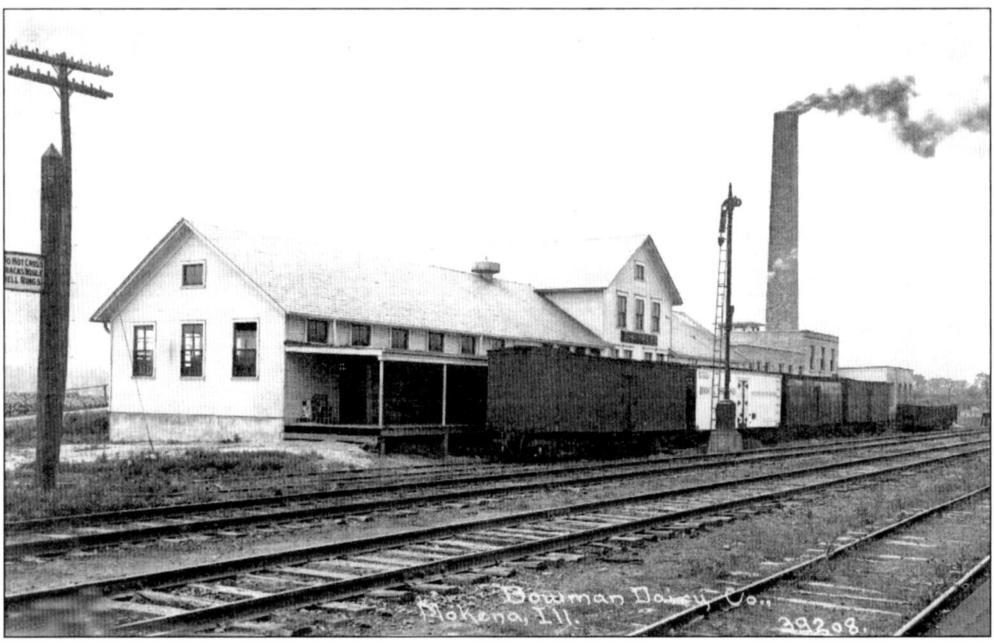

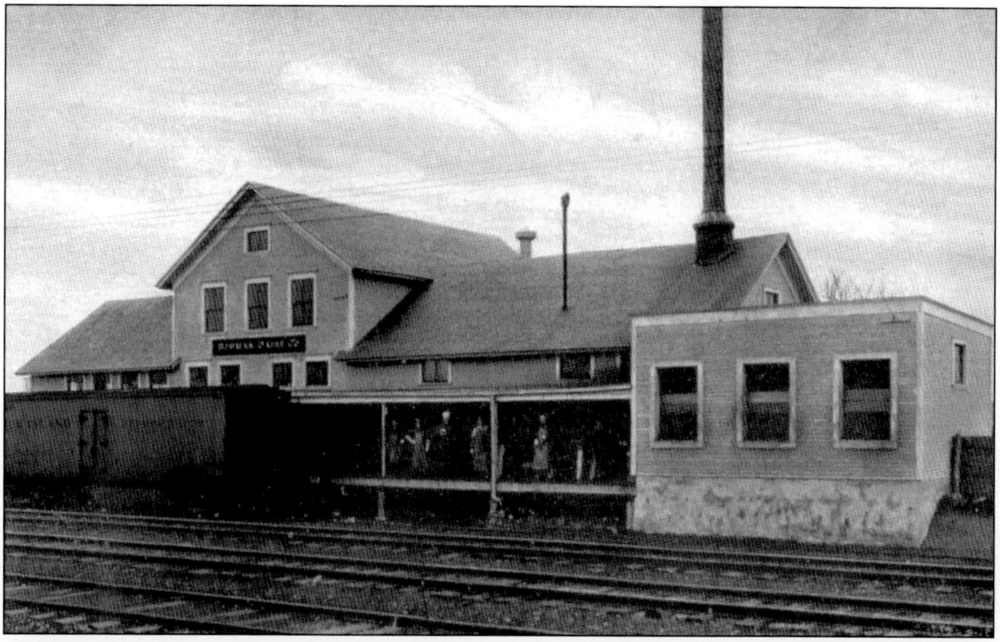

The Bowman Dairy Company, once an employer of over 3,000 Chicago residents and a leading supplier of dairy products in the Chicago area, was also one of Mokena's more flourishing enterprises. Located on Wolf Road adjacent to the Rock Island Railroad tracks, the bottling plant became an important operation in the area for many years. The photograph above shows the dairy plant looking south across the Rock Island tracks. Plant workers are standing on the loading dock, and a refrigerated railroad car is to the left. In the postcard below, workers are lined up between two freight cars for a picture along the dock platform. Notice the wooden Bowman Dairy Company crates stacked up behind the men.

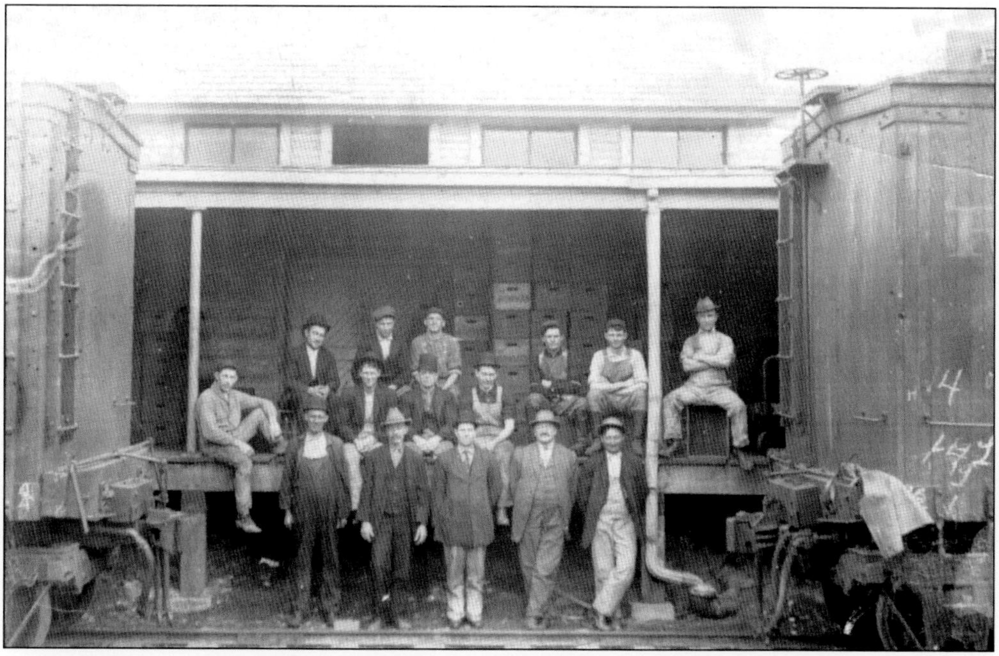

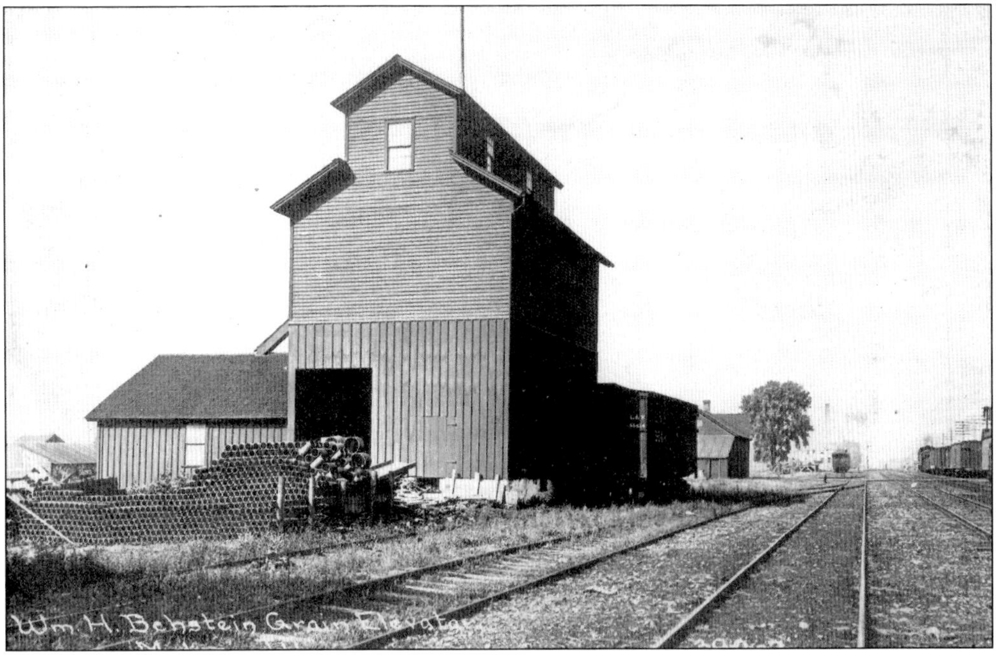

The grain elevator system became an important part of Chicago's growth in the 19th century. As the railroads expanded throughout the Midwest, farmers were able to get their crops from the prairies to the marketplace more quickly and efficiently. To tap into the Chicago market, a large grain elevator was constructed along the south side of the Rock Island Railroad tracks just east of Mokena Street.

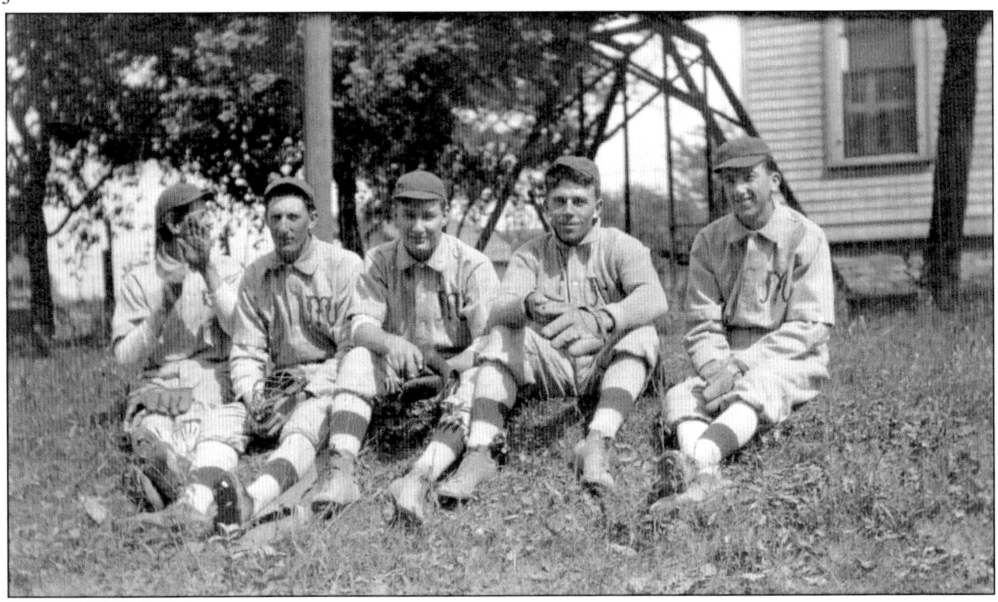

The sport that evokes more nostalgia among Americans than any other is baseball. In the early 20th century, numerous towns and rural communities across the country had baseball teams. This picture postcard, taken in 1911 in front of the Erickson-Benson farm, shows one such team from Mokena. From left to right are Lawrence Kohl, Charles Erickson, Andrew Schribiech, George Marti, and Christy Sippel.

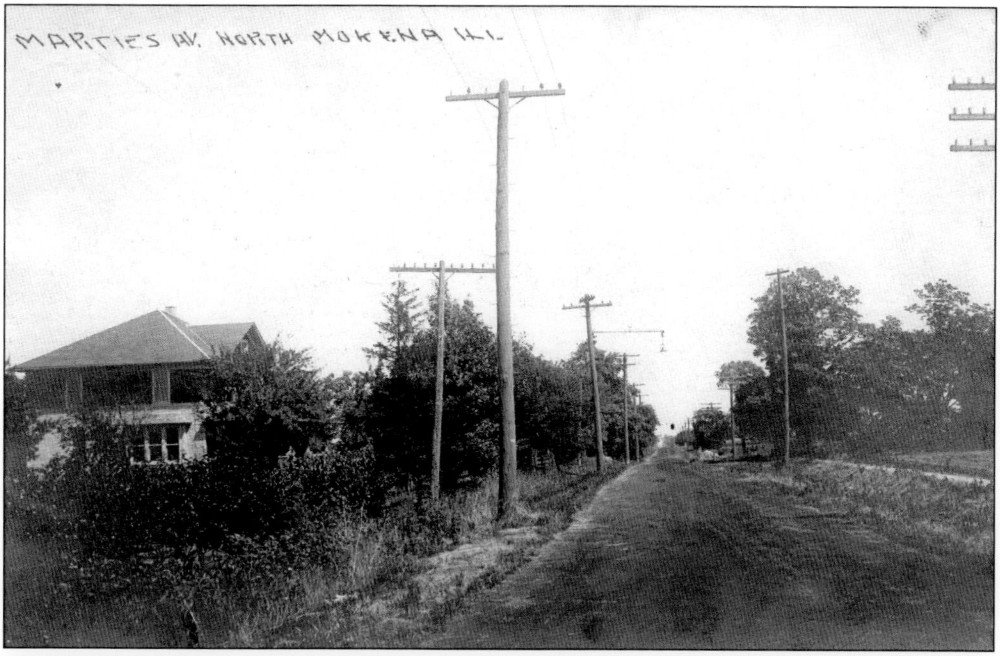

The arrival of the Rock Island Railroad led the village to become a major commercial center of the area, as farmers brought their grain to town and purchased supplies from local businesses. For many years Wolf Road was known as Marti Avenue and in 1930 was the first paved road in the village. This postcard photograph shows a view of Marti Avenue looking north.

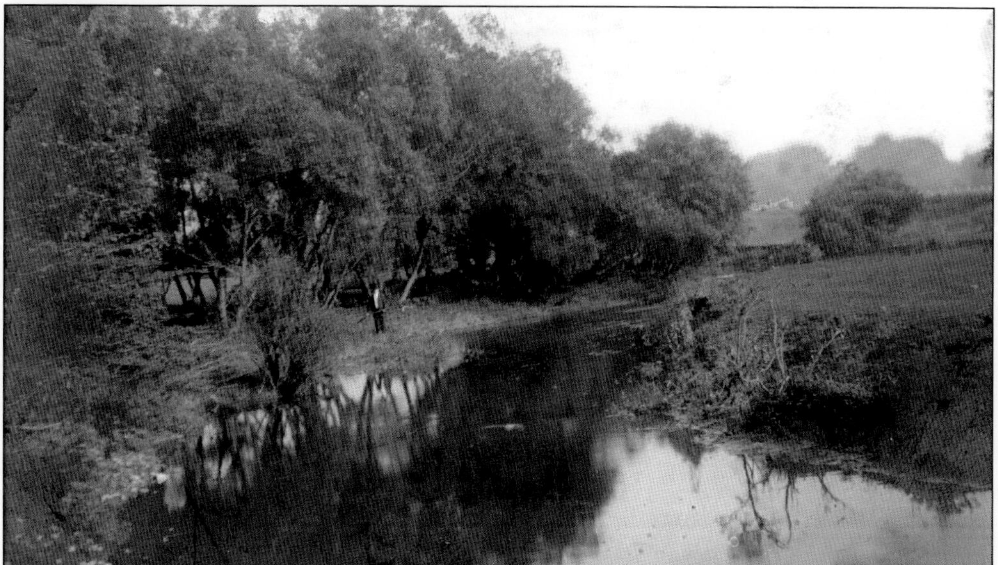

Hickory Creek has been recognized by many scientists as the gem of the Des Plaines River system. Hickory Creek flows southwest for nearly 21 miles, feeding into the Des Plaines River at Joliet. Following Route 30 much of the way, the creek flows through many southern communities, including Mokena, Frankfort, New Lenox, and Joliet. This postcard photograph from the early 20th century shows a section of Hickory Creek that flows just south of the old village of Mokena.

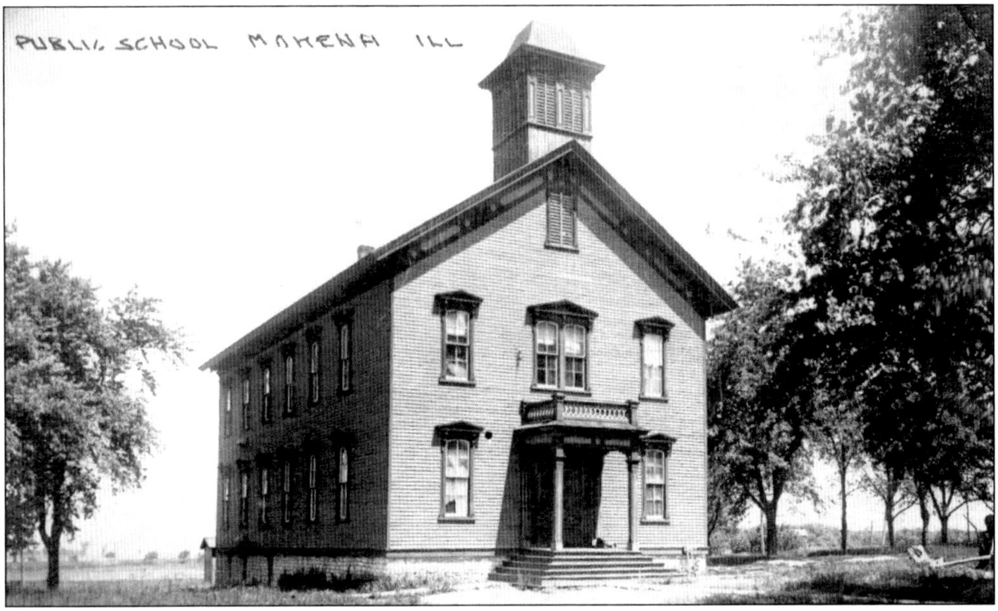

Mokena's first schoolhouse was a small frame building constructed in 1855 and was located on a village-owned section near the corner of Second and Union Streets. In 1872, a new two-story wood-frame building with a stone basement was constructed on the northwest corner of Front Street and Schoolhouse Road. The school grounds extended from Front Street on the south to First Street on the north. The school, shown in the above postcard photograph, served the needs of the village until the new Carpenter Street School was completed in 1929. Located at the corner of Carpenter and Division Streets, the Carpenter Street School shown in the postcard below operated until 1978 and now houses Mokena Village Hall.

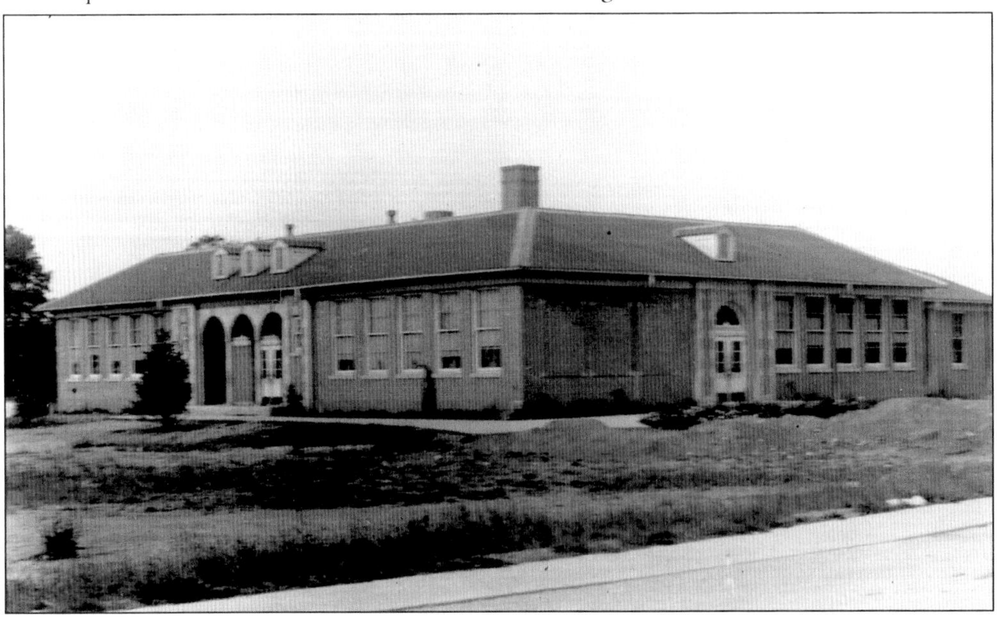

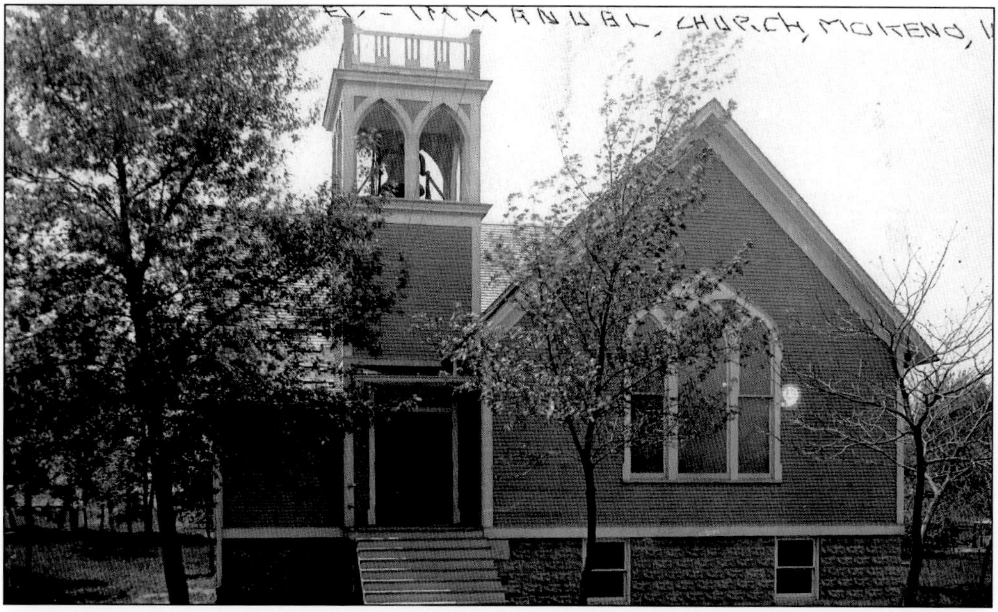

On November 4, 1850, the German Evangelical Lutheran Congregation was organized with 15 men listed as charter members. Johann George Geuther gave 20 acres of land near Eighty-eighth Avenue and St. Francis Road, and a small, wooden church was built. In 1915, the congregation decided to build a new church in the town of Mokena. This new church was located at Union and Cross Streets and served the congregation for nearly 50 years, when a new church was built on LaPorte Road and dedicated in 1966. From 1967 to 1978, the old church was used by the village of Mokena as a public library. After the library moved to a new building on 195th Street, the old church served as a civic center. The photograph above shows a view of the 1916 church. The photograph below is the LaPorte Road church. Today the congregation is called the Immanuel Evangelical Lutheran Church.

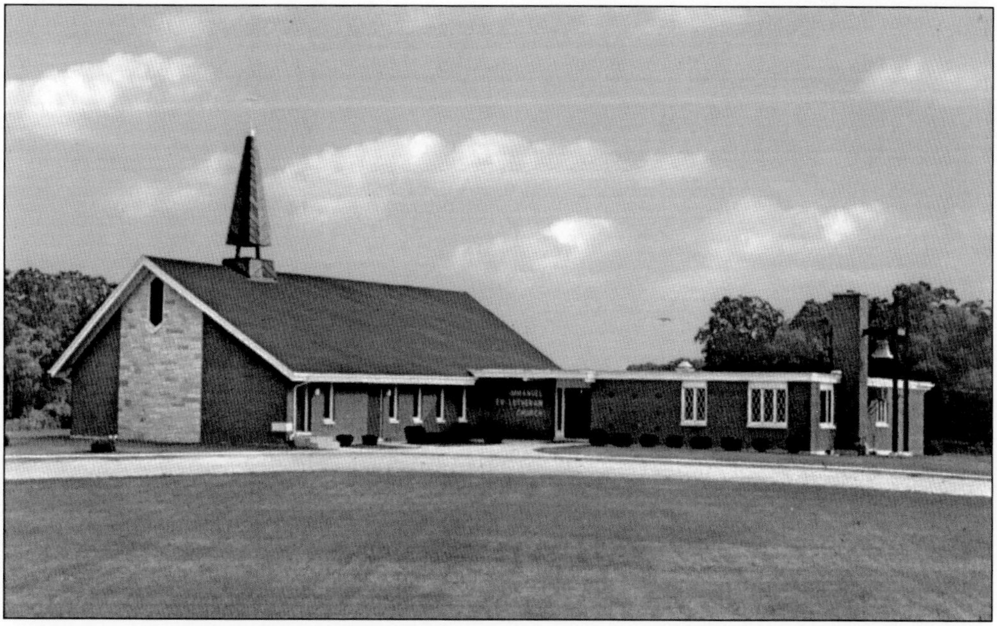

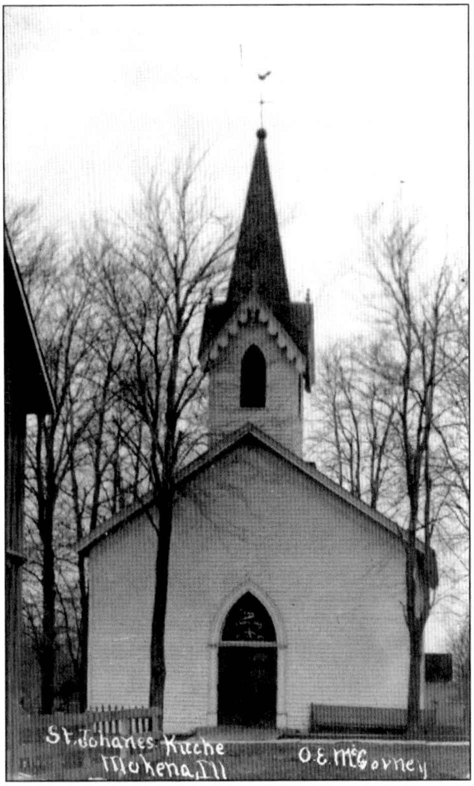

Settlers from Germany, Switzerland, England, and Sweden came to the Mokena area in the early 1830s. In the beginning, itinerant preachers held services in homes or in the schoolhouse. Rev. William Meyer became the first resident minister in January 1862. In March of the same year, 30 families formed St. John's German United Evangelical Church of Mokena. During the next six months, the first church was constructed and was dedicated on September 20, 1862. As the congregation grew, the old church became too small, and a new church was constructed and dedicated on April 16, 1923. The postcard photograph to the left shows the original church, and the postcard below shows a view of the second church, which today bears the name of St. John's United Church of Christ.

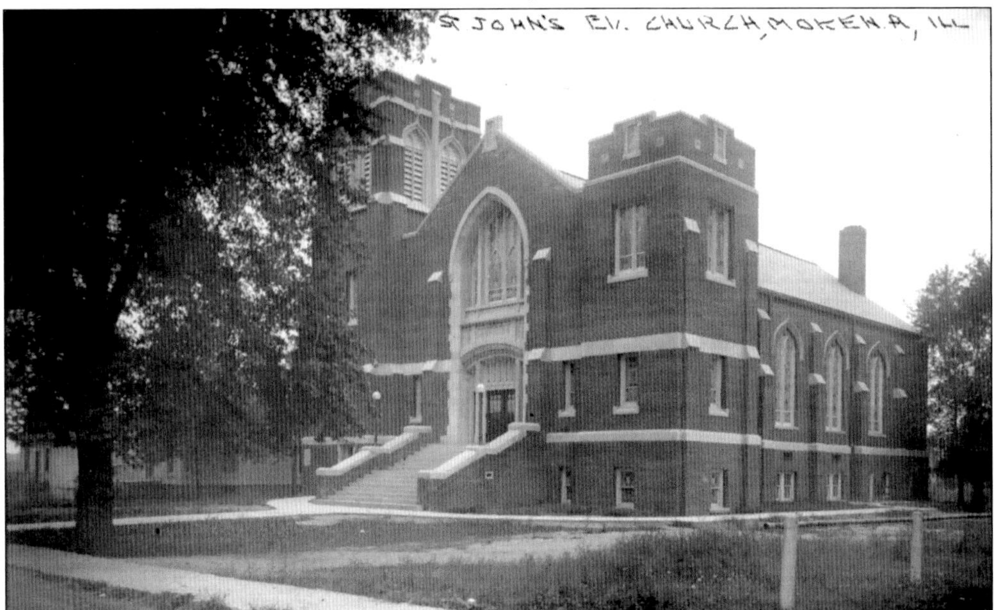

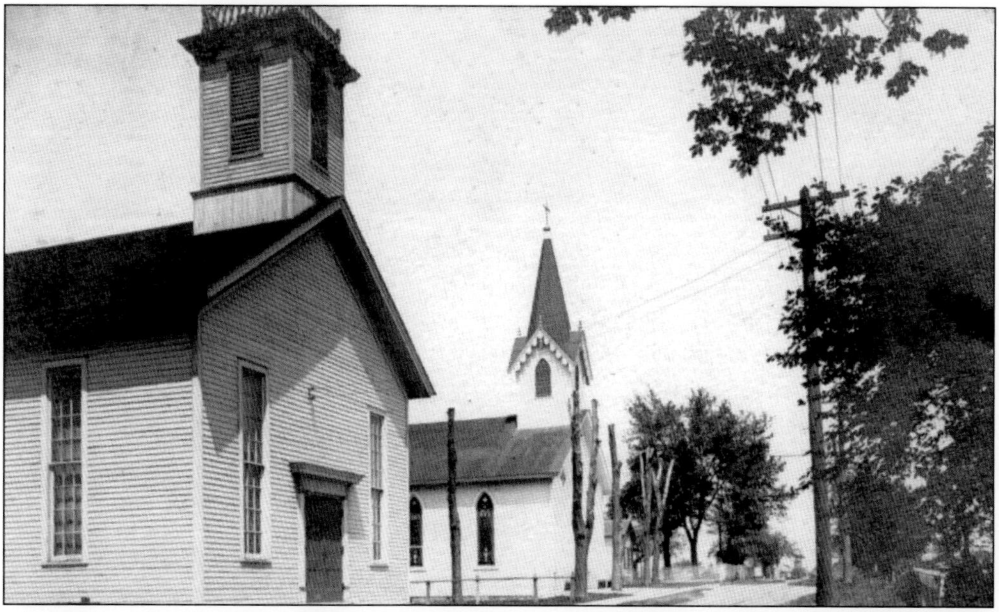

This picture postcard shows a view of two early churches in Mokena. In the foreground is the old Methodist church, which dates back to 1867. In 1954, the church was remodeled with a second floor and a beautiful new chapel to the east end. The church in the background is St. John's German United Evangelical Church, which was dedicated on September 20, 1862. This church was used until 1921, when the congregation needed a larger facility, and a new building was constructed on Second Street.

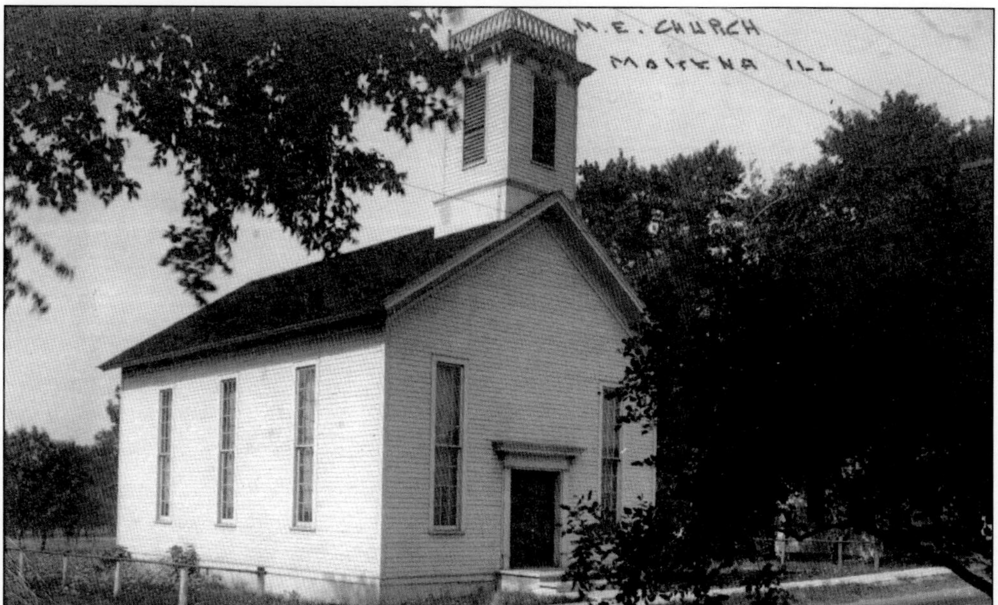

The Methodist church building dates from 1867 and is one of the oldest buildings in the village. The congregation was formed in 1867 with a suitable building dedicated in December of that year. For many years, the Baptists' congregation shared the facility on alternate Sundays. In 1954, the church was remodeled.

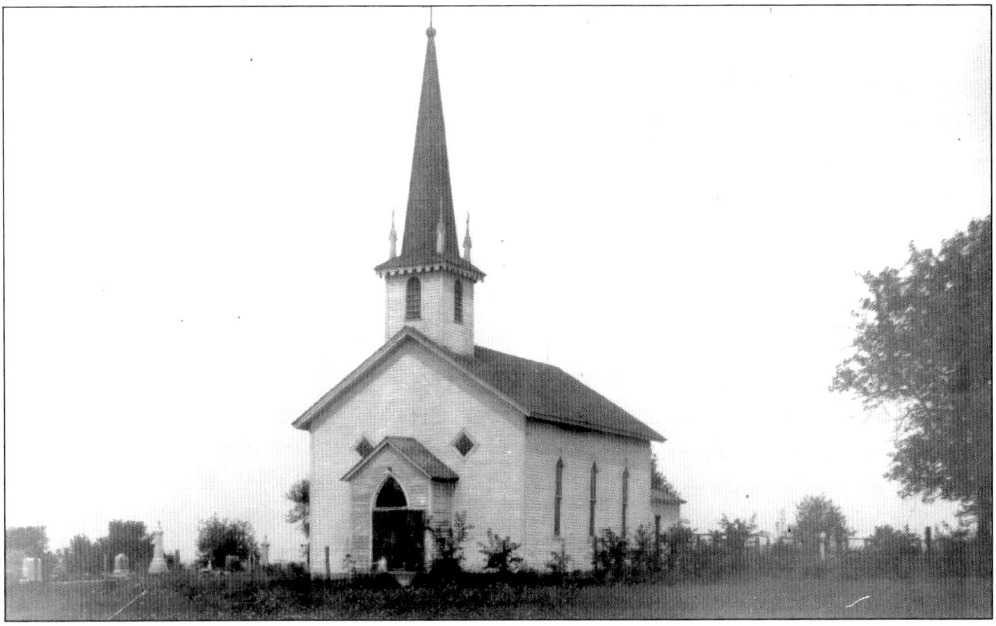

Mathias and Margaret Summers Ender, early pioneers who emigrated from Germany, donated land to help build a new parish. In 1860, the Enders deeded land to the diocese, and it was on this land that the old Catholic church was erected. The parish was begun in 1864 with Rev. Peter Fassbender as its first pastor. It was known as St. Mary's German Catholic Church and was nestled in St. Mary Cemetery just east of Wolf Road at 195th Street. Built in 1864 at a cost of $1,400, this white clapboard building with its tall steeple serves as a reminder of the rich history of the community. A parish hall was added in 1926, and in 1949, it was converted to a parochial school. In 1955, a new brick structure was built on 195th Street with a convent and a garage added in 1961 and 1962, respectively.

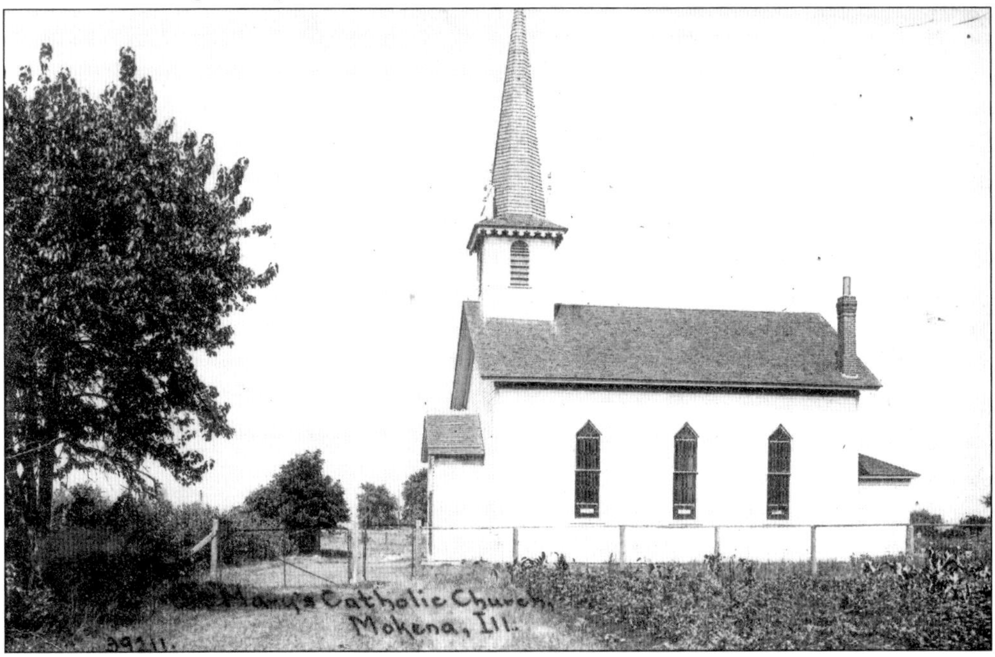

Seven

Channahon, Elwood, and Manhattan

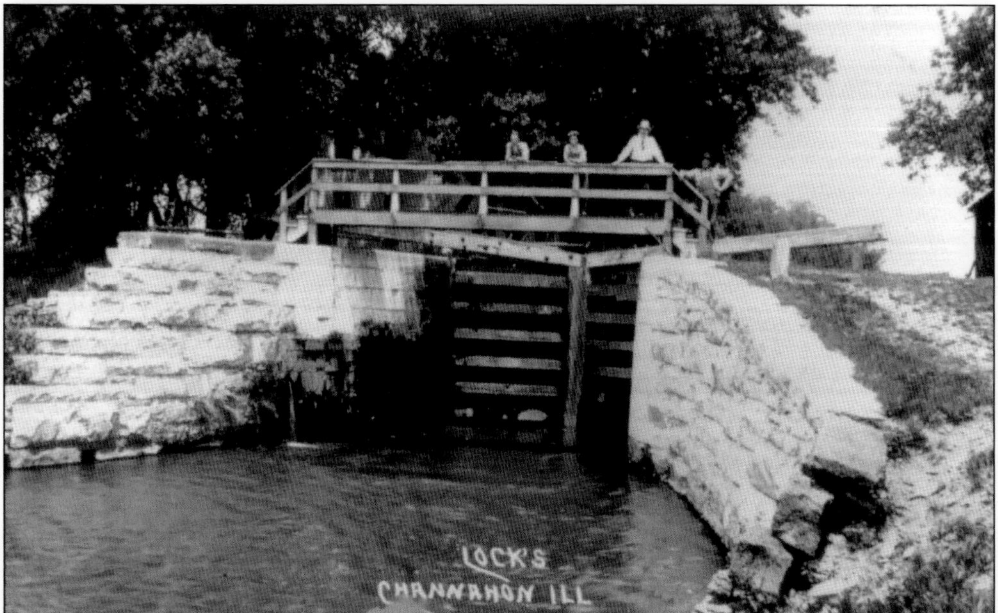

The growth of Will County can be directly traced to the building of the Illinois and Michigan Canal. Completed in 1848 and nearly 100 miles long, the canal was the final link in a national plan to connect different regions of North America via waterways. In this postcard, three people can be seen standing on the footbridge of lock No. 6 in Channahon.

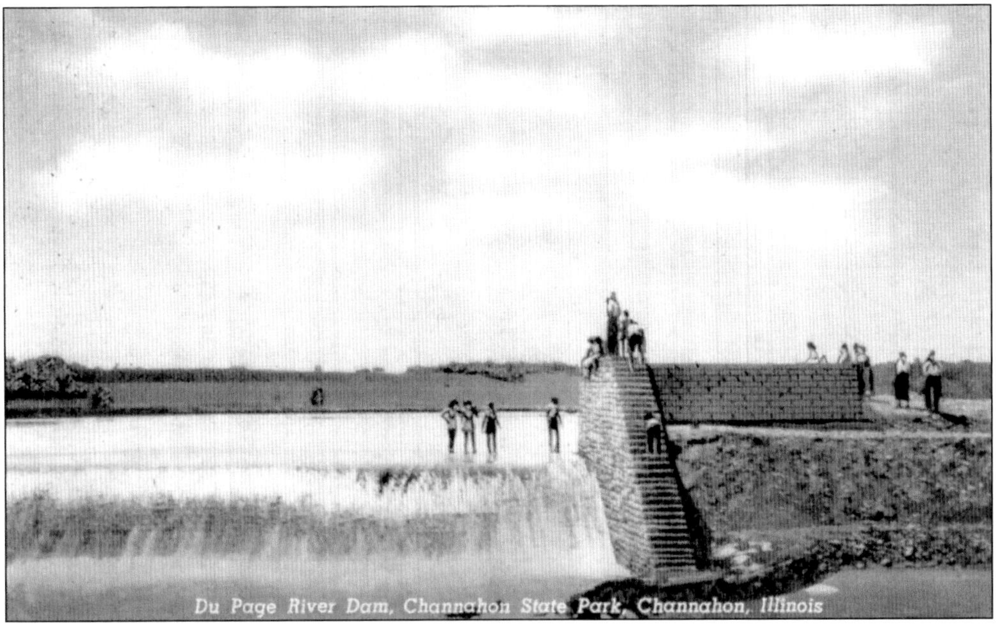

The Channahon Access first became a state park in 1932, known then as the Channahon State Park. This photograph postcard from the 1930s shows the DuPage River dam at Channahon State Park. The dam is located between lock No. 6 and lock No. 7 on the canal, and people of all ages today enjoy fishing the river and canal for bass, crappie, bluegill, catfish, and bullhead.

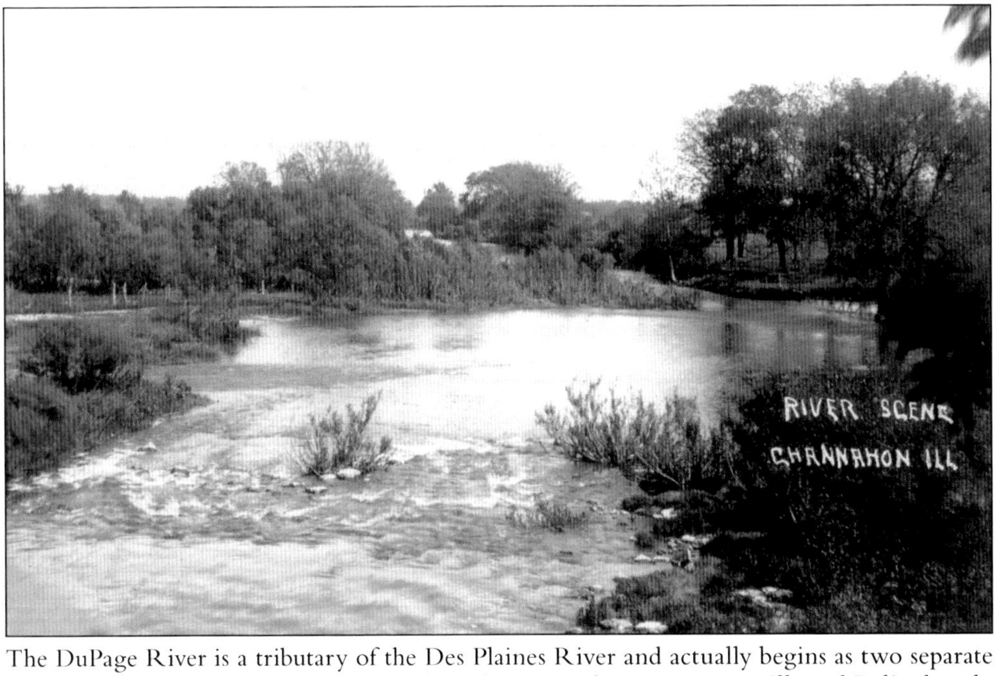

The DuPage River is a tributary of the Des Plaines River and actually begins as two separate streams. The west branch meets the east branch at a spot between Naperville and Bolingbrook. The combined DuPage River continues south from there through Plainfield, Joliet, Minooka, and Channahon before finally meeting the Des Plaines River. This postcard shows a photograph of the DuPage River in Channahon.

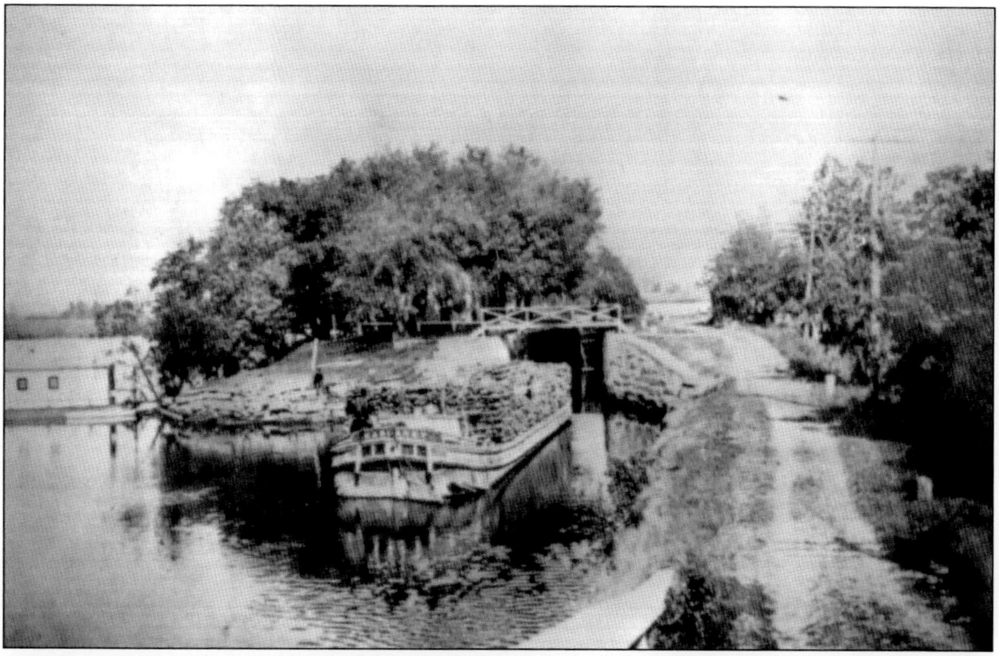

Lockport, Joliet, and Channahon were three towns that prospered in the 19th century because of the transportation network tying Will County with Chicago and the East Coast markets. Construction on the canal began in 1936, and the nearly 100-mile-long canal was completed 12 years later in 1948. This postcard photograph shows a view looking north toward lock No. 6.

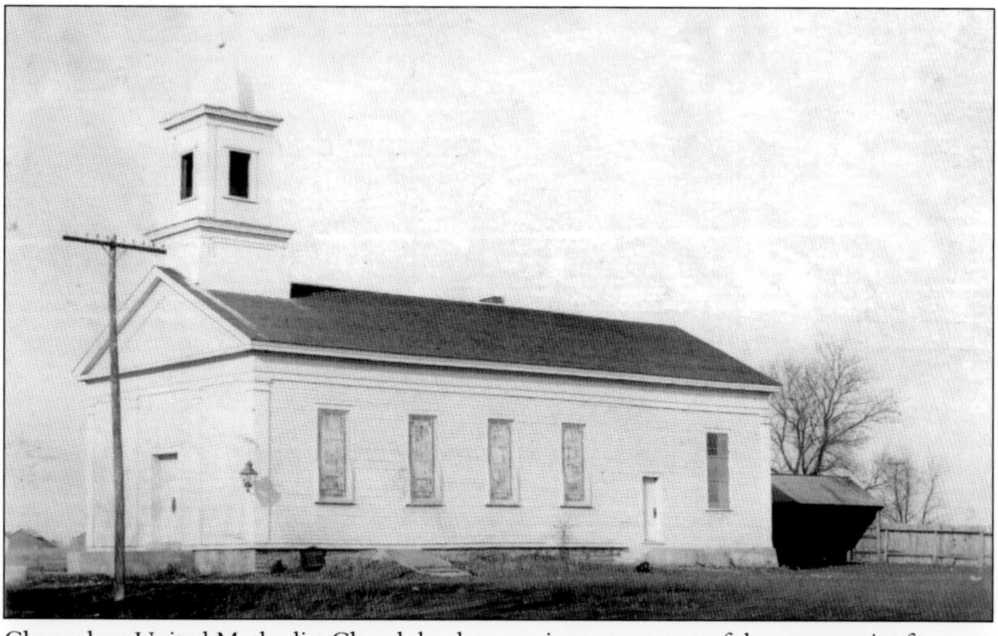

Channahon United Methodist Church has been an important part of the community for more than 100 years. In 1854, a wood-frame structure was built on the corner of West Eames Street (Route 6) and Sage Street. In December 1856, funds were raised for the purchase and installation of a new church bell. In 1875, an addition was put on the east end of the church for social functions. On March 19, 1926, the old church was struck by lightning and burned to the ground.

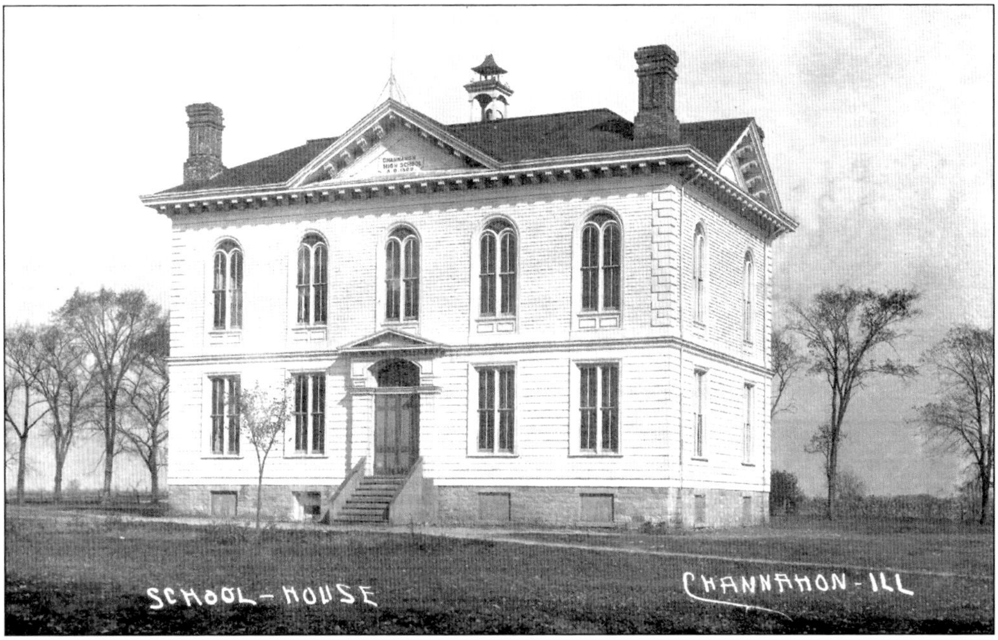

Six years before the village of Channahon was first laid out by Myrvin Benjamin in 1845, the first schoolhouse was built in the area. In 1869, an elegant and substantial two-story white frame building was erected on the southeast corner of Tyron Street and West Eames Street (Route 6). The school offered a primary and secondary school education. The two-story building, pictured in the above postcard photograph, burned in 1922. It was replaced in 1923 by a modest brick structure on the same corner shown in the postcard below. Channahon High School classes were discontinued in the building in 1947, when they were consolidated into Minooka Community High School. Today Pioneer Path School operates from the old building and serves the educational needs of students in preschool, kindergarten, and first grade.

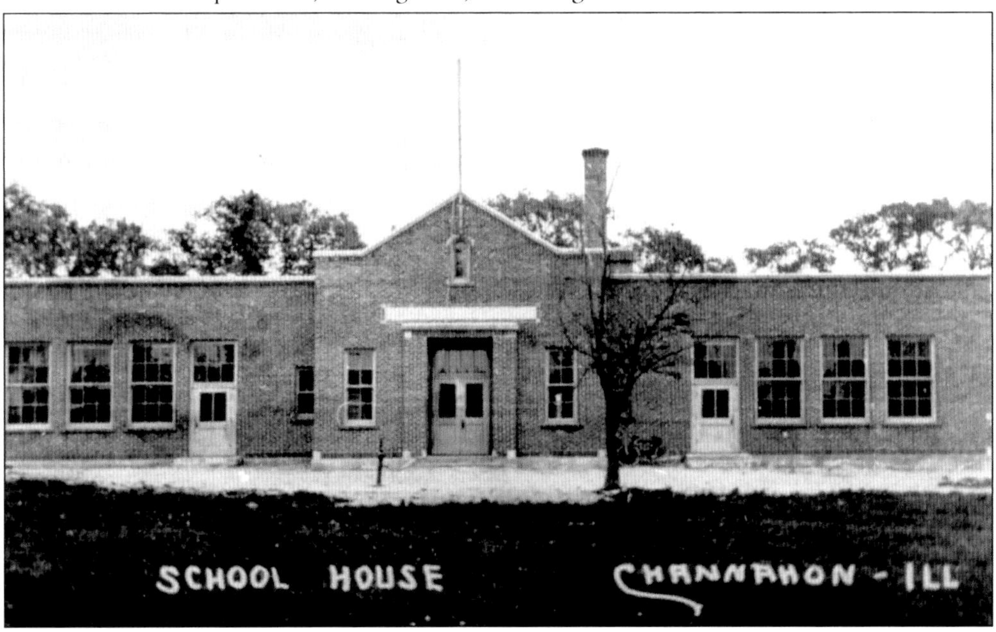

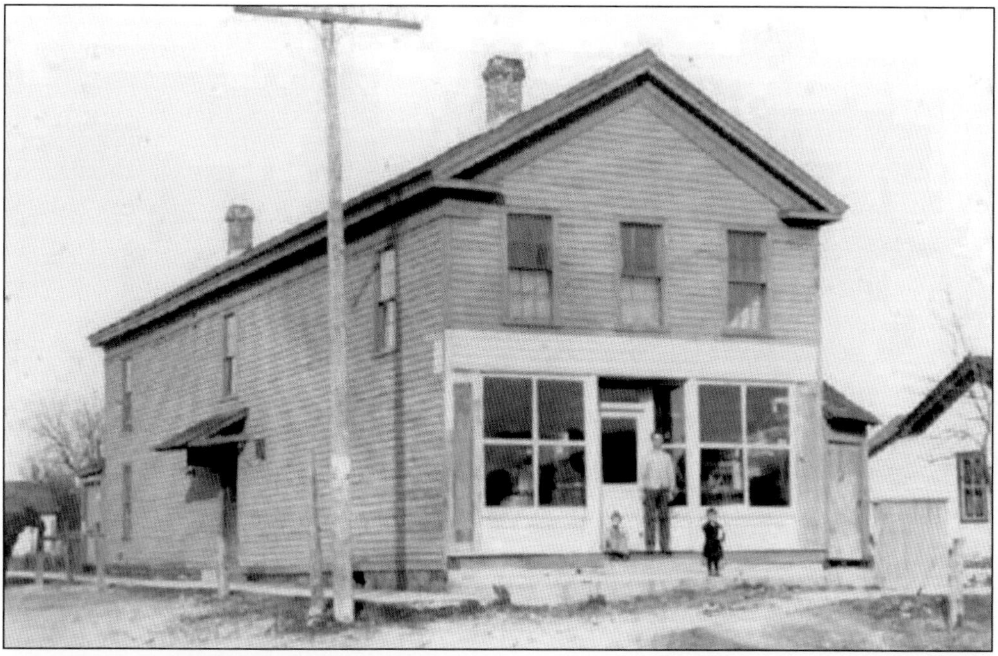

The village of Channahon was laid out in 1845 and called DuPage after the river that flowed through the area. When the village was organized, there were several thriving businesses, including four mercantile stores, two blacksmith shops, a wagon shop, a hardware store, two saloons, a hotel, and a grocery store, among others. The grocery store, located on the northeast corner of Canal and Bridge Streets, was known as Hulbert's General Store and was run by three generations of Hulberts. Shown in the above postcard, the Hulbert's General Store also housed the Channahon Post Office for many years. The postcard below shows the Masonic hall, which was located next door to Conroy's Tavern on the southeast corner of Fryer and Jessup Streets.

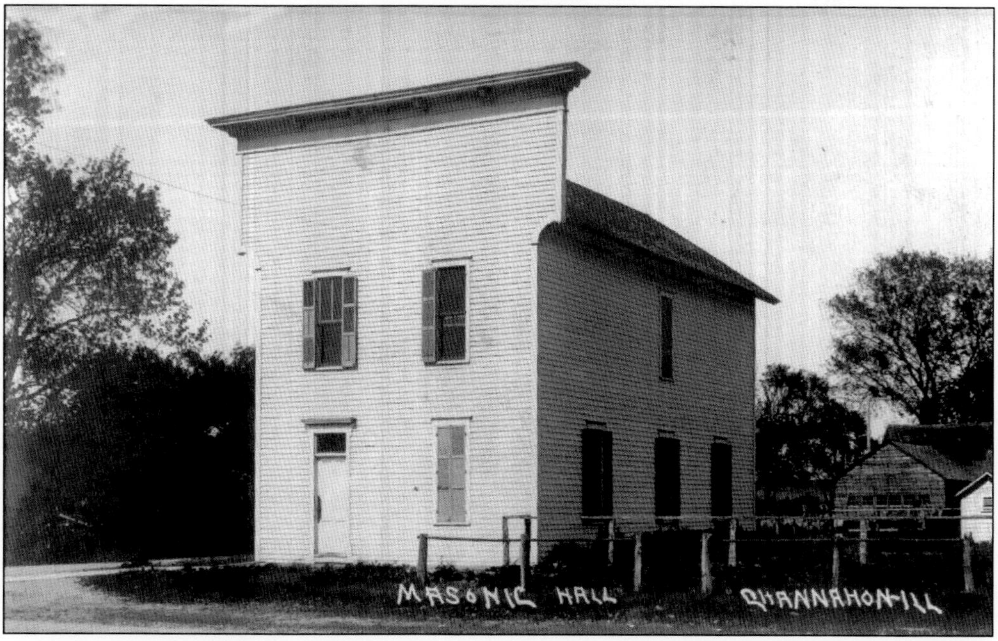

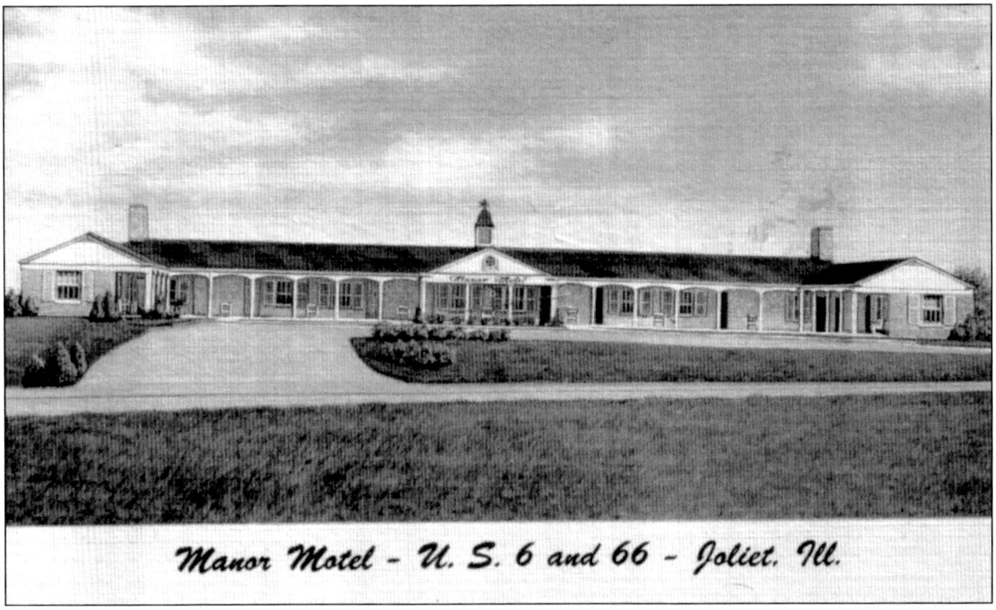

In 1940, Route 66 was realigned to pass through Plainfield and Channahon and bypass downtown Joliet. Located along the new Route 66 alignment in Channahon, the Manor Motel, built in the 1950s, offered the Mother Road traveler a nice place to spend the night. This linen-era postcard offers a panoramic photograph of the motel complex looking east from old Route 66.

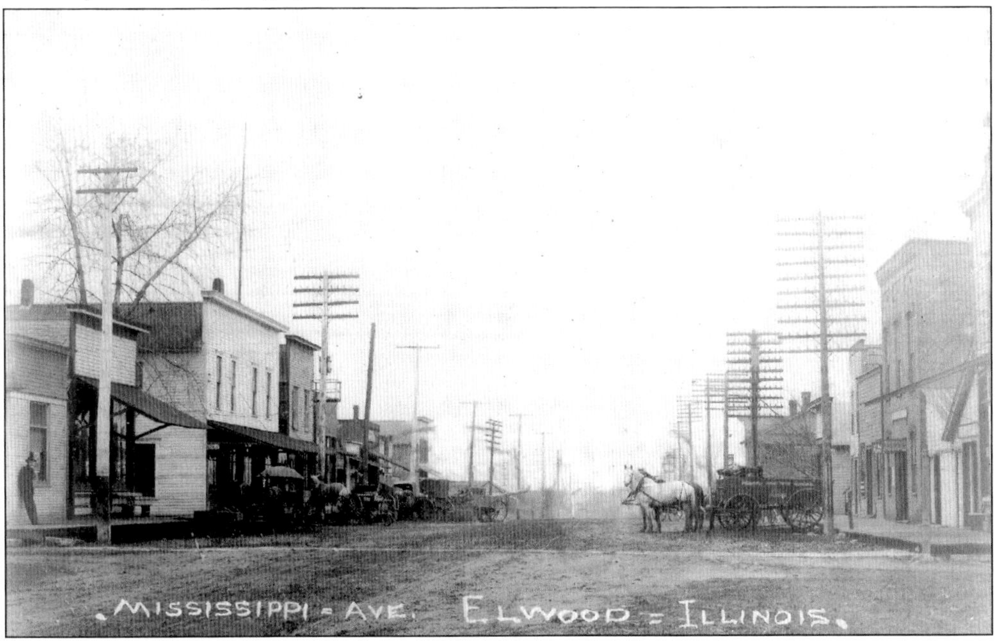

This postcard photograph from about 1909 shows a view of Mississippi Avenue looking east near Wood Street. On the south side of the street near the Alton station, the Rookery building, a confectionery store that was a favorite with children, can be seen. Across the street on the north side of the block are the wood-frame buildings that housed Richard Swan's Pool Hall, the confectionery and ice-cream parlor, Garland Blatt's Grocery Store, and, at the end of the block, John Larson's Grocery Store.

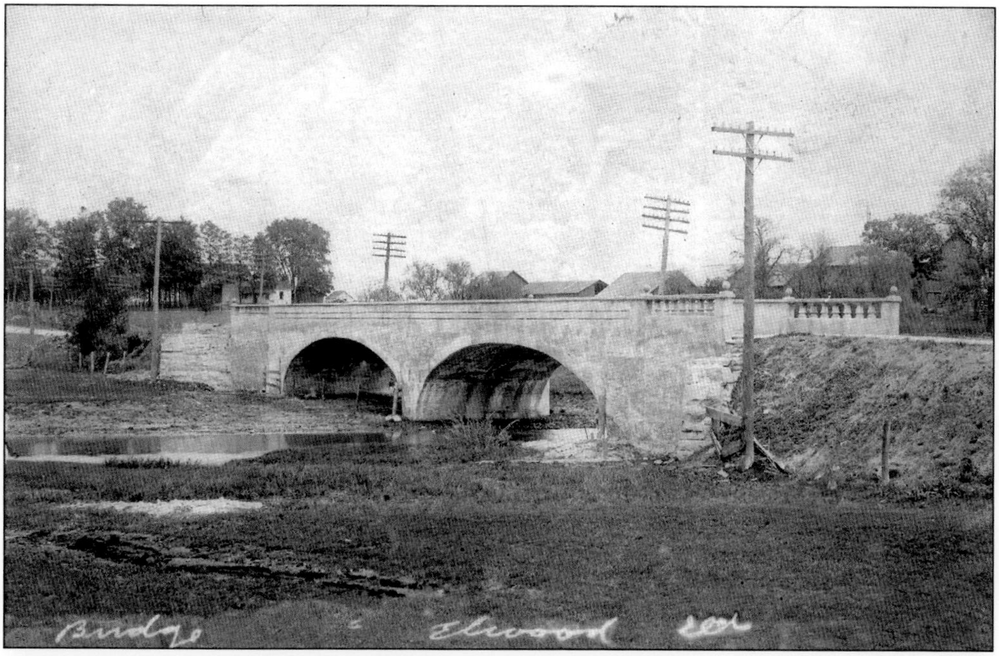

Jackson Creek is one of the largest tributaries to the Des Plaines River, covering nearly 55 square miles within Will County. Four communities reside partially or fully within the watershed, including New Lenox, Frankfort, Manhattan, and Elwood. This postcard photograph shows the old arch bridge on old Route 66 that crosses Jackson Creek in Elwood.

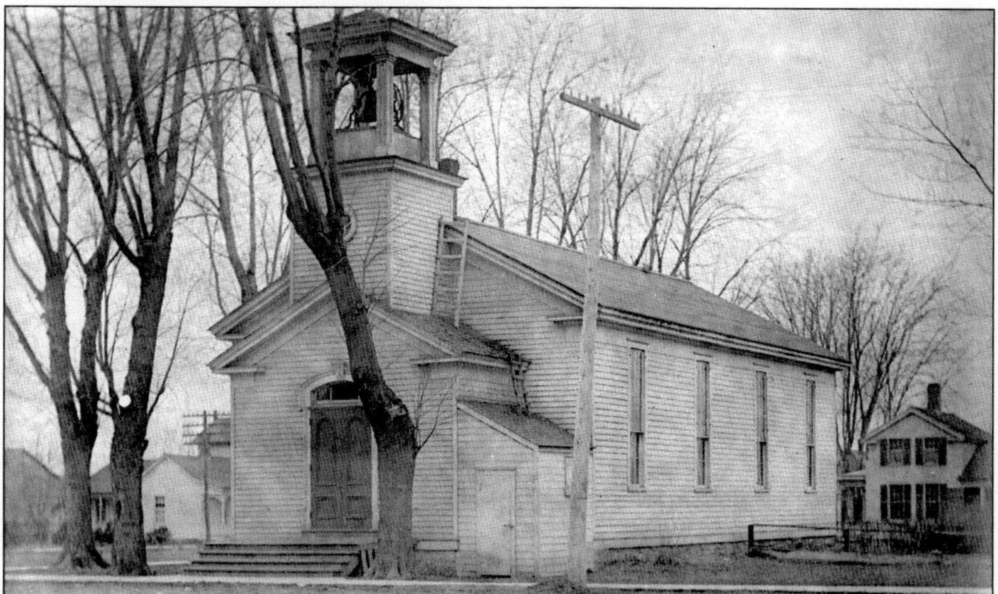

In 1852, the first Methodist church was built in a grove just west of the village of Elwood. By 1909, it was decided to replace the old church, and the cornerstone of the new building was laid on Sunday, September 12, 1909. On December 18, 1921, the Methodist church was completely destroyed by fire. This picture postcard shows the 1910 church located on the northwest corner of Chicago and Mississippi Streets.

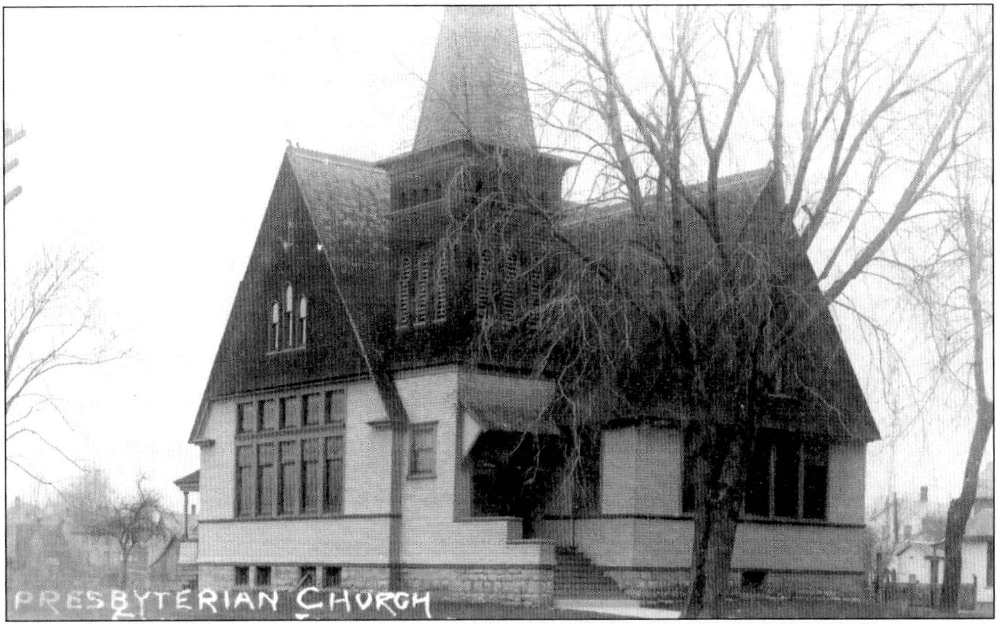

When the Presbyterians organized and first met, they used the old Baptist church for meetings until it was decided to construct their own parish. In 1895, construction of a new church, shown in this picture postcard, began on the northwest corner of Gardner Street and Chicago Avenue, and the building was dedicated in January 1896. Because of declining membership, the Presbyterian congregation merged with the Methodist church in 1965 to form the Elwood Community Church.

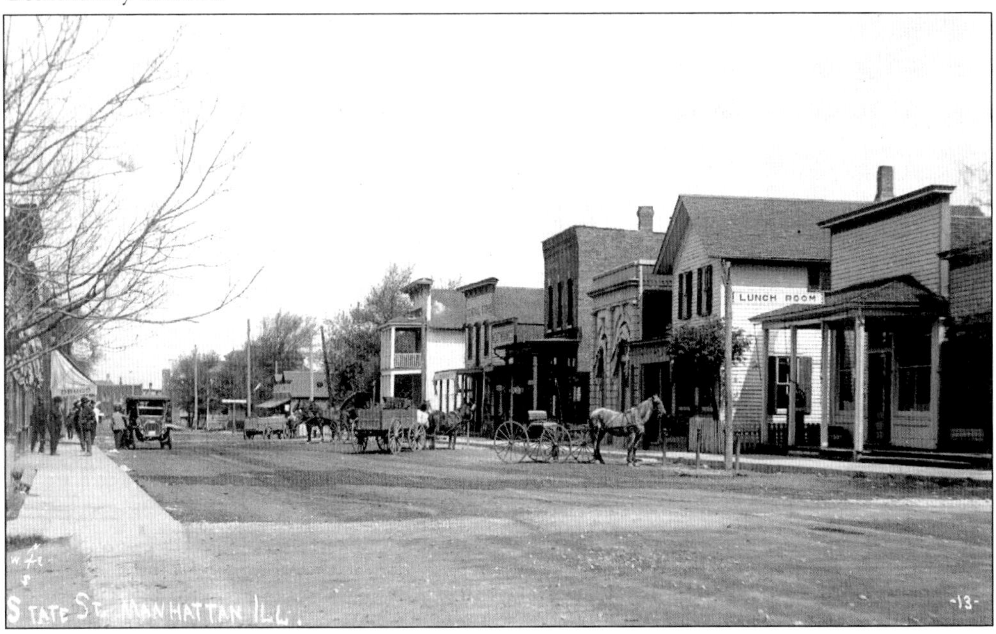

This postcard photograph shows a view of State Street in Manhattan looking north from First Street. Businesses located on the east side of the block, from right to left, include Fry and Hagen General Store, Fritz Gallinger Harness Shop, Citizen's Bank, Fehr and Smalley Hardware, A. H. Goodwin General Store and Meat Market, and the Vanderberg's Hotel and Boarding House.

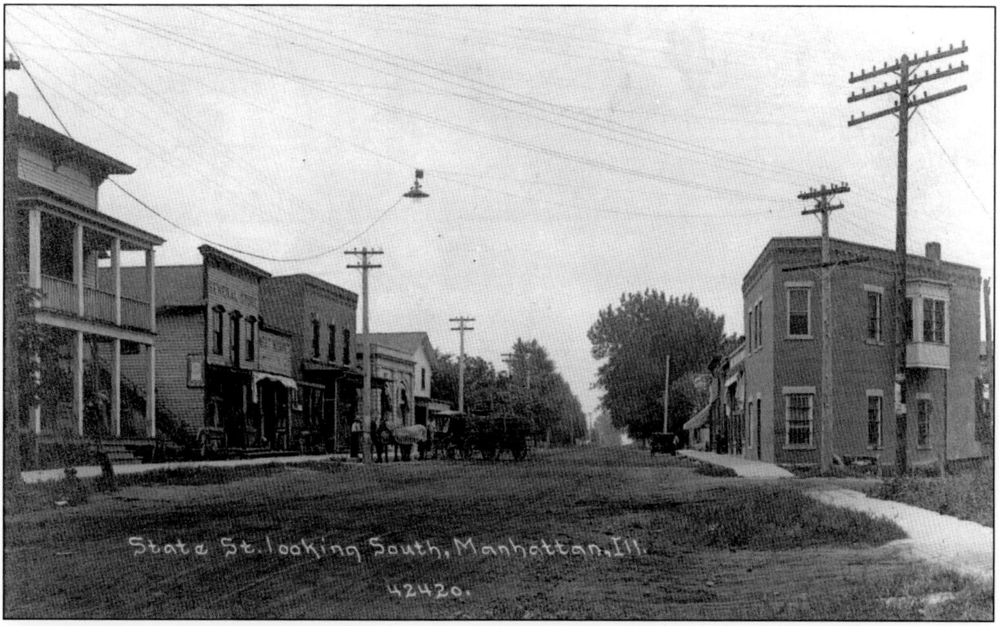

This 1910 postcard photograph shows a view of State Street looking south from the intersection of South Wabash Street. The triangular-shaped building on the west side of State Street was the Manhattan State Bank. The buildings along the east side of the street included the Vanderberg's Hotel and Boarding House, A. H. Goodwin General Store and Meat Market, Fehr and Smalley Hardware, First National Bank, and the Fritz Gallingher Harness Shop.

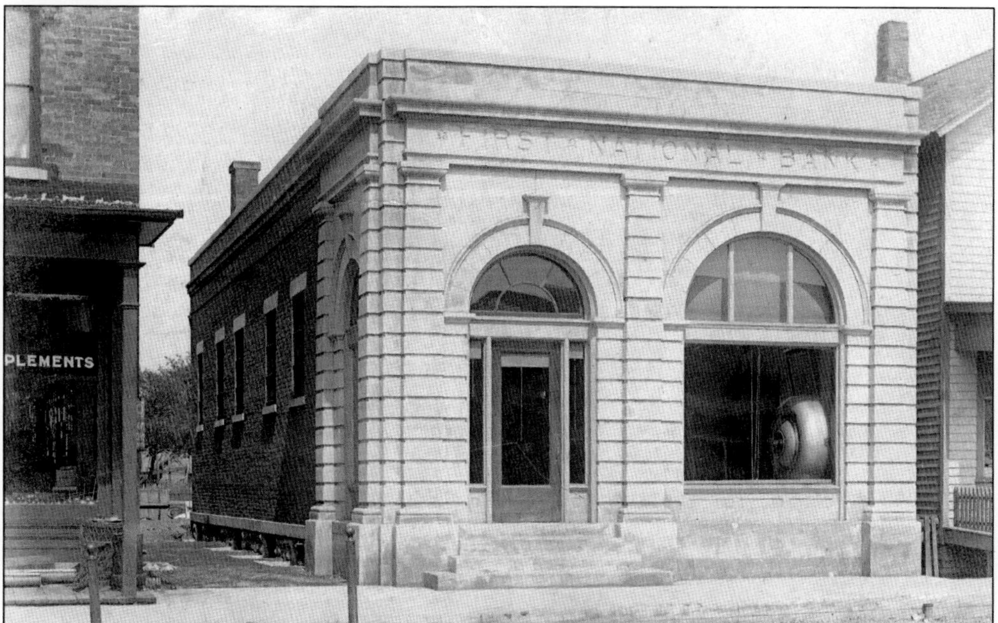

The First National Bank of Manhattan, charted on May 29, 1907, has served the community for over 100 years. Located on South State Street, between Wabash and First Streets, this picture postcard shows the old bank building looking northeast across State Street.

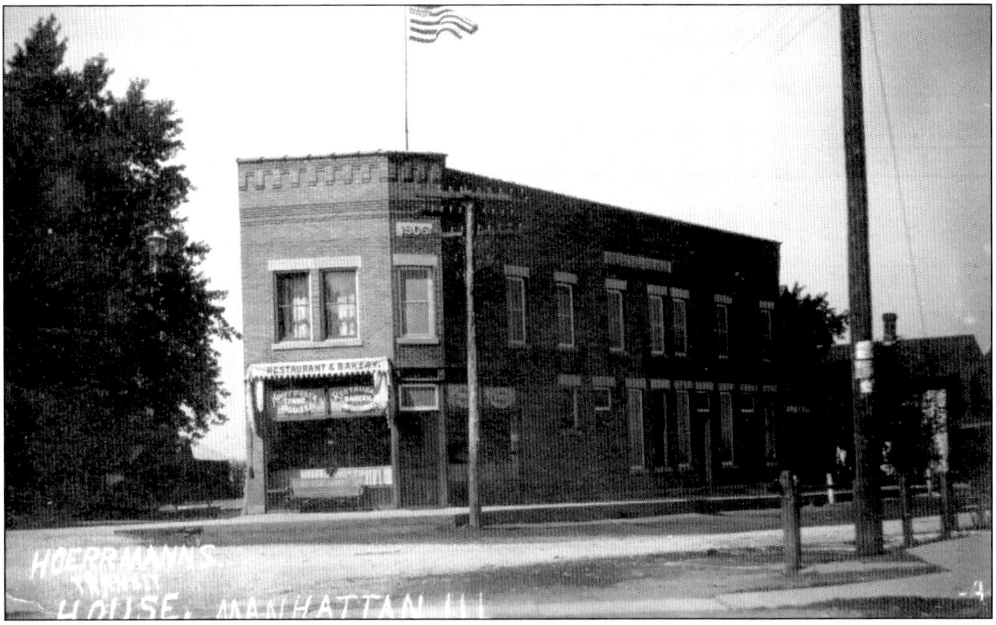

In 1895, Gustave Hoerrman and his wife started a bakery, and their sons and daughter worked in the business. The bakery and restaurant business, which included fresh delivery, became so successful that a two-story brick building was erected at the corner of West North Street (Monee Road) and State Street (Route 52) to accommodate the growth. In 1914, the building was enlarged, and a store building with flats was added.

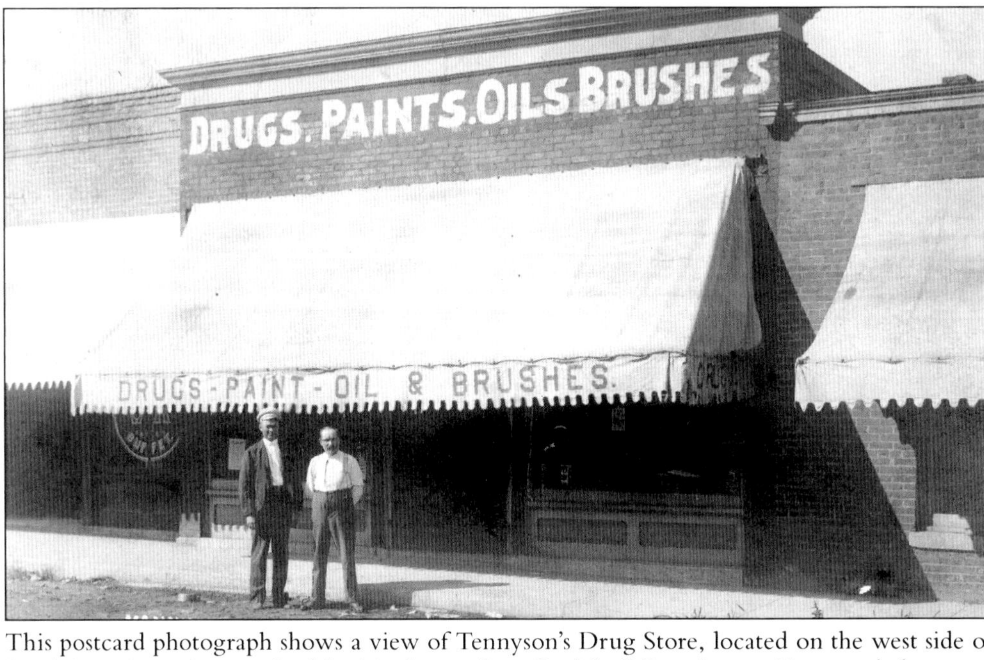

This postcard photograph shows a view of Tennyson's Drug Store, located on the west side of South State Street just south of the Manhattan State Bank building. August Tennyson's drugstore housed the town's first post office and public telephone. In later years, it became Sieffert Drug and Walter's Sundries. All businesses carried a variety of items, including drugs, paints, watches, shoes, and breads.

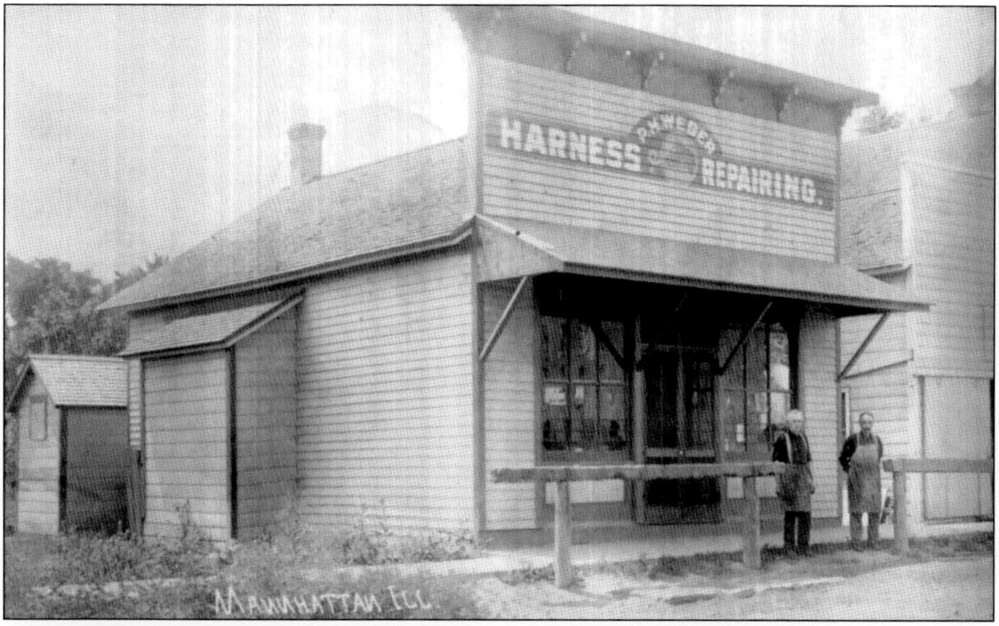

Pinnet Weber's Harness Shop was located just west of the Wabash Railroad tracks on the south side of North Street. Beginning in 1898, Pinnet and his brother Charles worked together in the business until 1908 when Charles and his family moved to Frankfort. The building stood vacant for a number of years and was eventually sold and turned into a tavern. In the 1960s and 1970s, the Murphys operated a Ford dealership at the same location.

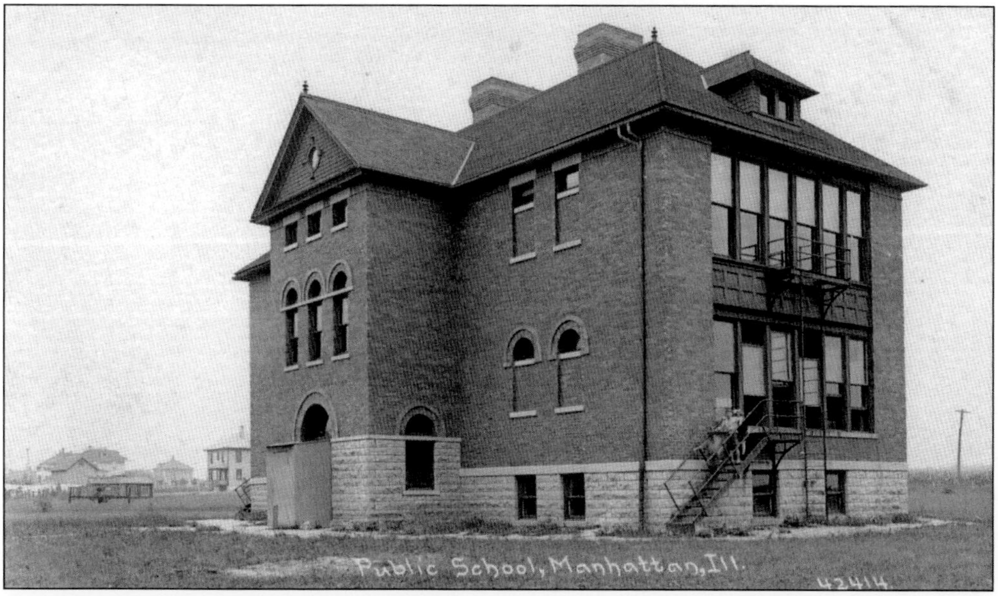

By 1870, there were eight separate school districts in Manhattan Township, and most school buildings were of the one-room wooden variety. In 1906, the Manhattan Township School District purchased land for a new schoolhouse, and two years later, a brick school building was erected south of town. This postcard photograph shows the 1908 brick school building prior to the 1915 additions. The building was demolished in 1964, when the Anna McDonald Elementary School was built.

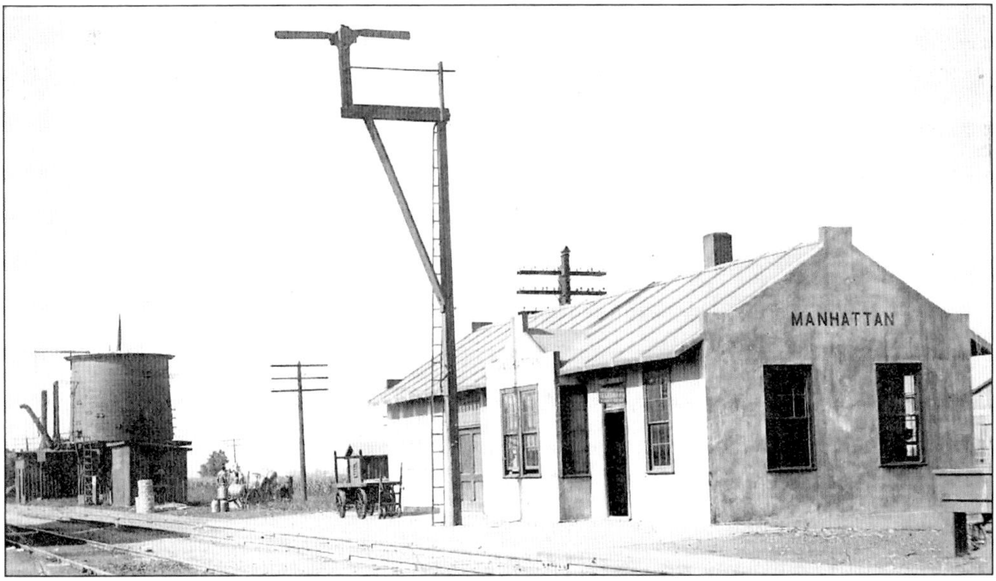

After the first Wabash Railroad depot burned down in 1907, a second railroad depot was built in the same location on Front Street on the west side of the tracks. The picture postcard above, looking south, shows the second depot to the right and the old water tank and waterspout to the left. Notice the signal pole and ladder in front of the depot. The mechanical signal arms were widely used as a method of communication to approaching trains. The postcard below shows a view looking north along the Wabash Railroad tracks. The new waterspout can be seen to the right of the approaching train.

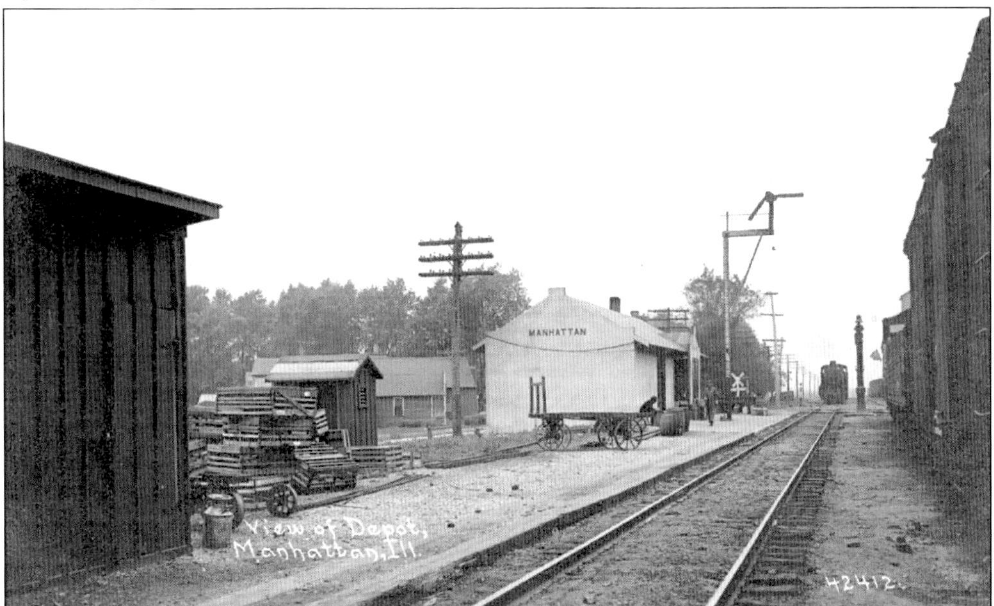

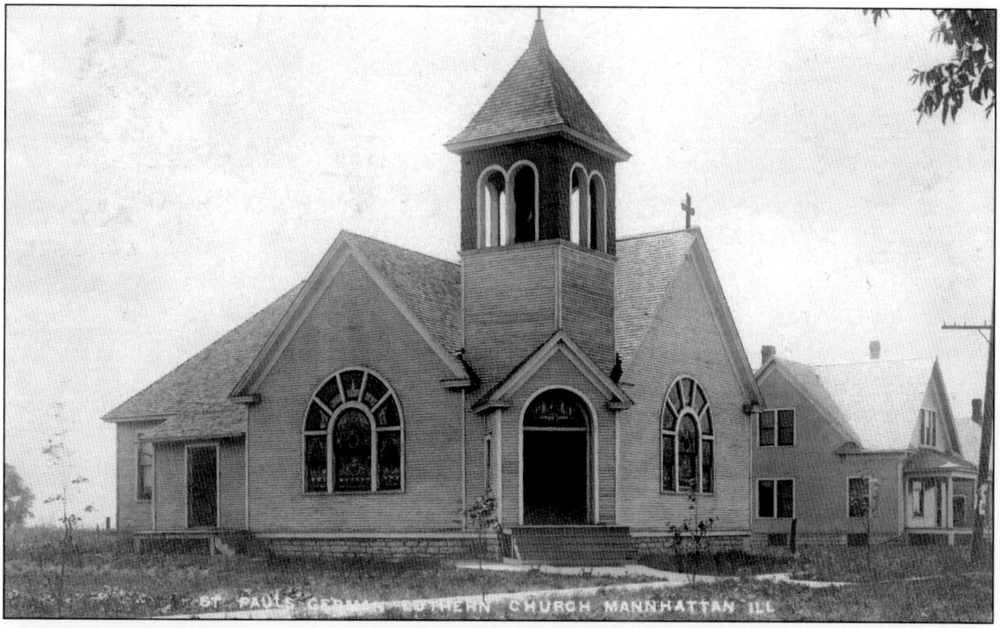

In 1903, 15 German families under the leadership of Rev. Carl H. Wittbracht, pastor of the North Peotone Church, organized St. Paul's Evangelical Luthern Church. In 1904, a church was built at Park and Whitson Streets on land donated by Sopia Heitman. Services were conducted in both English and German, and the "Luthern" was dropped from the name in 1934, after a merger between the Evangelical and Reformed Church and the Congregational Churches gave the church its current name of St. Paul's United Church of Christ.

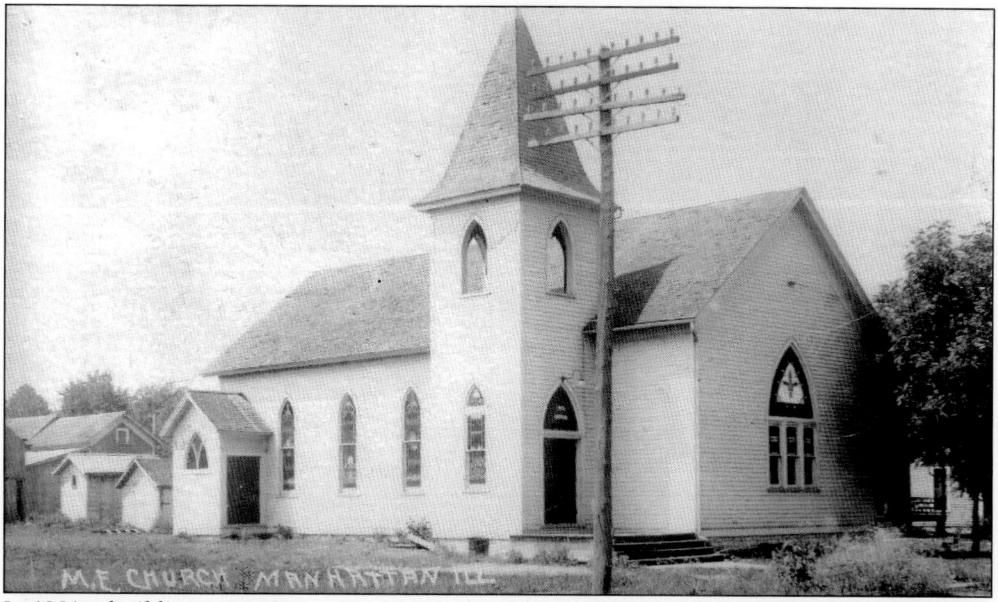

In 1881, a building committee was organized to select a site and erect a building for a Methodist congregation in Manhattan. In 1883, the church was built on a one-acre site near the southwest corner of North and Eastern Streets, and a parsonage was added in 1885. Fire damaged the interior of the church on December 16, 1917, and the following spring, the church was moved 50 feet to its present location and was reconstructed and redecorated.

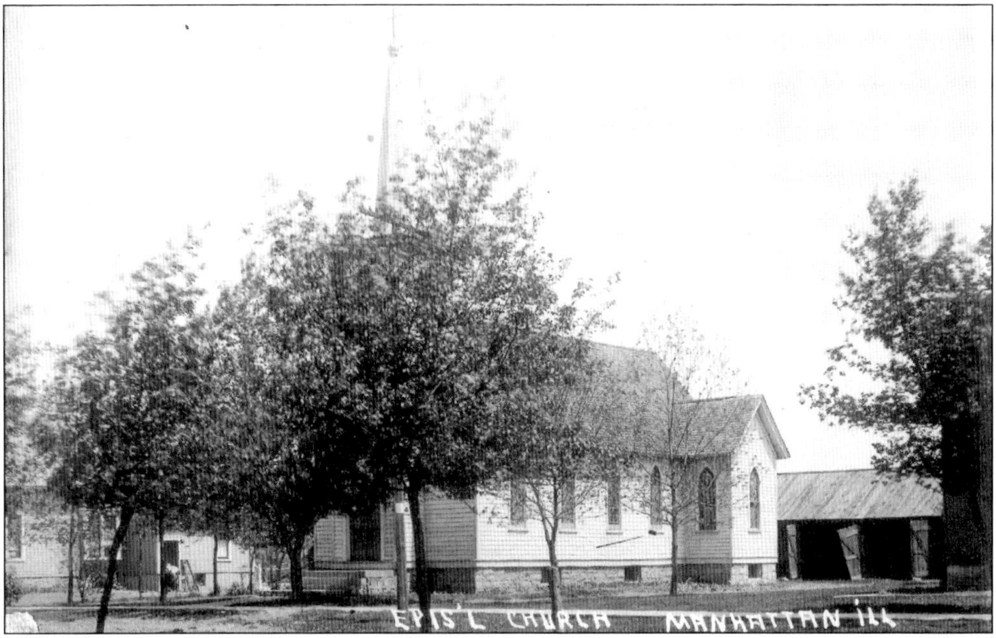

St. Paul's Episcopal Church was located at the intersection of Cedar and Monee-Manhattan Roads, near where the Manhattan Center Cemetery now stands. Founded in 1853, the church was established by Rev. Charles B. Stout with a congregation of 21. In 1897, the church was moved to Park Street in town and remained there until the congregation dwindled to the point that the church closed its doors in the early 1960s. The parsonage and church were sold in 1972.

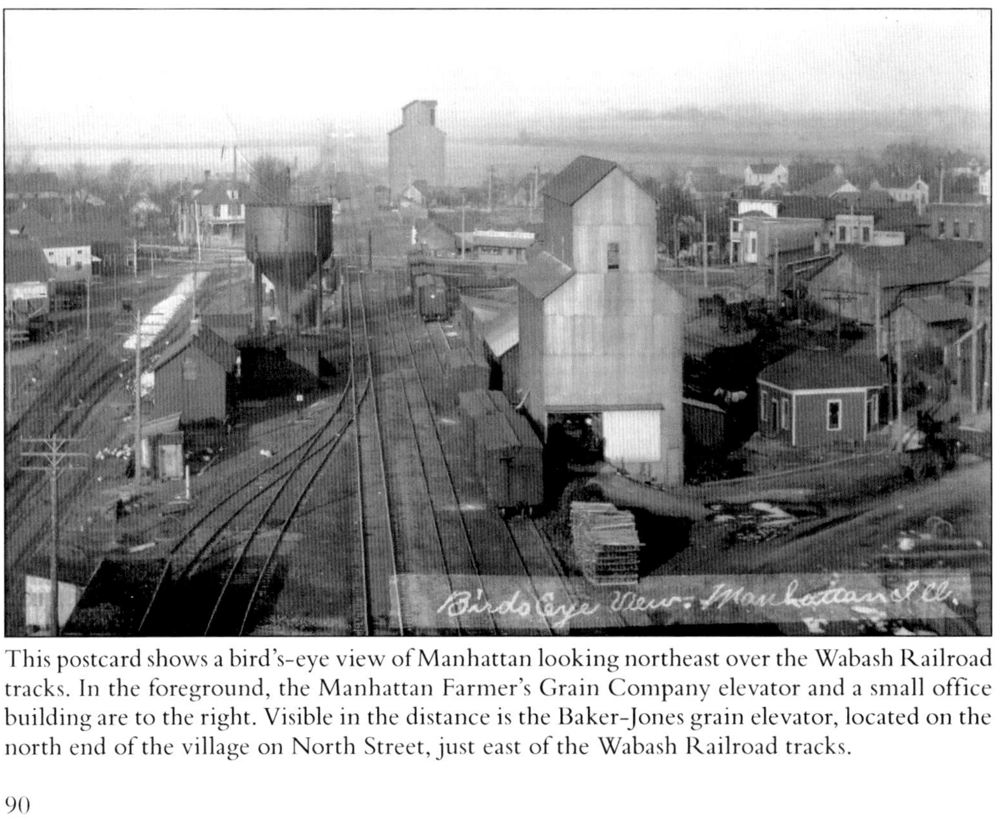

This postcard shows a bird's-eye view of Manhattan looking northeast over the Wabash Railroad tracks. In the foreground, the Manhattan Farmer's Grain Company elevator and a small office building are to the right. Visible in the distance is the Baker-Jones grain elevator, located on the north end of the village on North Street, just east of the Wabash Railroad tracks.

Eight

Wilmington and Symerton

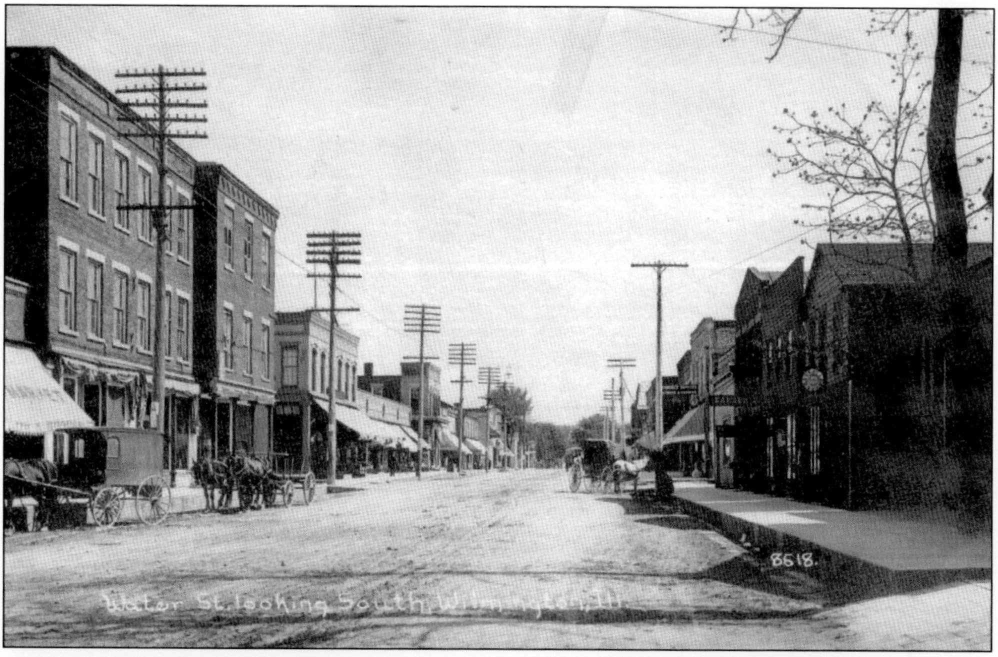

This postcard photograph shows a view of Water Street looking south near Van Buren Street in the early 20th century. Buildings and businesses visible on the east side of the street include Vander Bogart Meat Market, the Commercial National Bank, and Bennett Dry Goods and Furniture Store. On the west side of the block, the Carl Markert Jeweler Shop and the Whitmore Hardware Store can be seen.

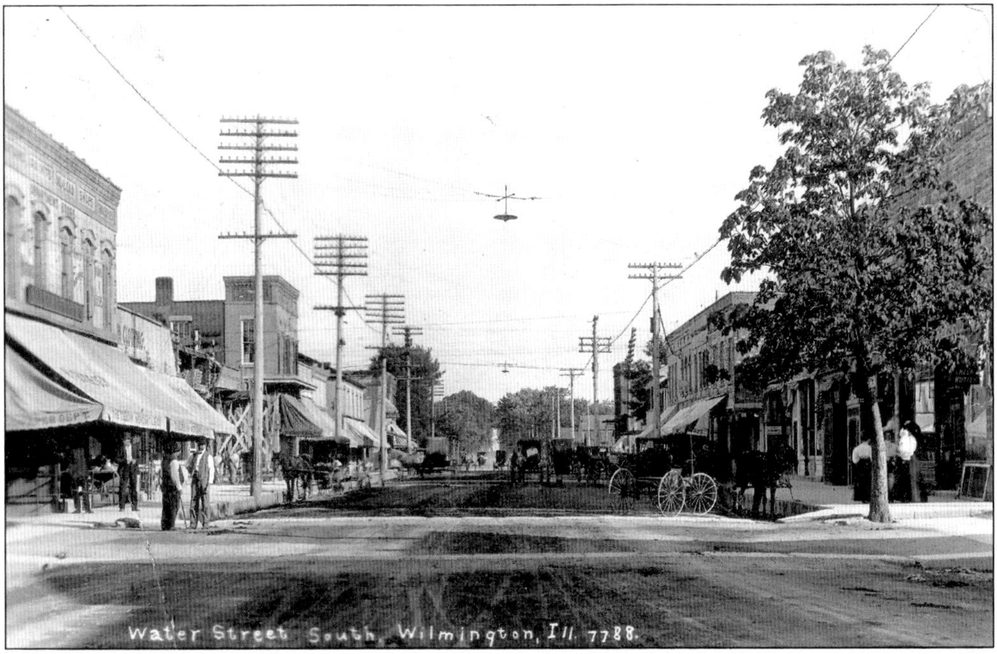

Looking south on Water Street from the Jackson Street intersection, a number of noteworthy buildings and businesses are visible. On the left, the Bennett Dry Goods and Furniture Store with its large awning can be seen. On the right, the old Eagle Hotel (Schroeder Hotel) is visible on the northwest corner of Water and Baltimore Streets.

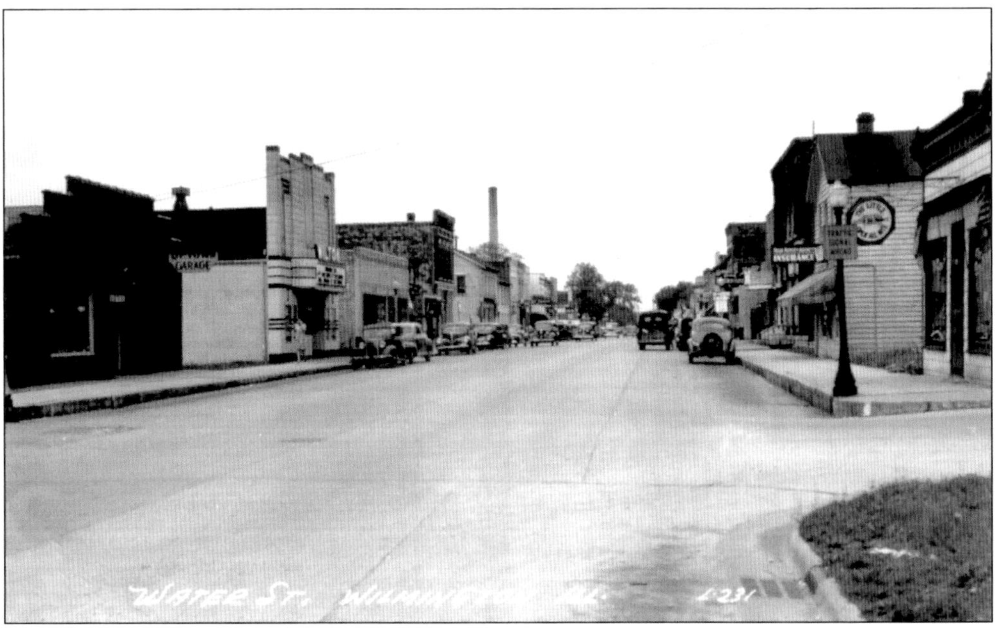

Looking north on Water Street near the Jefferson Street intersection in the 1940s, the Wilton Theatre is visible on the west side of the street. On the right is the Little Pig Restaurant, with a sign that reads, "Best in the Midwest—Open all Nite." Next door to the restaurant is the Felix Keeley Insurance Agency. Today both buildings are gone, and this corner serves as a parking lot for the Grundy County Bank.

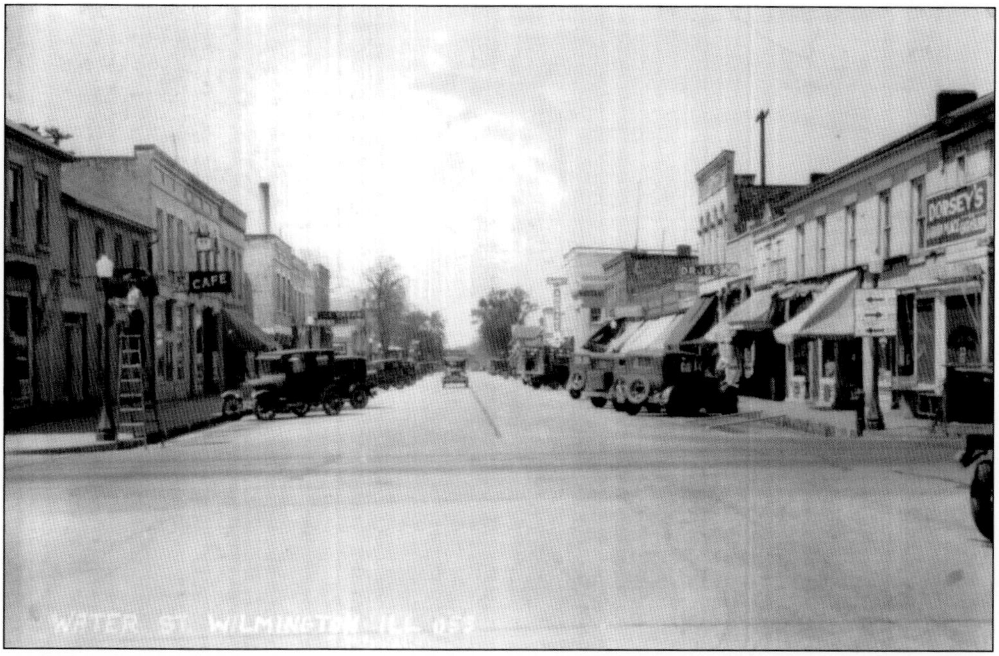

Looking north on Water Street from Bridge Street in the late 1920s, a few noteworthy businesses can be seen in the postcard. On the left, the man on the ladder is directly in front of the old Eagle Hotel. As the oldest building in Will County, it has been an important part of the history of the town. Other businesses located on this block include Barry's Hardware, Dorsey's Hotel, and a variety of drug, ice cream, and bakery businesses.

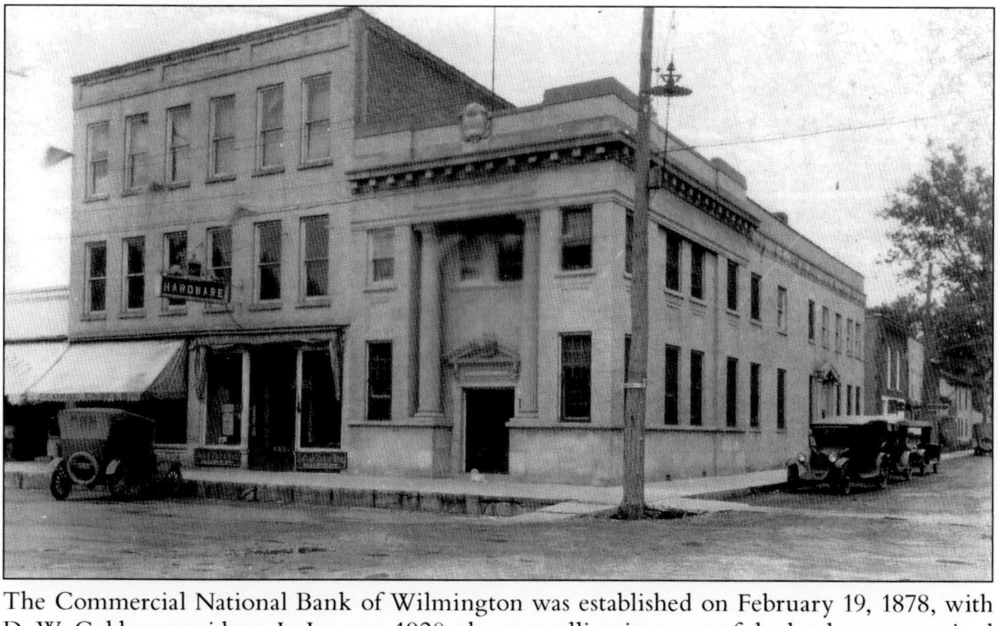

The Commercial National Bank of Wilmington was established on February 19, 1878, with D. W. Cobb as president. In January 1920, the controlling interests of the bank were acquired by George and F. W. Woodruff. Later that year, the Commercial National Bank moved into a new two-story, brick-and-stone structure on the northeast corner of Jackson and Water Streets. After serving the community for nearly 55 years, the bank went through liquidation in 1936.

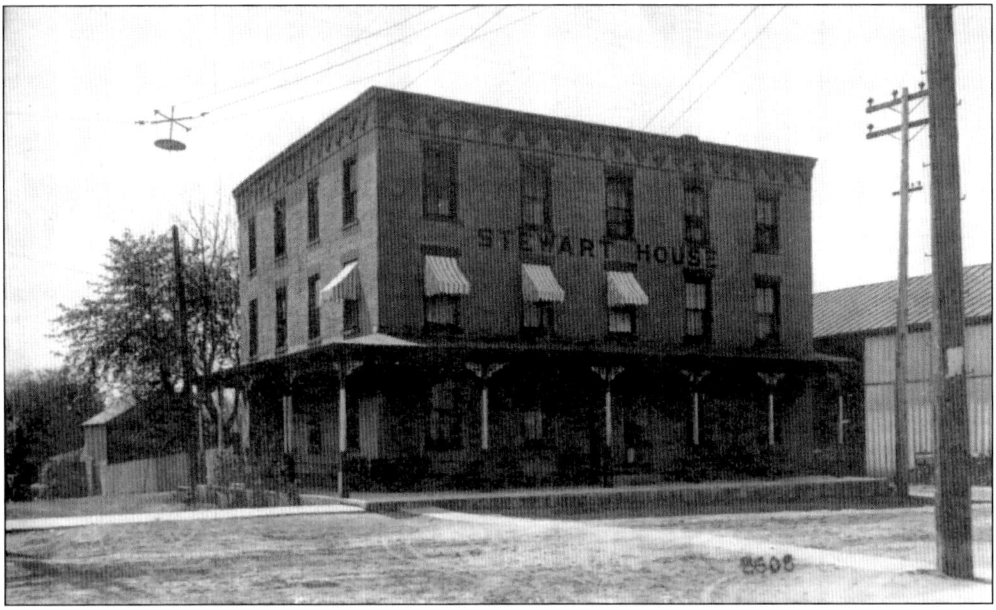

Located on the northwest corner of Van Buren and Water Streets, the three-story brick hotel known as the Stewart House was constructed by Peter Stewart in 1854. Stewart was one of Wilmington's most influential early citizens and was an ardent abolitionist who helped organize the Underground Railroad in the area and gave fugitive slaves safe harbor in the hotel. By the 1970s, the building began to deteriorate, and it was demolished on October 20, 1972.

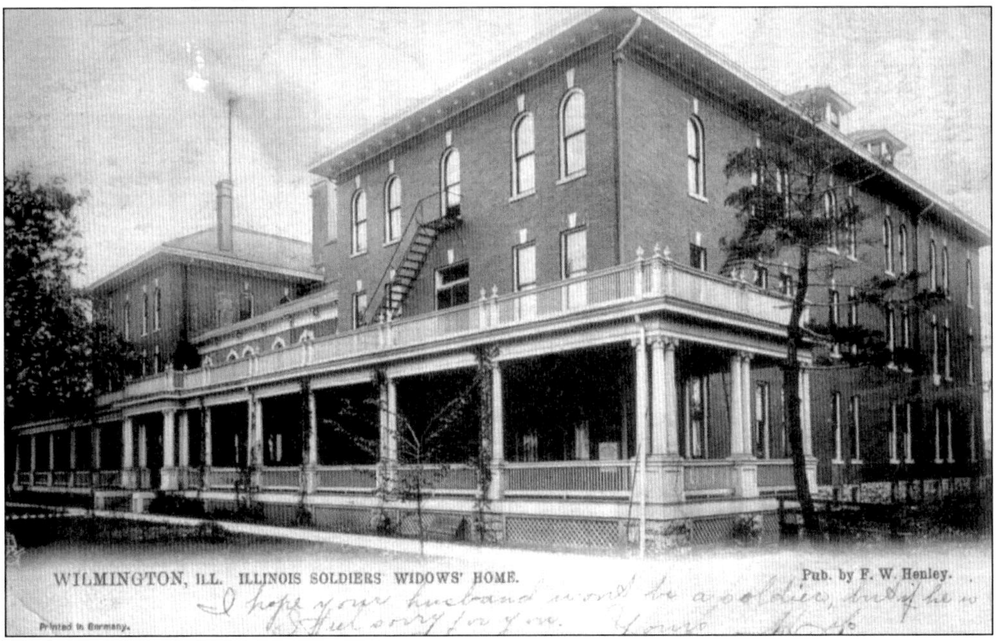

The Soldiers' Widows' Home was founded by the Woman's Relief Corps, Department of Illinois, in 1895. The home was the only one of its kind in the United States and was beautifully located on the west bank of the Kankakee River. The home, including a hospital, accommodated 112 members. In 1963, the ladies were moved to Quincy, and the buildings were used for a state boys' home as part of the Illinois Youth Commission program.

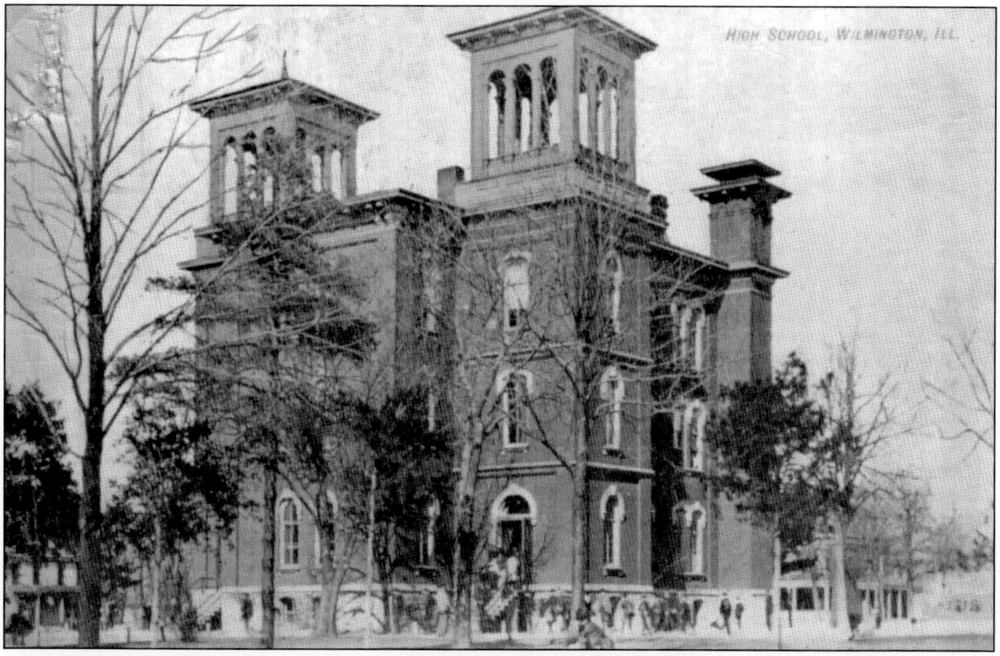

Education in Wilmington can be traced back to the late 1830s when a small private school was started in the Steward home. In 1869, the city council appropriated $30,000 for the construction of a building to house nearly 700 students. This postcard photograph shows the three-story, four-tower brick structure that served the community until it was torn down in 1936. This school building was located where Booth Central Elementary school is now.

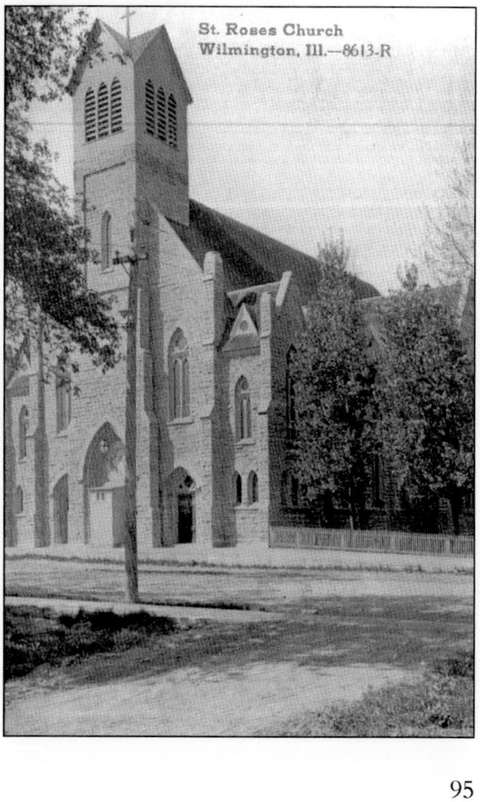

In 1851, the parishioners of St. Rose began construction of a small church building that was completed in 1855. In 1865, they built a larger church, but this soon became too small for the congregation. In 1883, construction began on a new church, on the southwest corner of South Kankakee and Wabash Streets, with a seating capacity of 700. The large stone church cost approximately $45,000 to build, and the first mass was sung on Christmas day in 1886. For over 150 years, the St. Rose Parish has served the Catholic community of Wilmington.

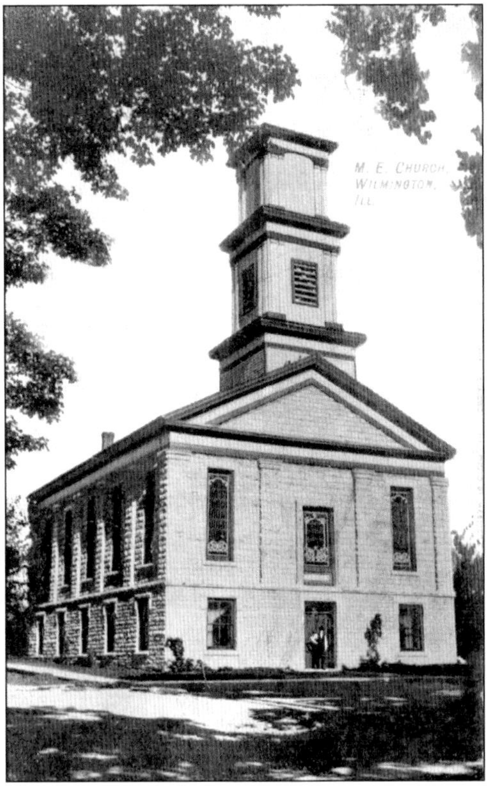

Located today on the southeast corner of Jefferson and South Kankakee Streets, the old Methodist church was first established in 1837 by a Methodist pioneer preacher named Stephen R. Beggs. In 1840, a small building that was to be used for many years as a parsonage was erected, and in this building, services were held until 1857, when the limestone church was constructed. In 1969, the Wilmington Public Library Board purchased the old native stone Methodist church.

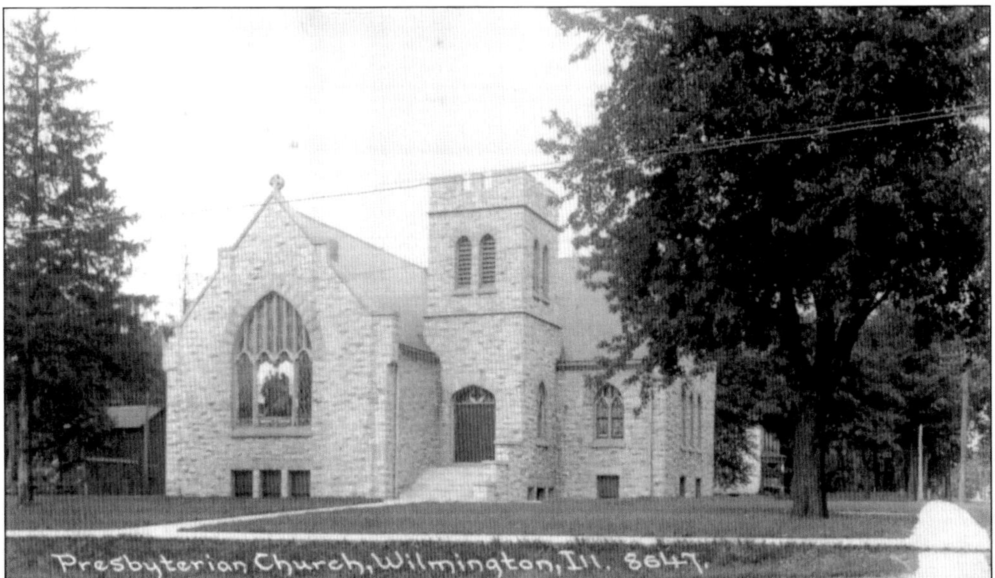

The early settlers of Wilmington were religious people. In 1838, the Presbyterian Church was organized by Pastor J. G. Porter, and a small church was built in 1840. Small additions were made to the original structure over the years to accommodate growth. The present First Presbyterian Church, located on the northwest corner of North Kankakee and Van Buren Streets, was constructed using local limestone in 1902 and 1903.

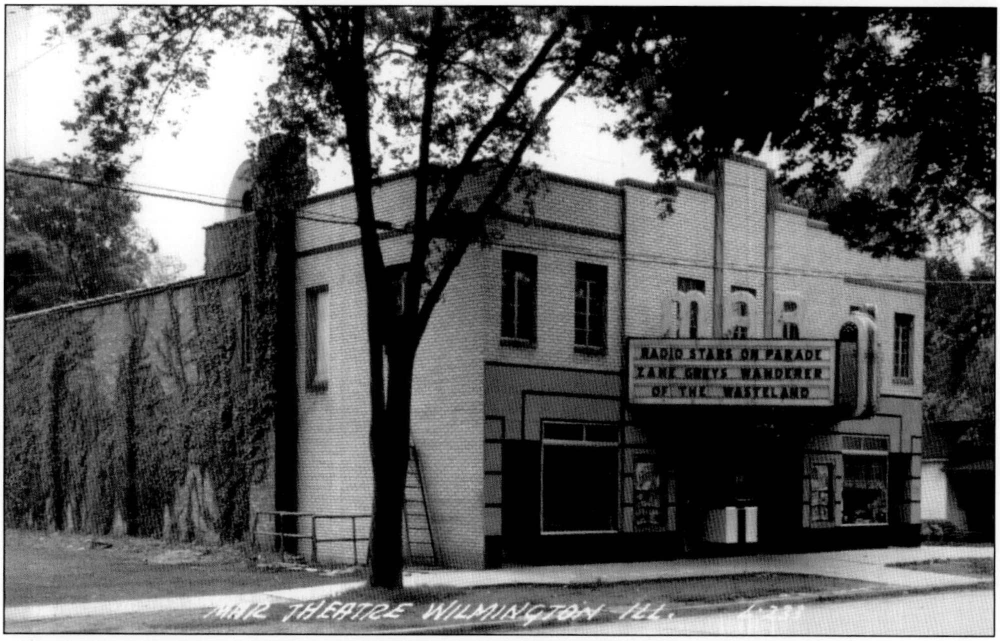

Located on South Main Street, the Mar Theatre opened for business on June 15, 1937, during the Great Depression. The Butcher brothers conceived the idea in 1935 and completed construction of the art deco–style building two years later. Today the first-run theater looks much as it did when it first opened. This picture postcard from 1945 shows the front of the theater looking east from Main Street. Notice the marquee advertising RKO's late summer release of *Radio Stars on Parade.*

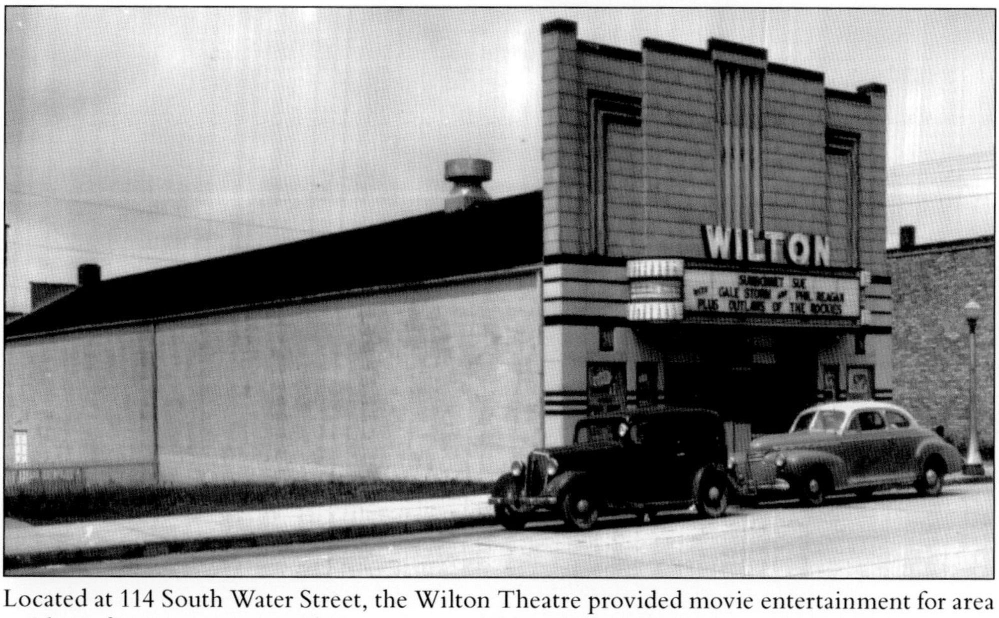

Located at 114 South Water Street, the Wilton Theatre provided movie entertainment for area residents for many years. Looking west across Water Street, the movie marquee advertises the 1945 musical comedy *Sunbonnet Sue*, with Gale Storm and Phil Reagan. The second feature is the western *Outlaws of the Rockies*, with Charles Starrett and Tex Harding. After the Wilton Theatre closed, the building was home to other businesses, including the Old Theatre Antique Mall.

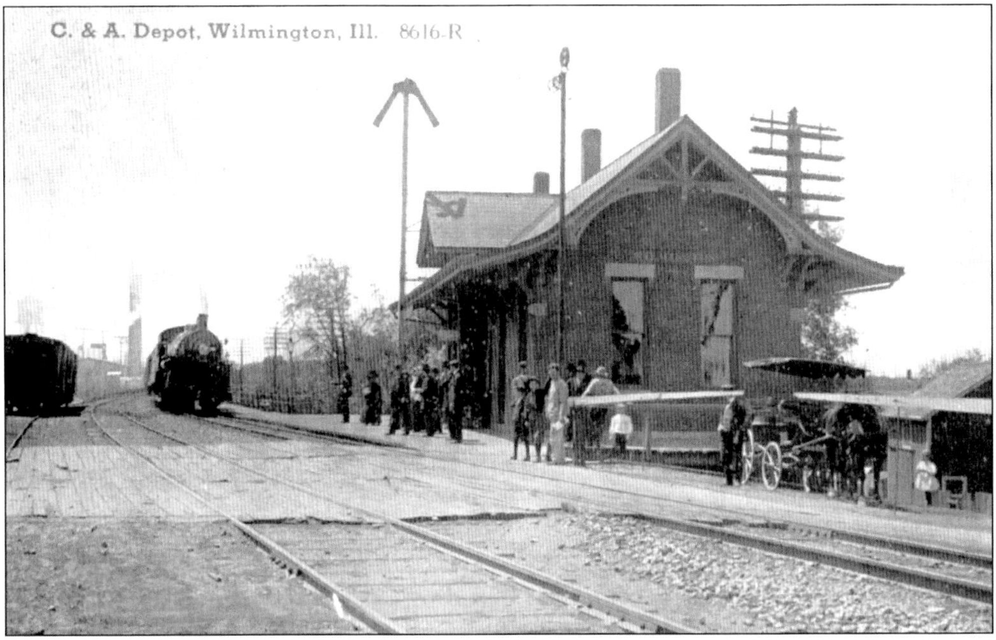

The Chicago and Alton Railroad line was completed through the newly incorporated village of Wilmington in 1854. In the spring of 1869, a large depot was constructed and completed north of the tracks on the southwest corner of Chicago and Kankakee Streets. This picture postcard shows the depot looking west from Kankakee Street.

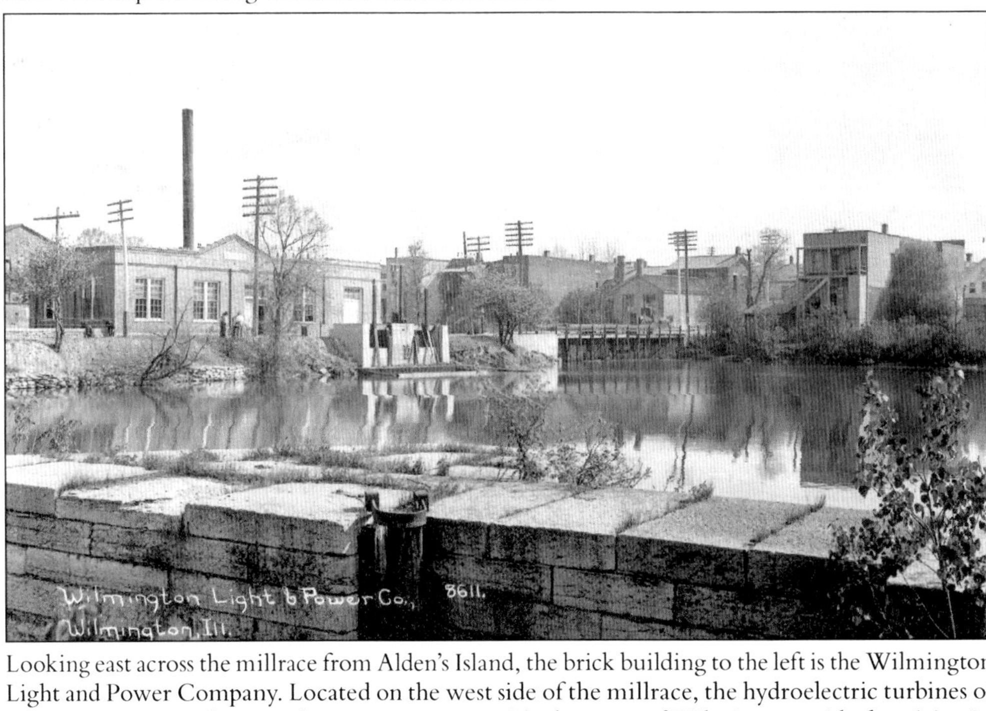

Looking east across the millrace from Alden's Island, the brick building to the left is the Wilmington Light and Power Company. Located on the west side of the millrace, the hydroelectric turbines of the power company harnessed river power to provide the town of Wilmington with electricity. In the 1870s, the Kankakee Navigation Company built a series of dams and locks to help navigate and create waterpower. In the distance, directly behind the Eagle Hotel, dam No. 2 is still visible.

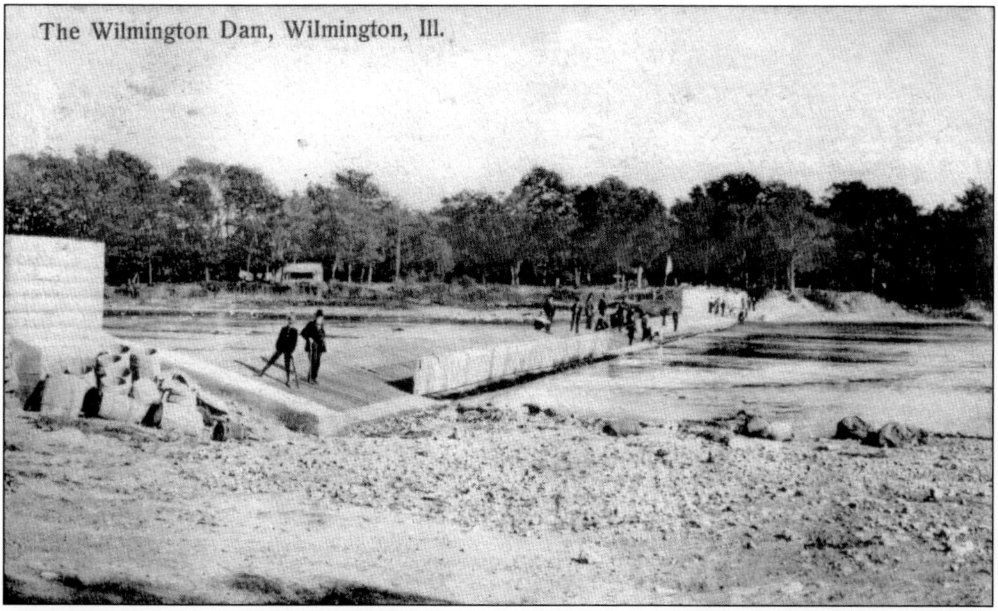

Long before settlers arrived in Will County, the Kankakee River was used as a means of transportation and exploration. After settlement, the first persons to utilize the Kankakee River were those who valued it as a source of power. Those individuals built dams and mills for processing grains and cutting timber. Many of the 19th-century dams were constructed from wood and did not hold up to the occasional ice jams and floods that are common on the river. The postcard photograph above is a picture of the Wilmington dam looking west across the Kankakee River during construction. Completed in October 1904, the construction of the dam was part of an overall river improvement project. The postcard photograph below was taken from the same location on the east bank of the Kankakee River on Alden's Island and shows the completed dam.

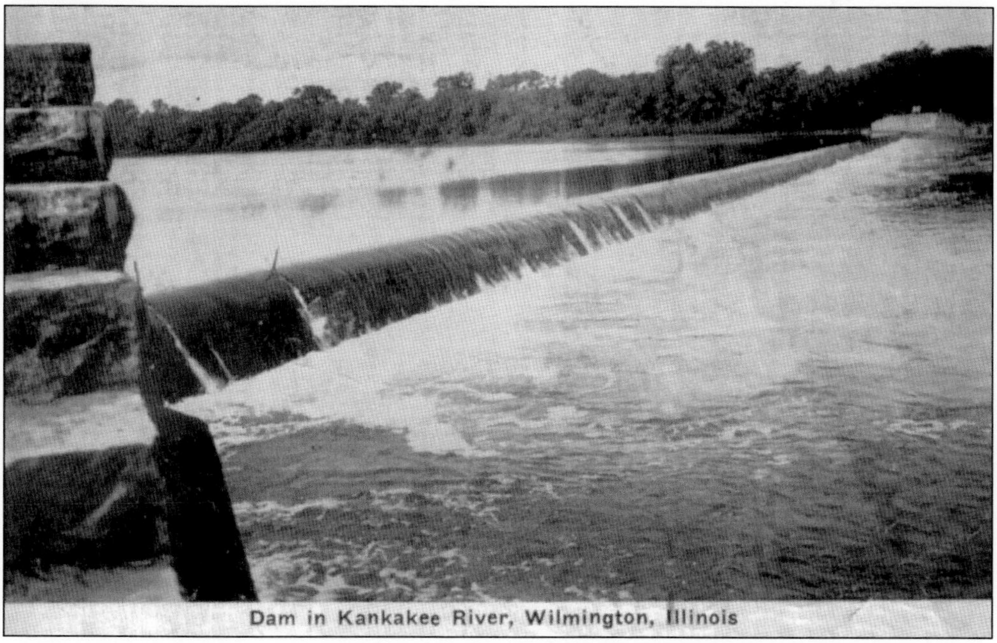

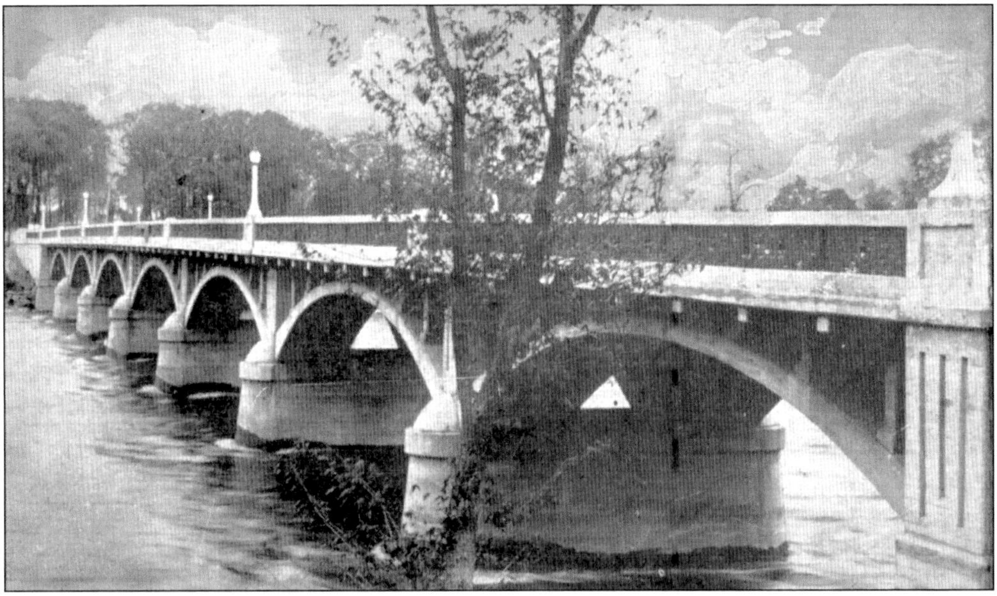

In the spring of 1867, an ice jam and flood destroyed the first bridge over the Kankakee River in Wilmington. It was replaced by an iron wagon bridge, which served area residents until modern road building created the need for a new bridge. Under the direction of supervisor Nicholas Engels, a concrete seven-arch bridge was built in 1920 and 1921 and was known as the Engels bridge. The modern road crossing the bridge was known by a variety of names, including the Will Rogers Highway and Route 66. The postcard photograph above shows a view of the newly constructed Engels bridge. The postcard below shows a view of the old, iron wagon bridge looking west across the Kankankee River. Today just south of the modern bridge, one can still see the remains of the rock abutments that were part of the old wagon bridge used to cross the river.

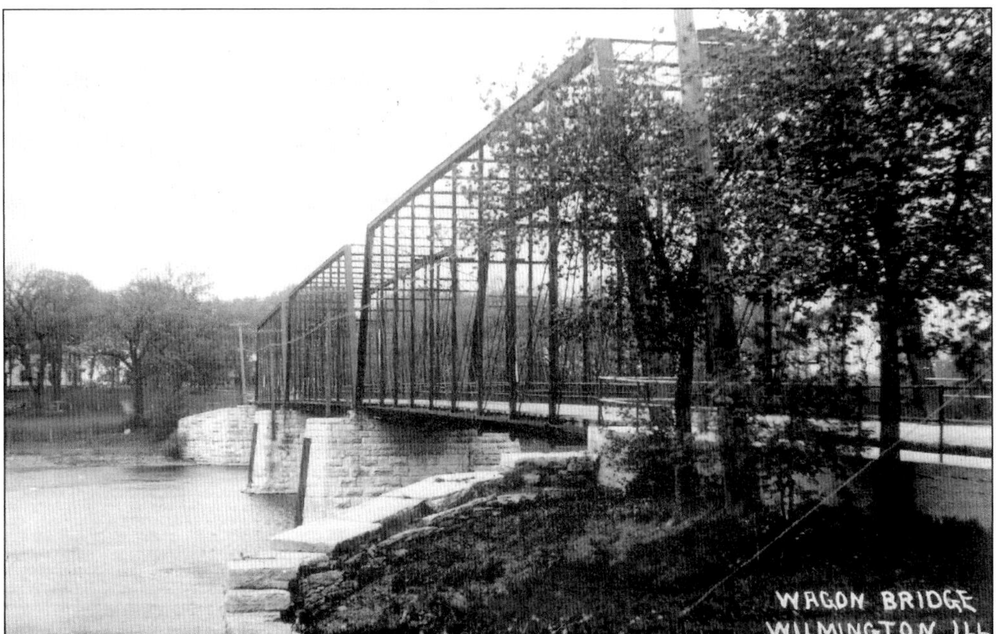

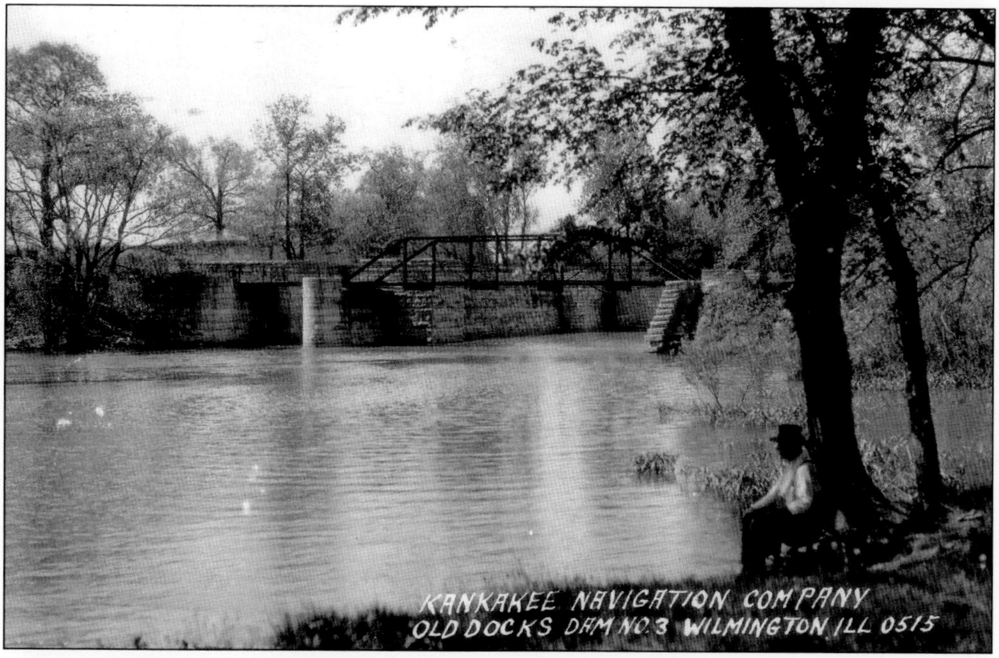

Upon its completion in 1848, the Illinois and Michigan Canal included a feeder canal built through to the Kankakee River in Wilmington, but the river was too shallow for most boats. In 1871, eastern investors created the Kankakee Navigation Company, which repaired and improved the old dam and eventually constructed five lock and dam combinations on the river.

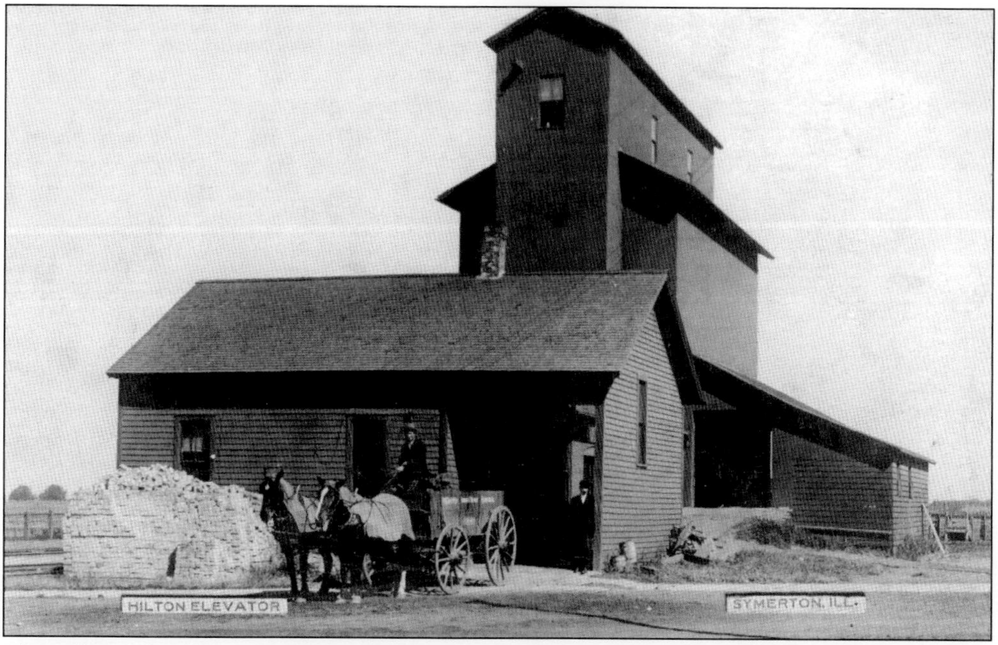

The village of Symerton was started when the Norfolk and Western Railway was built in 1878. This postcard shows the Hilton elevator along the east side of the Wabash Railroad tracks on Commercial Street in the early 20th century. A. N. Hilton operated the elevator from the early 1890s to 1914, when it was sold to William Murray.

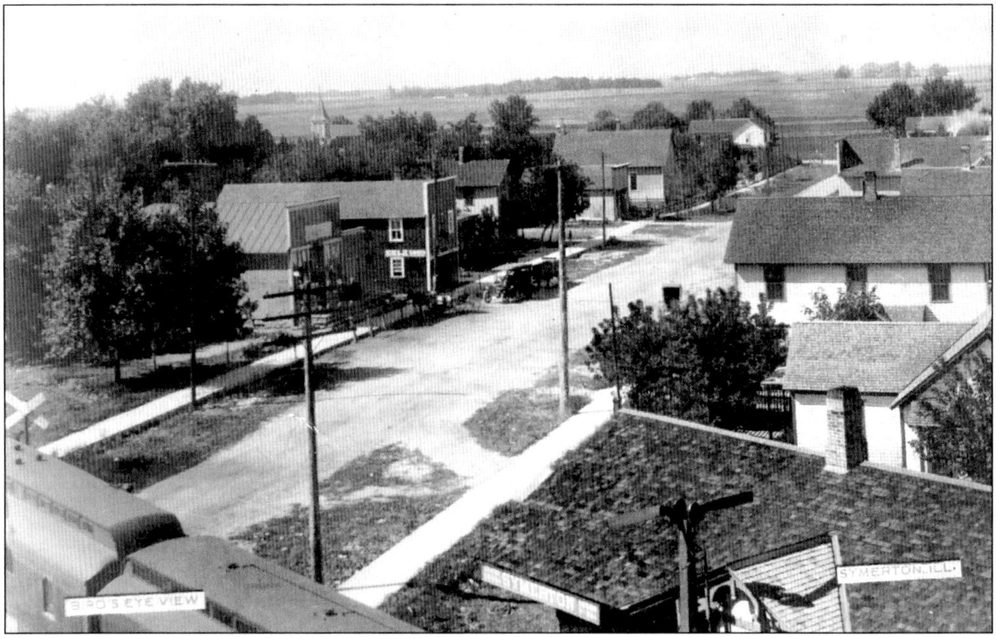

Symerton, located in Florence Township, is about four miles east of the town of Wilmington and about 40 miles from the city of Chicago. The Norfolk and Western Railway was constructed in the east-central part of the township in 1878 and 1879. Within two years, the Wabash Railroad took it over from the original builders. It was during this time that the village of Symerton was started. Since its incorporation in 1904, Symerton has remained a small agricultural town. The picture postcard above shows a bird's-eye view looking east of Commercial Street. The photograph below shows a similar view of Commercial Street just west of the railroad tracks. In both photographs, the Symerton depot can be seen on the right. Built in 1881 by the Wabash Railroad, this classic wood structure represents a typical 19th-century small-town railroad depot.

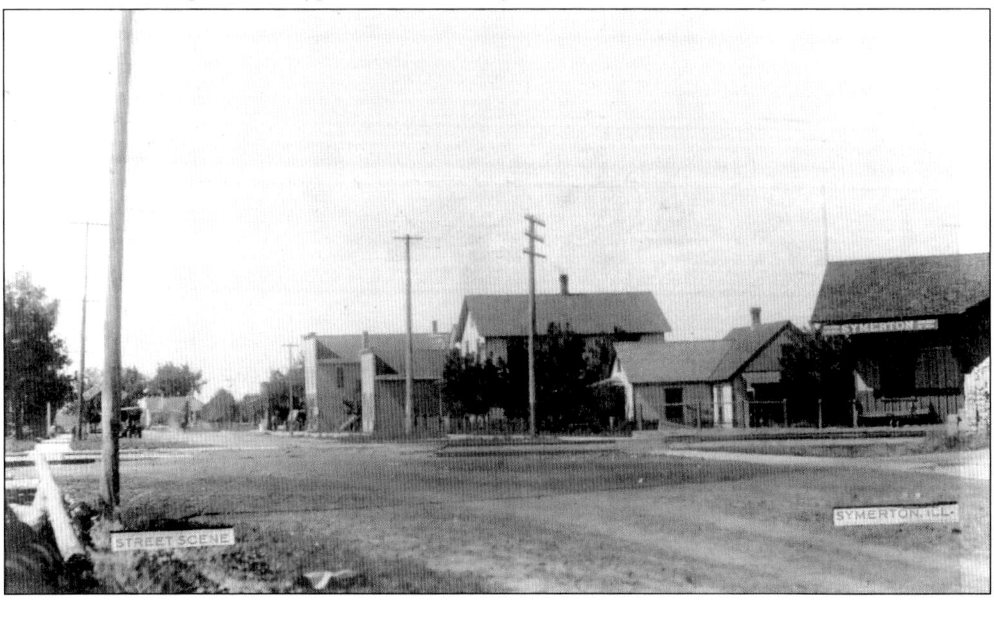

Nine

Braidwood, Custer Park, and Torino

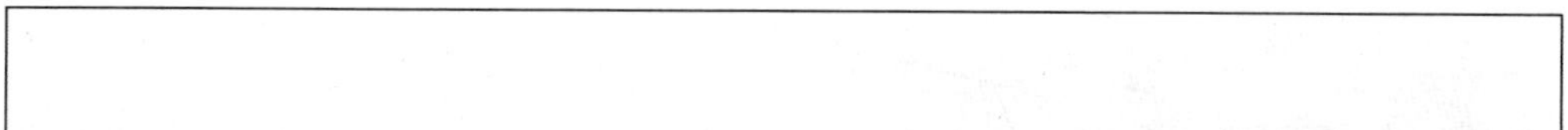

In this photograph taken from the rooftop of city hall, four of Braidwood's early churches can be seen. In the distance, the tall spire of the Catholic church is on the corner of Main and School Streets. Across the street, the Methodist Episcopal church is visible. In the center of the photograph, the Presbyterian church is on the corner of Main and East Street (Lincoln Street).

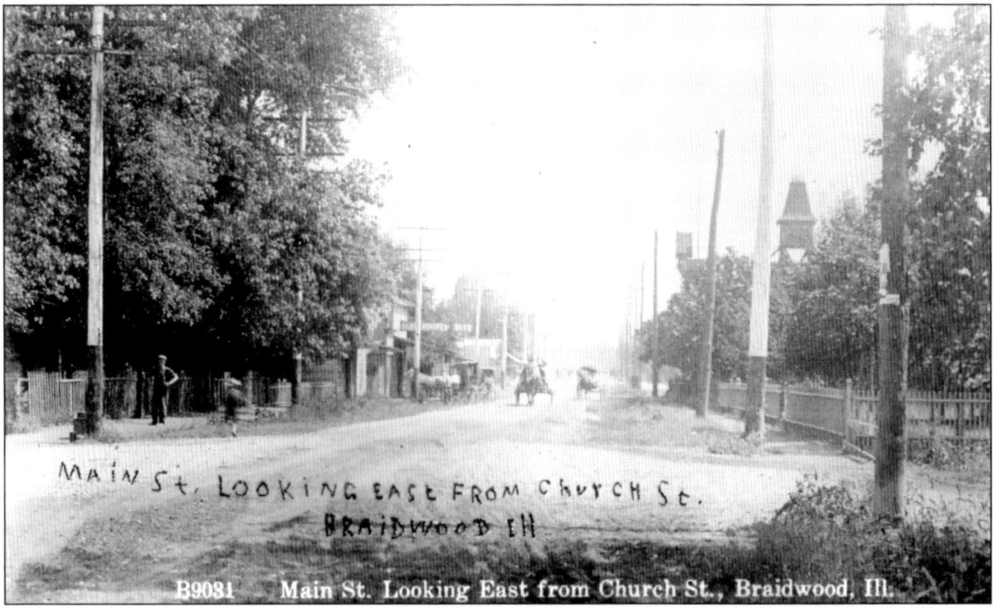

This picture postcard shows a view of Braidwood's Main Street looking east toward Center Street from E Street. Visible on the south side of the block is city hall, and directly across the street, the sign for the Batista Perona tavern can be seen. Notice the electrical lines. Beginning in 1894, Braidwood was one of the first towns in the area to build and operate a municipal light and power plant.

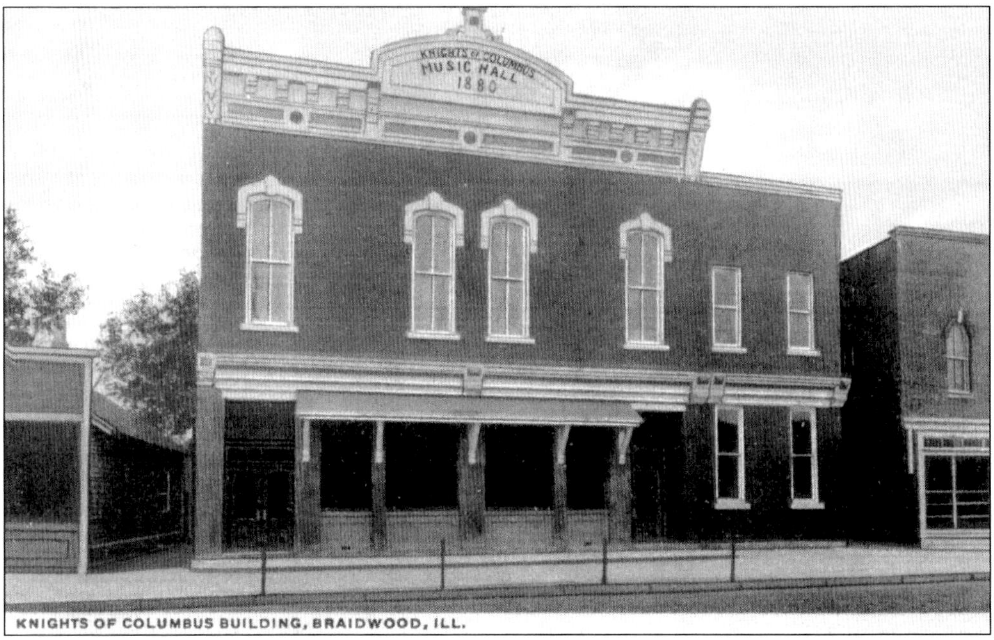

Located on the south side of Main Street was the two-story brick structure known as the music hall. Built in 1880, the building had a double storefront and an upstairs ballroom and auditorium. The double stores on the ground floor were occupied for many years by the Chicago, Wilmington, and Vermilion Coal Company as a store and business office. In 1919, the property was acquired by the Braidwood Knights of Columbus.

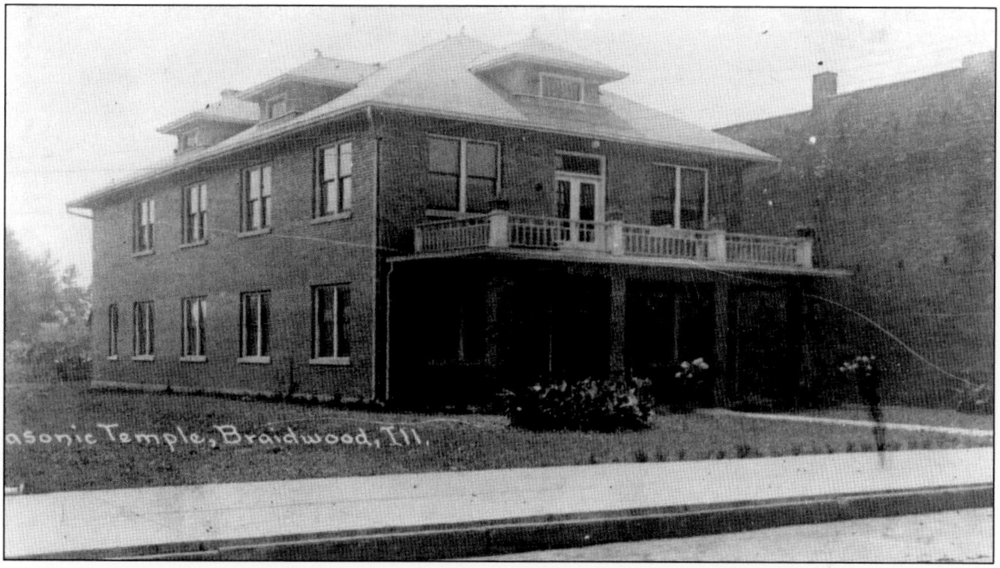

Freemasonry in the United States is as old as the country, and Masonic lodges are found in many communities across America. As the Braidwood-Coal City area was settled, the Braidwood Lodge No. 704 came into existence. Chartered in 1873, the first meeting place of the lodge was a two-story frame building located on Main Street, just west of the present Masonic temple. In 1914, a two-story brick building, designed by John H. Barnes, was constructed just east of the old building.

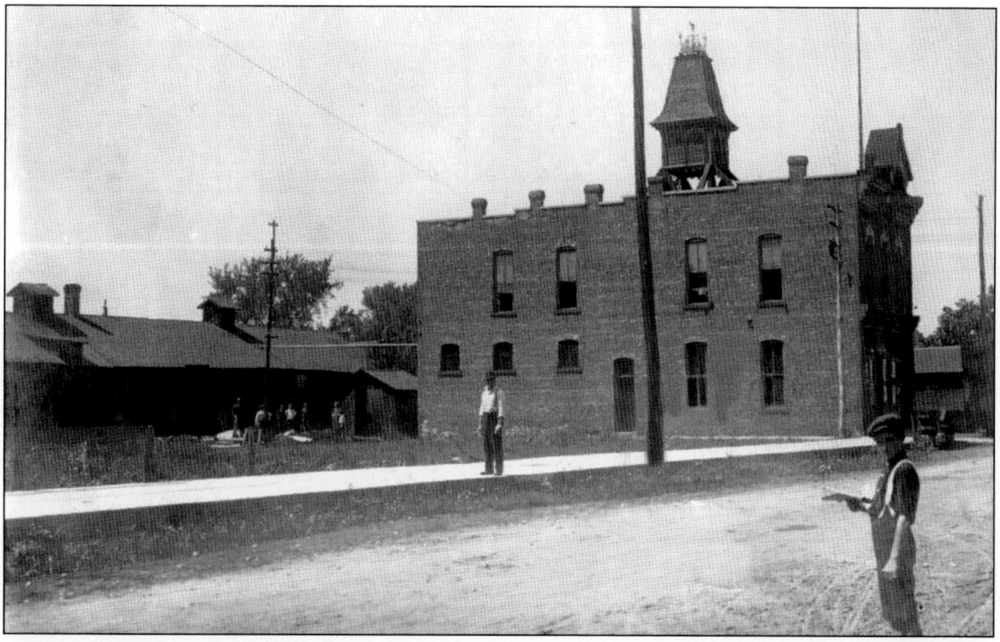

The first Braidwood City Hall was located on the east side of South Center Street. Attached to the building was a small jailhouse, and a fire station was built nearby. In 1885, a new city hall was constructed and was considered one of the finest buildings in the area. The two-story structure shown in this postcard housed the council chambers, the city clerk's office, and an upstairs library. The ground floor of the building contained the courtroom and the jail.

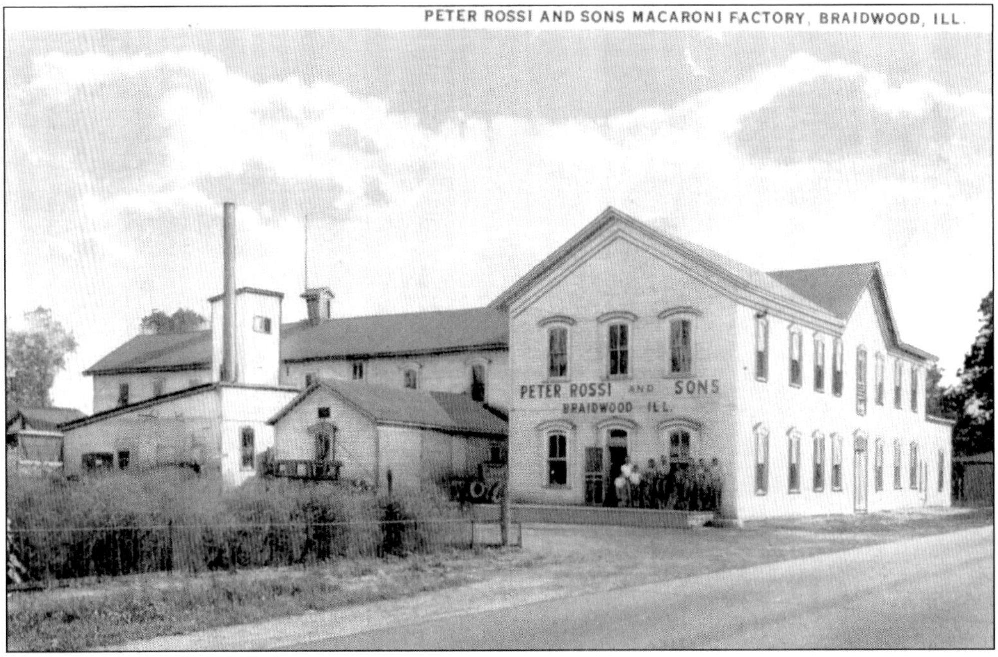

Peter Rossi Sr. came to the United States from Italy in the late 1870s and began manufacturing macaroni in a small factory on Fourth or Hall Street east of Division Street. At this time, it was the first factory of its kind outside Chicago. As the business grew, in 1898, Rossi purchased the old Broadbent Hotel, located on the south side of Front Street near the Alton depot, and extensively remodeled the building to serve the company's needs. In business for nearly 100 years, the Rossi and Sons Macaroni Factory was one of the oldest industries in the community. Braidwood became known throughout the macaroni industry as "the Little Macaroni Capital of the Big Macaroni World." The postcard above shows the factory building, and the postcard below shows a company truck used to deliver the products to area vendors.

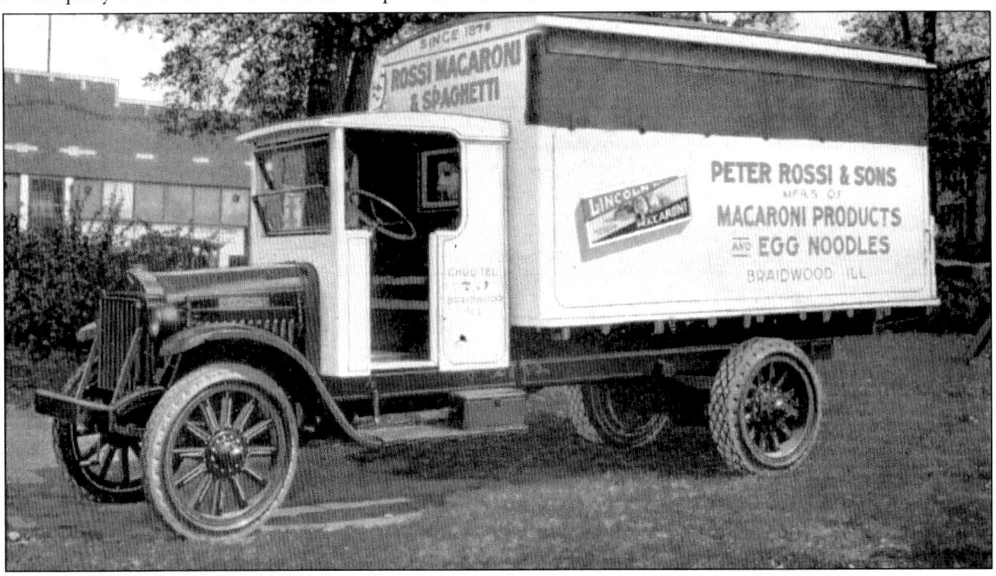

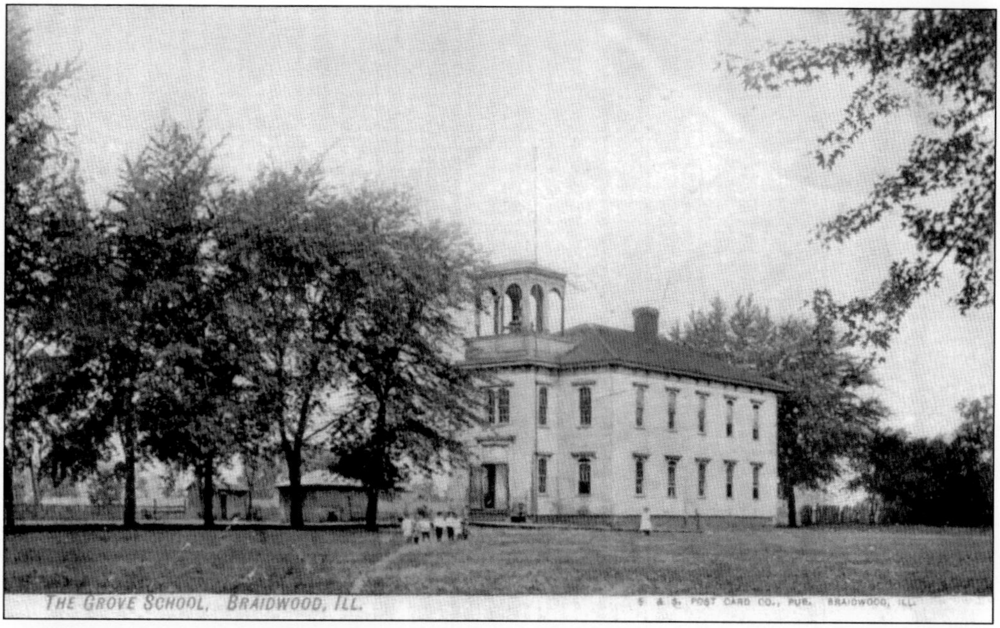

Located on School Street just south of Main Street, the Grove School was built in 1870 to accommodate students living in the newer section of Braidwood. The two-story wood-frame structure was built with a high belfry and two large classrooms on each floor. The school educated pupils in the area until 1905 when it was closed. It was torn down in 1915. Today Reed-Custer Intermediate School occupies the land on which the old Grove School was located.

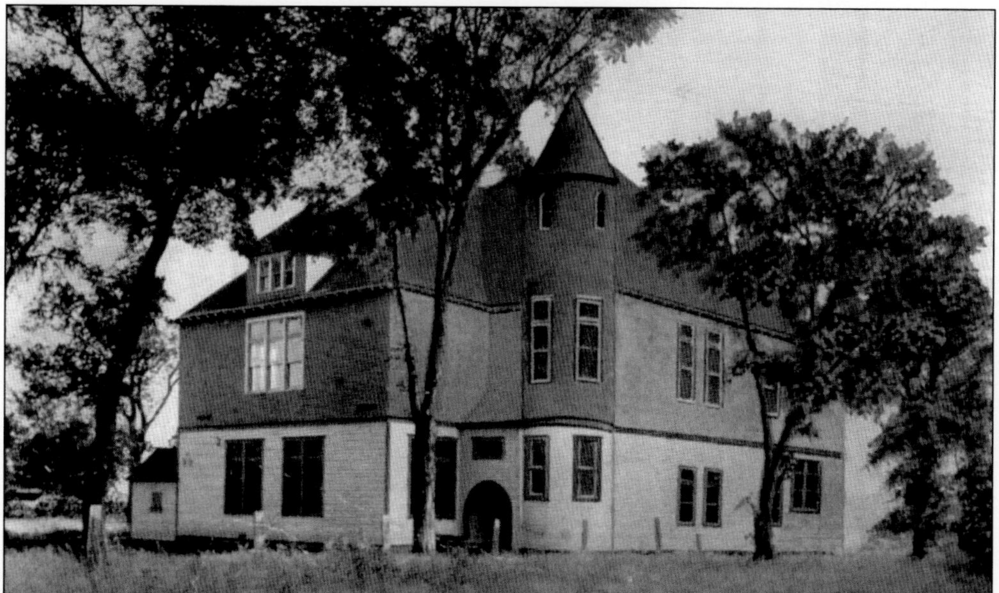

The first East School was built in 1870 on the west side of East Main Street just south of the railroad depot. The school was built to accommodate children living in the southeastern part of the town. Destroyed by fire in the late 1880s, the school was soon rebuilt on a large lot that stretched from East Main Street to French Street. The building continued to be used as a school until 1952 when a new brick grade school was opened.

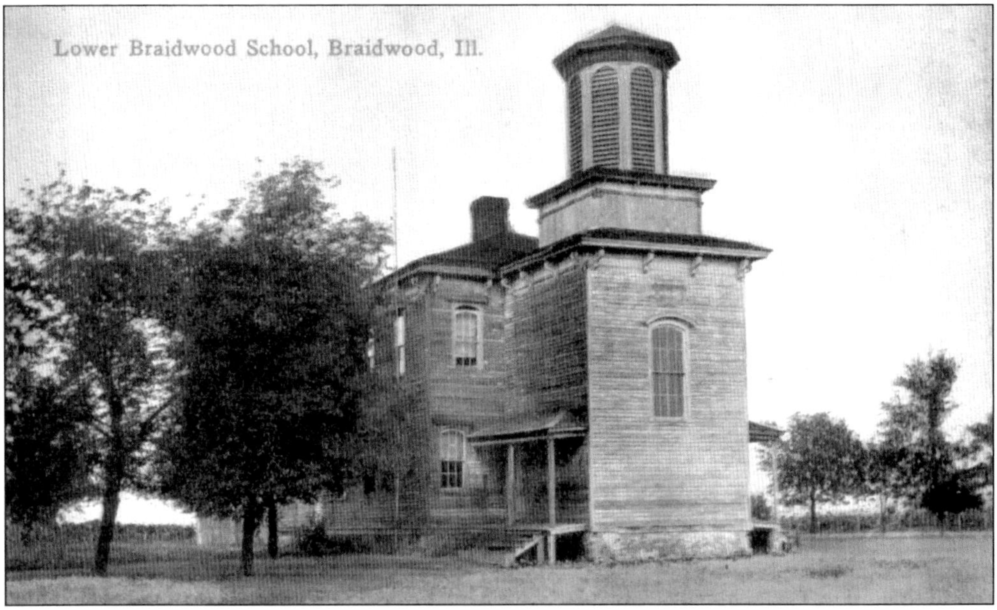

Located on land near Center Street just north of Fifth Street, the Lower Braidwood School was built in 1871 to accommodate the miners' children. The two-story wood-frame school had six rooms, a double stairway to the second floor, and a high belfry on the south end of the building, which housed a large school bell. By the early 1930s, the school building was in need of major repairs and was razed in 1934.

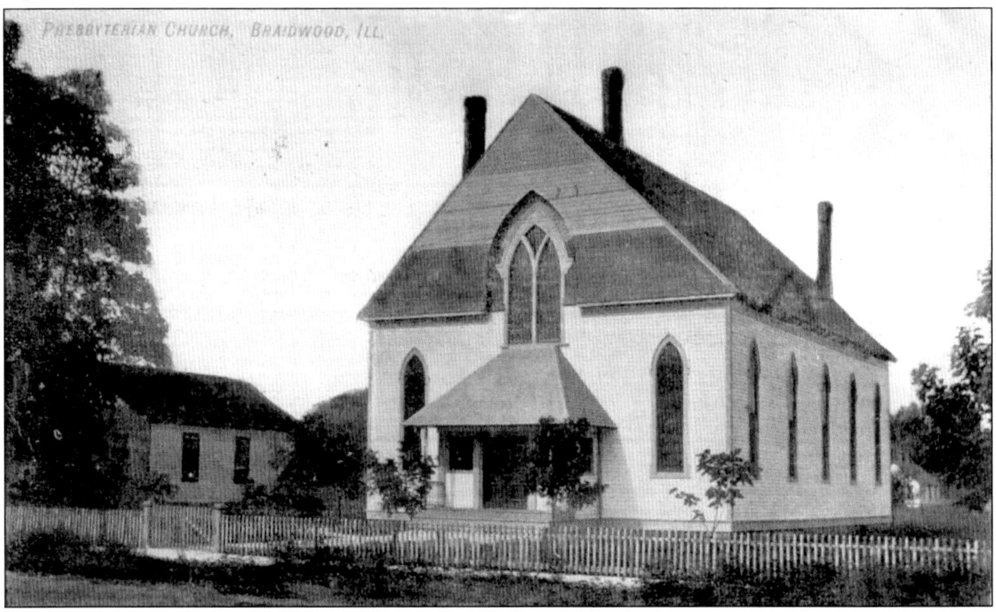

The early Presbyterians established the First Presbyterian Church in 1872 under the direction of Rev. E. R. Davis. As the first minister of the church, he helped supervise the construction of a spacious edifice near the southwest corner of E Street (Lincoln Street) and Main Street. Construction of the new church began in 1873, and the edifice was dedicated in 1875. In 1946, the Methodist Episcopal congregation merged with the Presbyterians and purchased the old church and property.

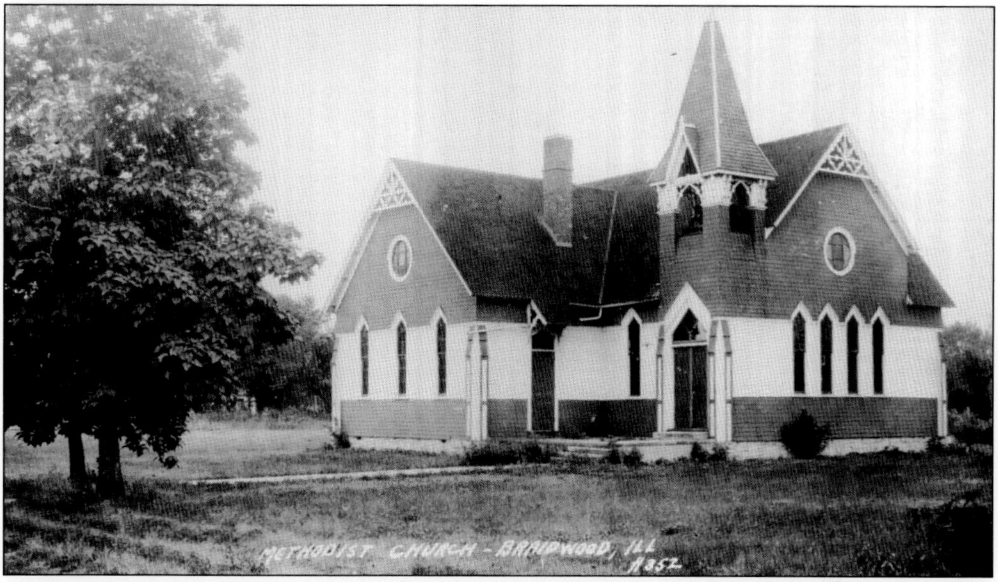

Located on the southeast corner of Main and School Streets, the Methodist Episcopal church was one of the oldest parishes in Braidwood. Organized in 1867, the congregation held its early services in one of the city schools. By 1869, the congregation had financed and constructed one of the first modern church edifices in the area. In 1950, the church building and grounds were sold to the Presbyterian Assembly and used for various functions until 1954. The old church building was razed in 1955.

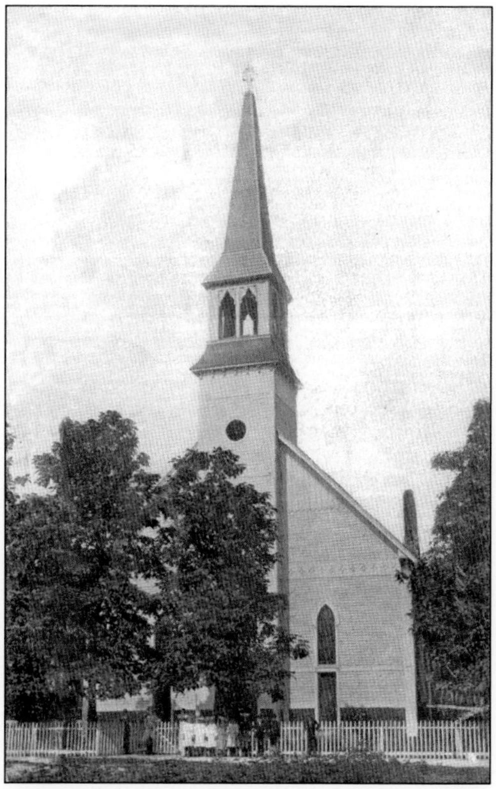

The first Catholic church was erected in Braidwood in 1869 and was located at the north end of Walker Street near Fifth Street. Fire destroyed this first church in 1887, and within the year, a new site was chosen on the southwest corner of Main and School Streets. A modern church structure was built there in 1888. In 1911, lightning struck the steeple, causing a fire to destroy the church. The following year, a new church, without a high steeple, was built on the same site.

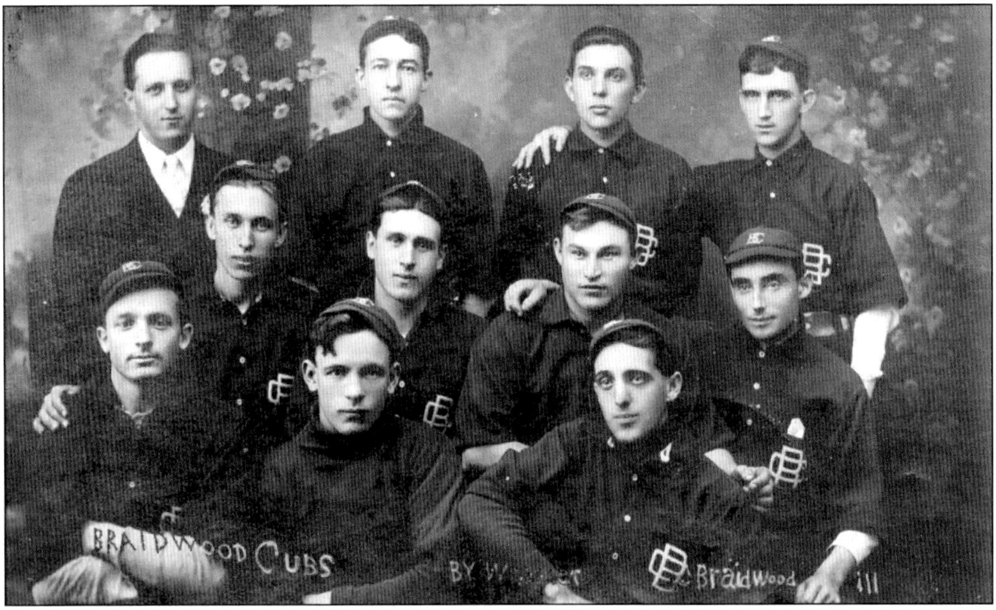

Between 1902 and 1912, the city of Braidwood had one of the most successful amateur baseball teams in northern Illinois. Known as the Cubs, the team was limited by funds and equipment in the early years when playing games in nearby towns, including Diamond, Coal City, Braceville, and Godley. When the Cubs disbanded, other teams followed, including the Lincoln Macs and the Braidwood Grays.

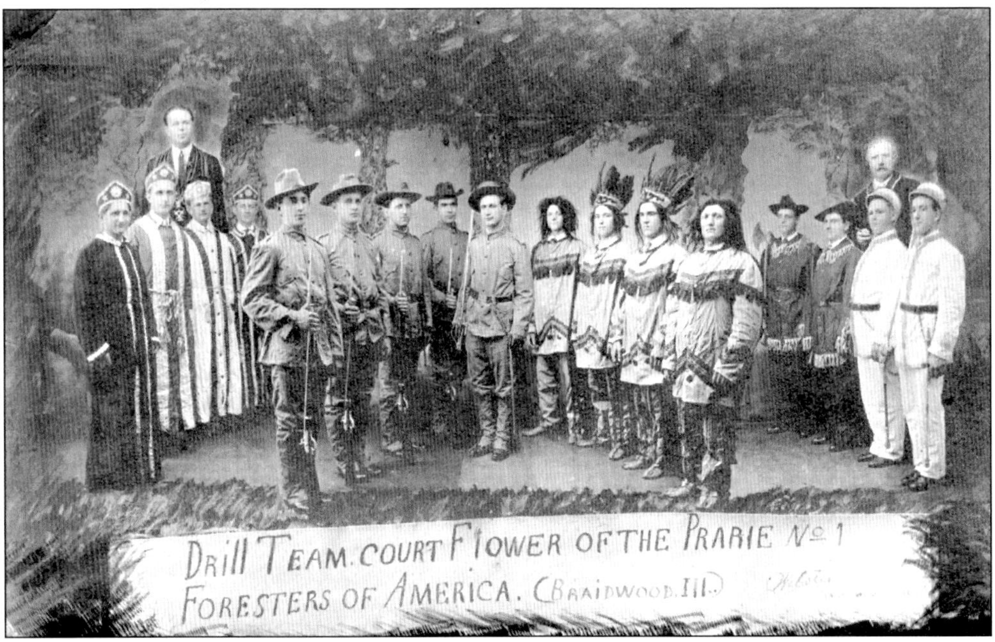

The Foresters of America, with ritualistic work based on the Robin Hood legend, was a popular organization in America during the late 19th century. The local Court Flower of the Prairie organized in 1876 as a branch of the English order and eventually seceded to form an independent lodge. As the oldest chapter in the state of Illinois, it was given the Number One Chapter designation and operated in Braidwood for many generations.

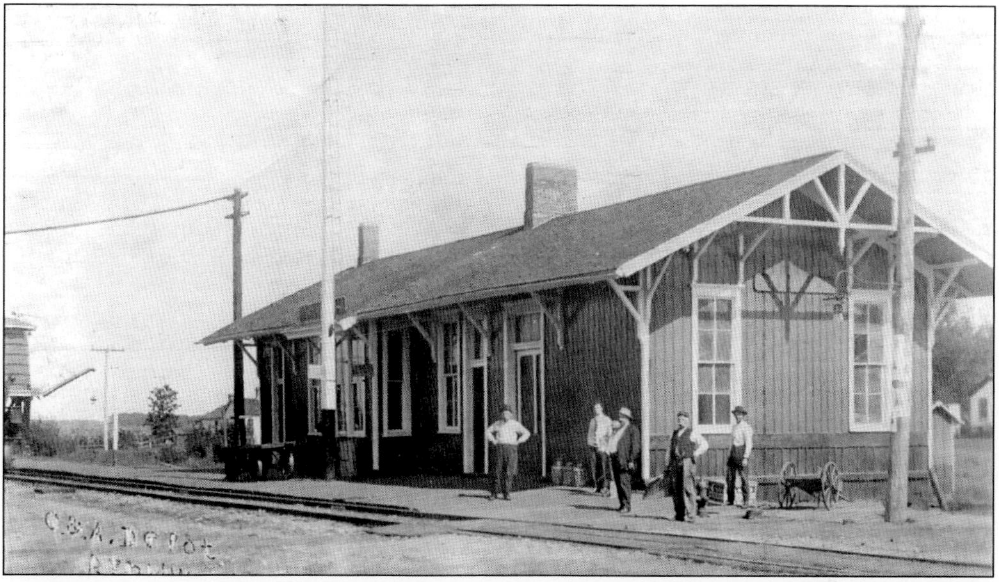

Braidwood, a town named for James Braidwood, a Scottish emigrant who sunk the first shaft for the Chicago and Wilmington Coal Company, was incorporated nine years after William Henneberry discovered coal in the area in 1864. Braidwood soon became a major coal supplier to Chicago and other communities via the St. Louis, Alton and Chicago Railroad, which ran through the town. In 1882, the Braidwood railroad depot was constructed just south of the tracks near Front and Main Streets. Although this was not Braidwood's first railroad depot, it was the town's third and still stands. In November 2008, the owner of the depot, John Kotara of Berkot's Super Foods, donated the structure to the City of Braidwood. The city's current plan involves moving the depot to the corner of Main and Center Streets in town where it will thrive as a historic landmark.

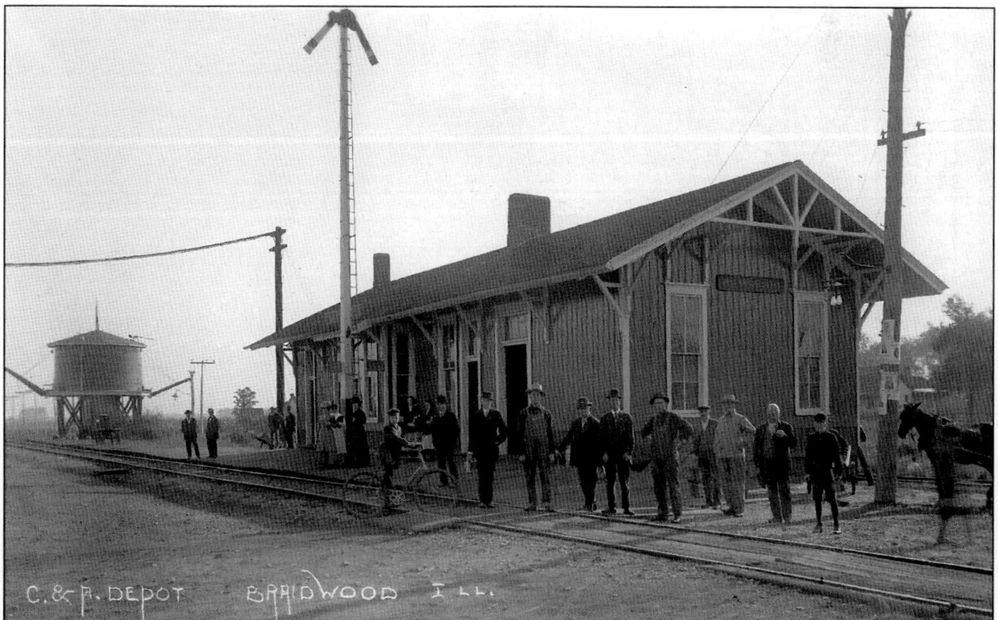

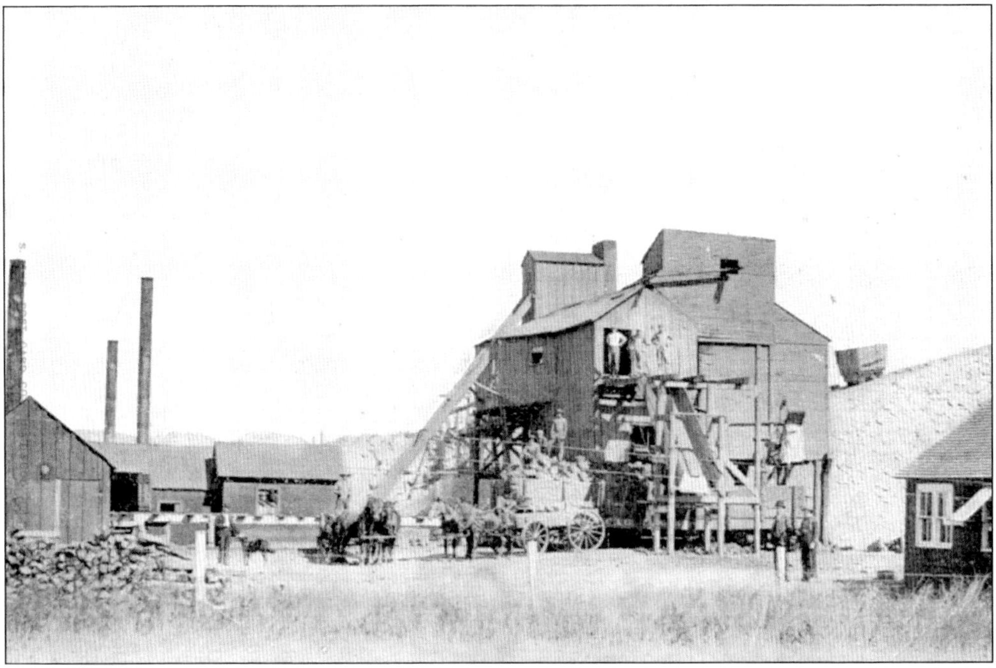

Coal has been mined in 76 counties in Illinois. More than 4,500 coal mines have operated since commercial mining began in Illinois about 1810, and fewer than 30 are currently active. The town of Braidwood was developed during the coal mining boom from 1870 to 1910. This picture postcard shows the Murphy, Keenan and Company coal mine in Braidwood.

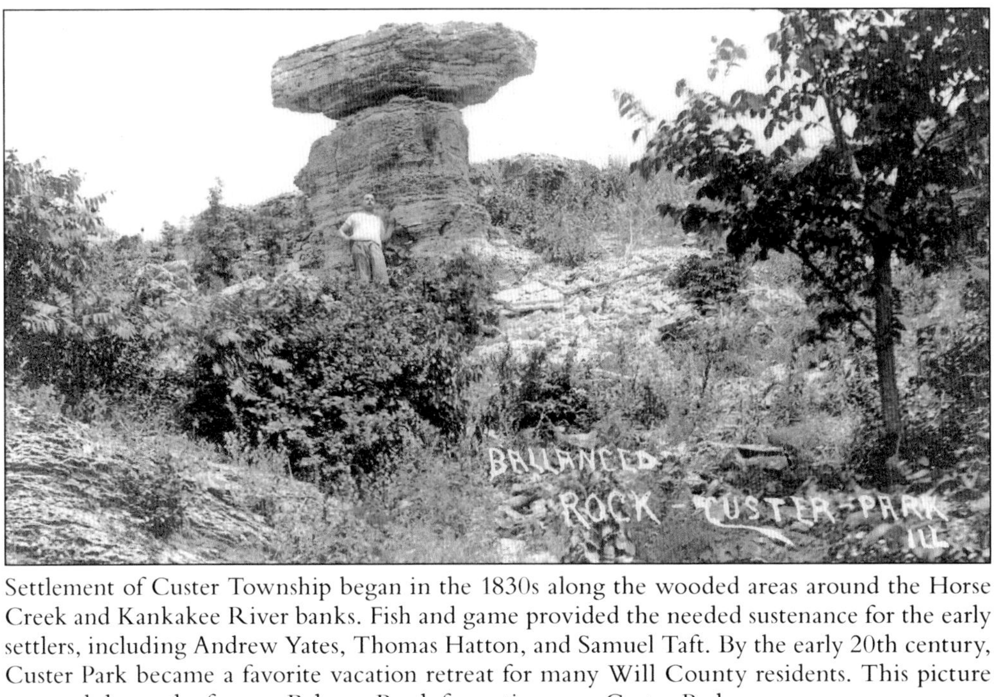

Settlement of Custer Township began in the 1830s along the wooded areas around the Horse Creek and Kankakee River banks. Fish and game provided the needed sustenance for the early settlers, including Andrew Yates, Thomas Hatton, and Samuel Taft. By the early 20th century, Custer Park became a favorite vacation retreat for many Will County residents. This picture postcard shows the famous Balance Rock formation near Custer Park.

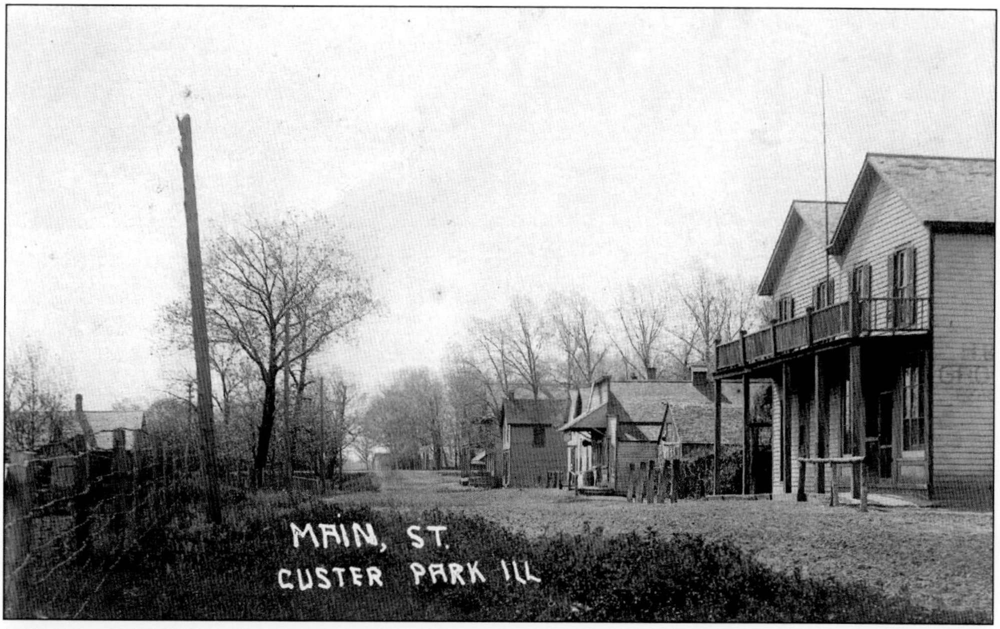

When coal was discovered in Braidwood, the residents of the eastern portion of Reed Township, who did not like the newly arrived immigrant miners, petitioned to be set off as a separate township. The board voted in favor, and the 18 western sections remained Reed Township. The 26 sections to the east had to find a new name. With Lt. Col. George Custer and the U.S. 7th Cavalry's 1876 Battle of the Little Bighorn still in the minds of residents, the new township was named in his honor. The Kankakee River and the Wabash Railroad, which came through the township in 1880, provided the area with general transportation needs. The postcard above shows Main Street in Custer Park, and the photograph below shows the Wabash Railroad. The hotel to the left was built and owned by Camben Knight in the early 1880s. The hotel was sold to Art Shinaberger in 1885 and was known for years as Shinaberger's Hotel.

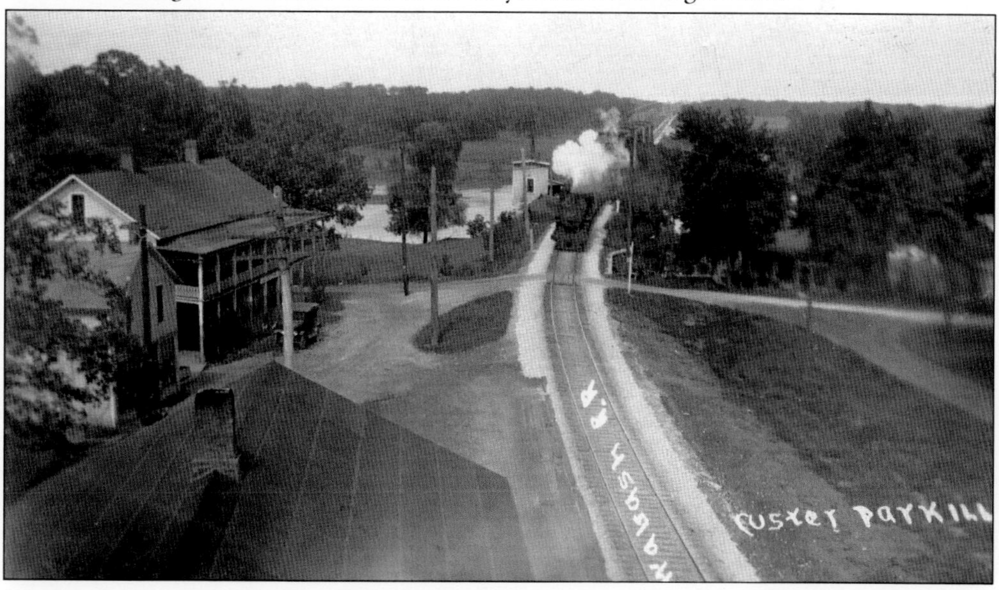

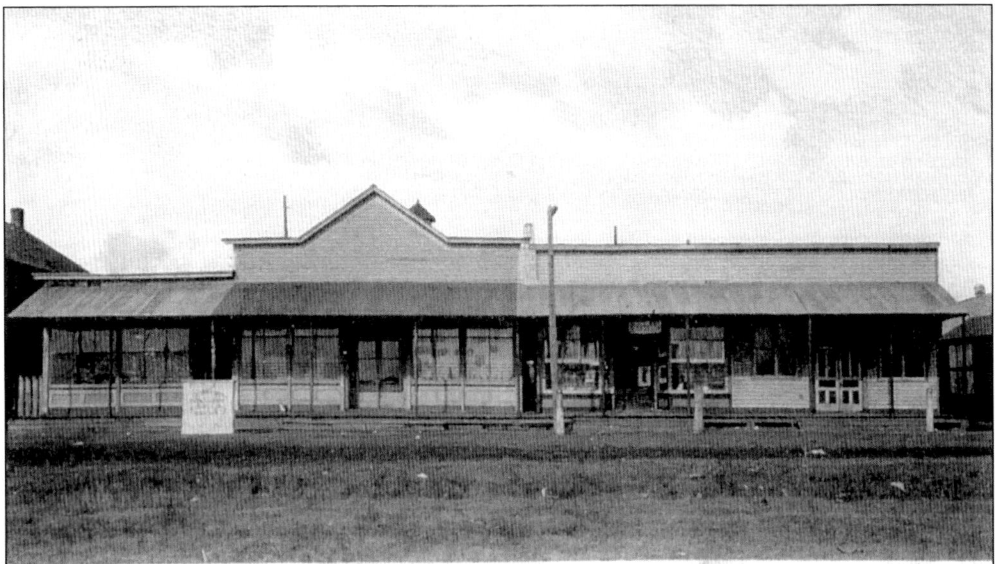

636. Motta's Store, Main Street. Torino, Ill.

The extensive coalfields in northern Illinois were discovered in the 1860s, and within 20 years, coal mining had reached its peak in the county. With the influx of immigrants working in the mines, many boomtowns exploded in size as miners flocked in from the eastern states and southern and eastern Europe. Located in Reed Township, the town of Torino was one such boomtown. Incorporated in 1905, Torino's population was mostly Italian mine workers. The town had nearly 100 buildings, including an icehouse, two grocery stores, a livery stable, a butcher shop, a general store, and a dance hall. By the 1930s, Torino was considered a ghost town, and the last store building collapsed in 1952. Today the site of Torino is covered by the cooling lake of the Braidwood Exelon Nuclear Power Plant. The postcard above shows the Motta General Store, and the postcard below is of the home of Alexander Skinner, superintendent of the Torino mine.

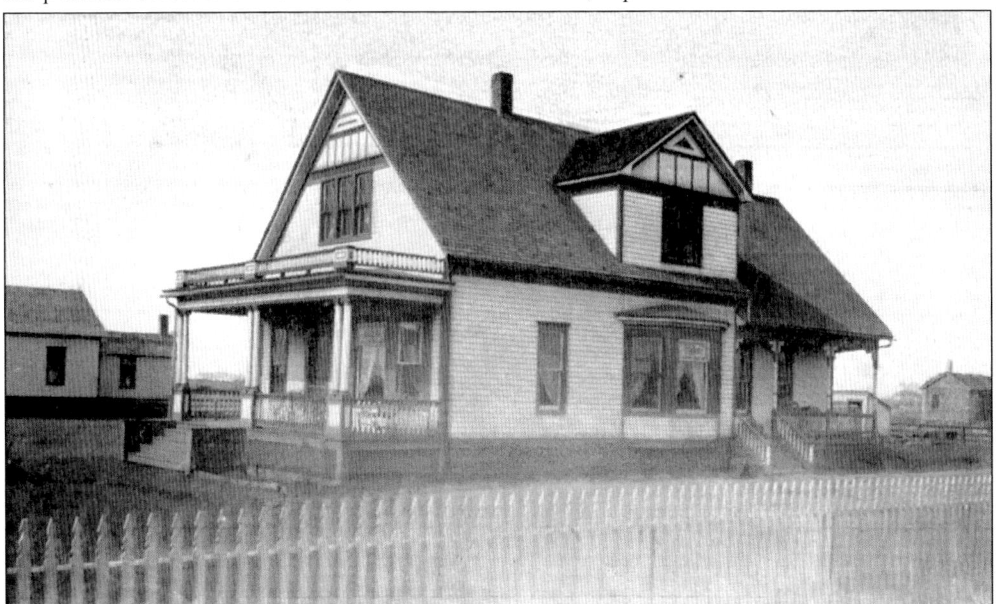

639. Home of Superintendent Skinner, Torino, Ill.

Ten

Peotone and Crete

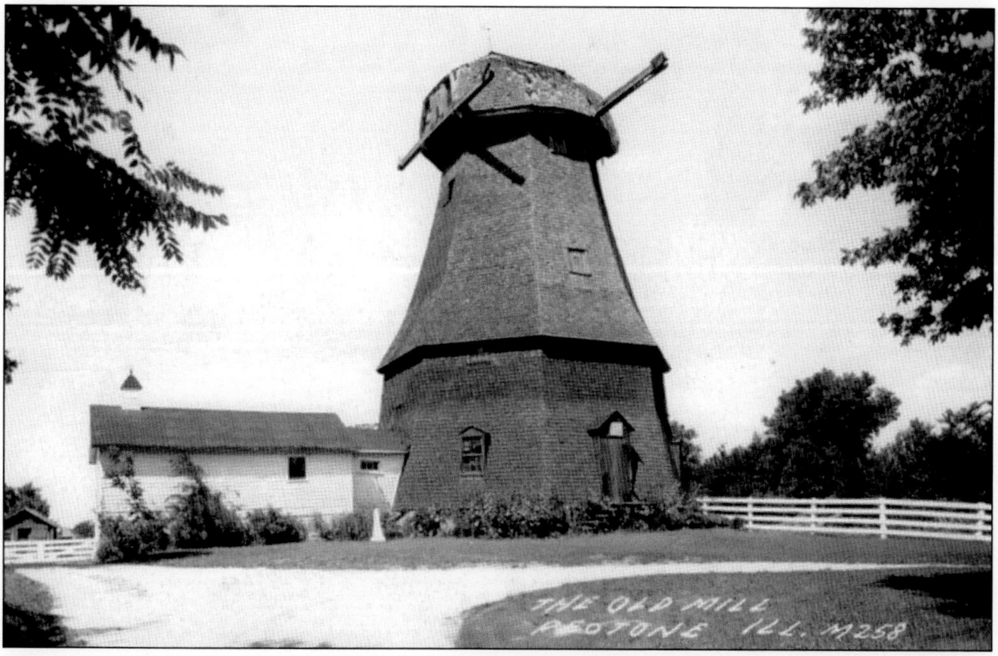

The village of Peotone was established in 1856 and soon grew to become an important farming community. As there was no reliable source of water to provide the power necessary for grinding grain, Henry A. Rathje and his father, Frederick, began construction of a windmill in 1871. By 1900, competition from other mills and new technology caused the mill to close. The H. A. Rathje Mill was designated a Will County historic landmark on January 18, 2002.

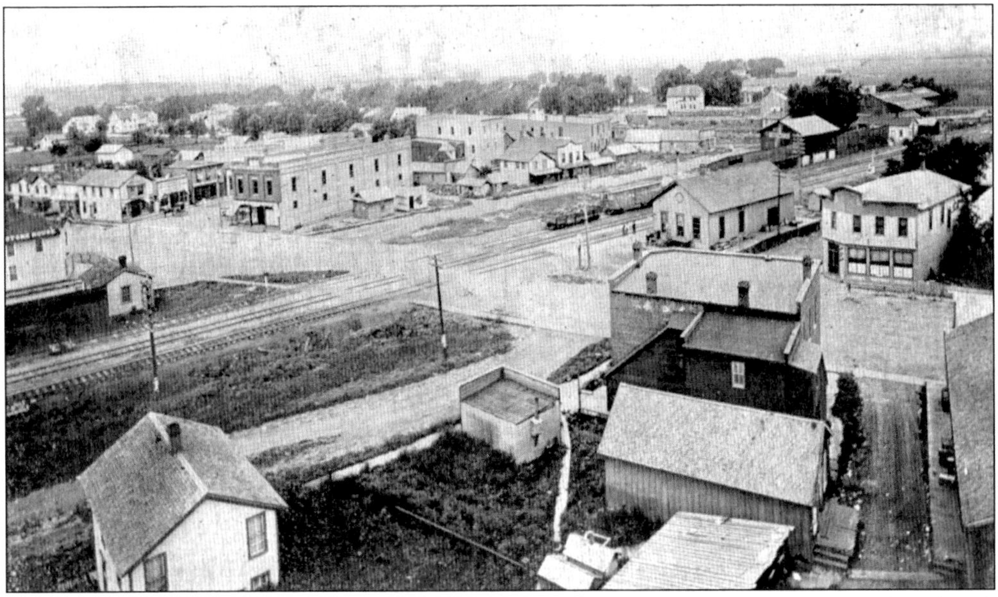

The settling of the township began in 1855 on land purchased from the Illinois Central Railroad, and the village of Peotone was laid out the following year by David Goodwille. The population of the town grew over the next decade, and the town was incorporated in 1869. This postcard shows a bird's-eye view of the town. The tracks of the Illinois Central Railroad and the depot can be seen in the middle of the photograph, and the business district along Second Street can be seen in the distance.

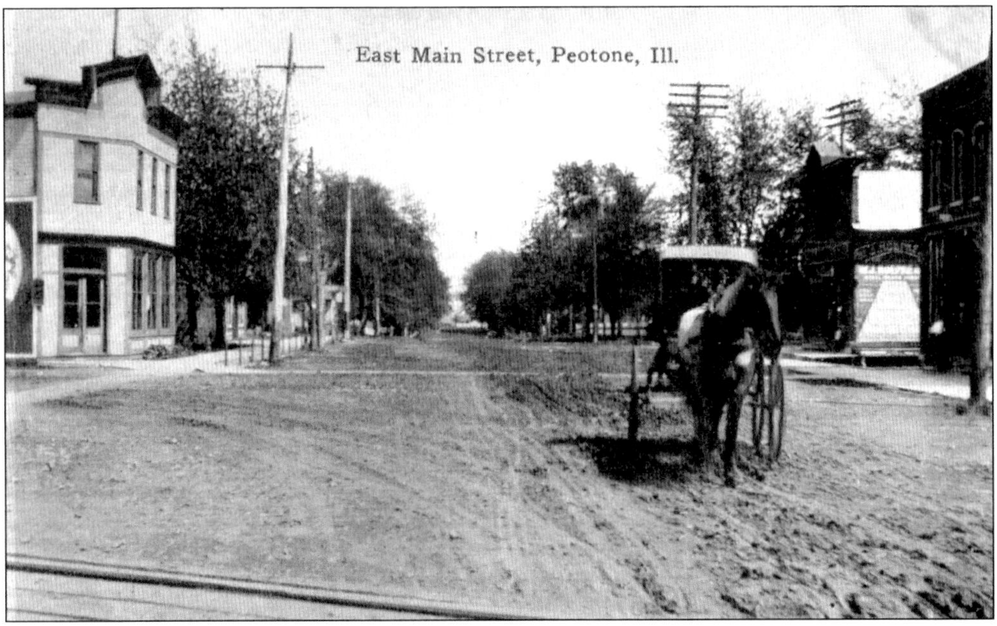

By the 1880s, the business district was located along Railroad Street, and many businesses between Main and North Streets used ramps and platforms to transport goods to and from the railroad cars. By 1890, the business district began to shift west to Second Street, and the nature of Railroad Street changed. This postcard shows a view of Main Street looking east from the Illinois Central Railroad tracks. The building to the left is Louis Schmidt's Saloon.

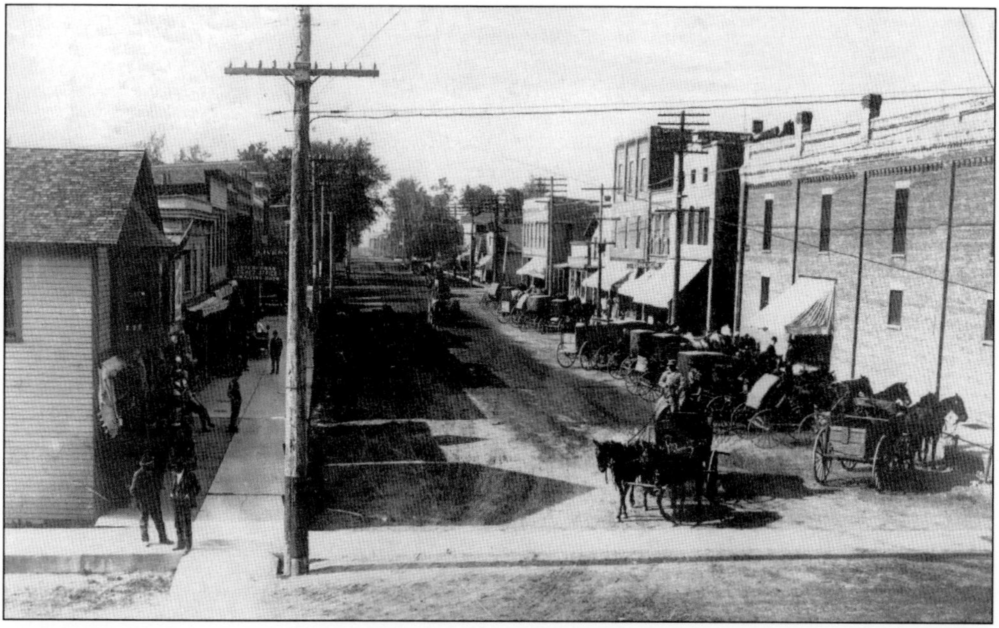

Both picture postcards show views of Second Street looking north from Main Street. Businesses visible along the west side of the block include Koenning and Behrens Men's Clothing Store, Ed Storch's Barber Shop, Lester's Bakery, Schroeder and Poppenhagen's Saloon, and George Grice's Restaurant and Ice Cream Parlor. The interurban trolley, which ran through Peotone from 1907 until 1927, also used the building for a ticket office and waiting room. The interurban sign can be seen in the middle of the block in the above picture. On the east side of the block, the Frederick Schroeder building is on the right at the corner. The two-story brick building next door is Gebhardt's Meat Market followed by A. J. Foster and Company Drug Store and the Frahm and Fletcher Dry Goods Store. Today this section of Second Street and sections of Main and East North Streets are part of the downtown Peotone historic district.

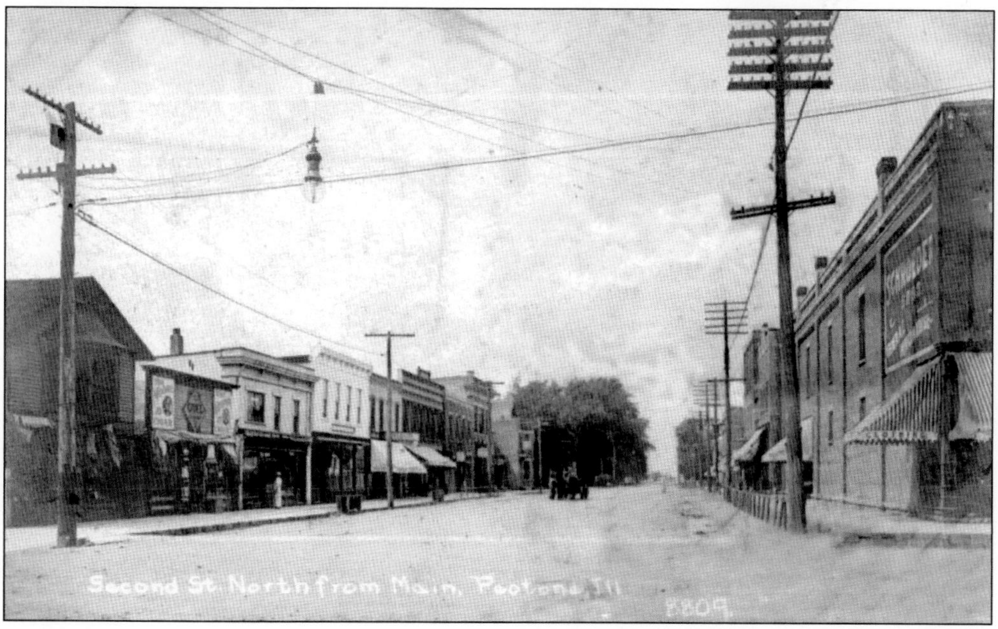

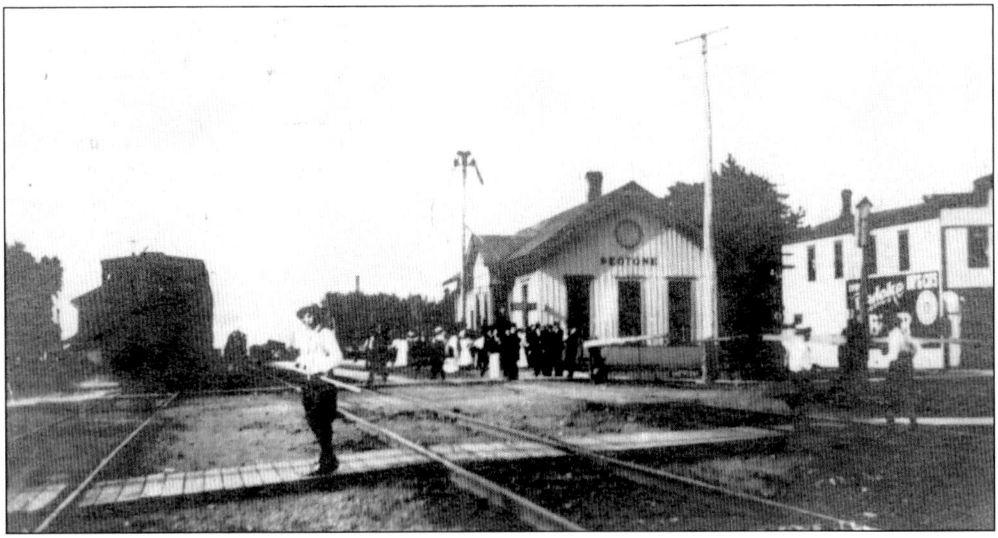

The Illinois Central Railroad was charted in 1851 to take advantage of the federal land grant of 1850 and built a north–south line in Illinois from Cairo to Chicago. This provided the catalyst for growth in the central and southern regions of Illinois, attracting thousands of settlers and laying the foundations for agricultural, industrial, and urban development. This postcard looks north of the railroad depot in Peotone just east of the Illinois Central Railroad tracks near Main Street.

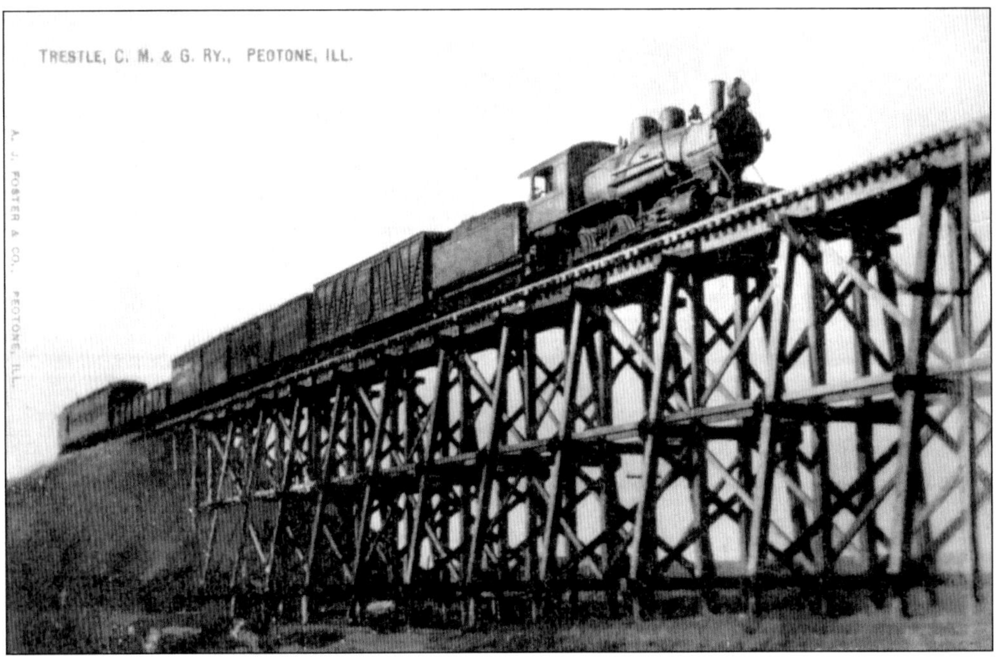

The Illinois, Iowa and Minnesota Railway served the Will County communities of Joliet, Manhattan, Wilton, Andres, and Peotone. In June 1908, the Illinois, Iowa and Minnesota Railway changed its name to the Chicago, Milwaukee and Gary Railway Company. This picture postcard shows a Chicago, Milwaukee and Gary Railway train on the original timber trestle over the Illinois Central Railroad at Peotone. Over time, the original timber trestle in Peotone was replaced by a steel-plate girder bridge.

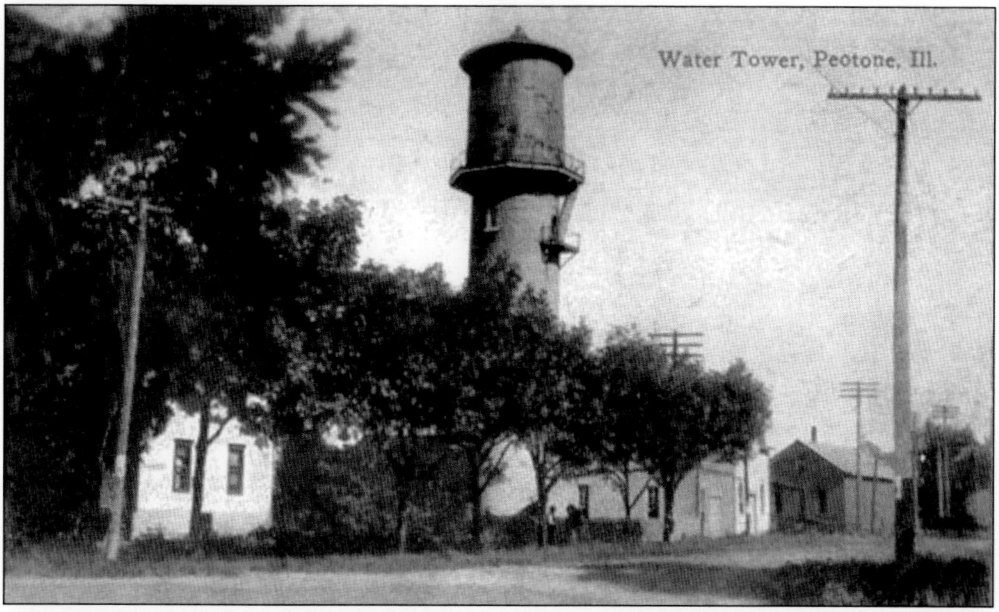

The Peotone water tower was built in 1895 and included a 2,000-barrel tank built on the top of a 70-foot round brick tower. Located near the corner of Main and Third Streets, the old village hall is the second building from the right under the water tower. The wooden water tower collapsed in January 1914, sending 2,000 barrels of water below. It was replaced with a modern steel tank on the brick tower. In 1990, the water tower was torn down.

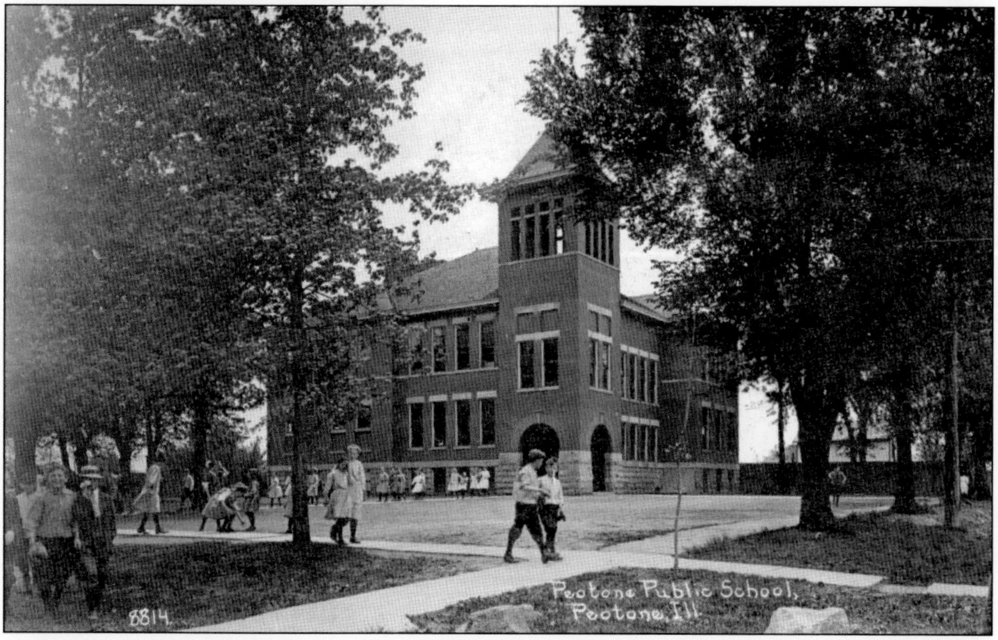

Located on the corner of West and Wilson Streets, the Peotone brick schoolhouse was dedicated in September 1901. A gymnasium and auditorium were added onto the east side of the building in 1927. A fire later destroyed the old building, including all the school records, and the loss was estimated at the time to be nearly $95,000. The school was rebuilt and housed all the grades until a new high school was completed in 1955.

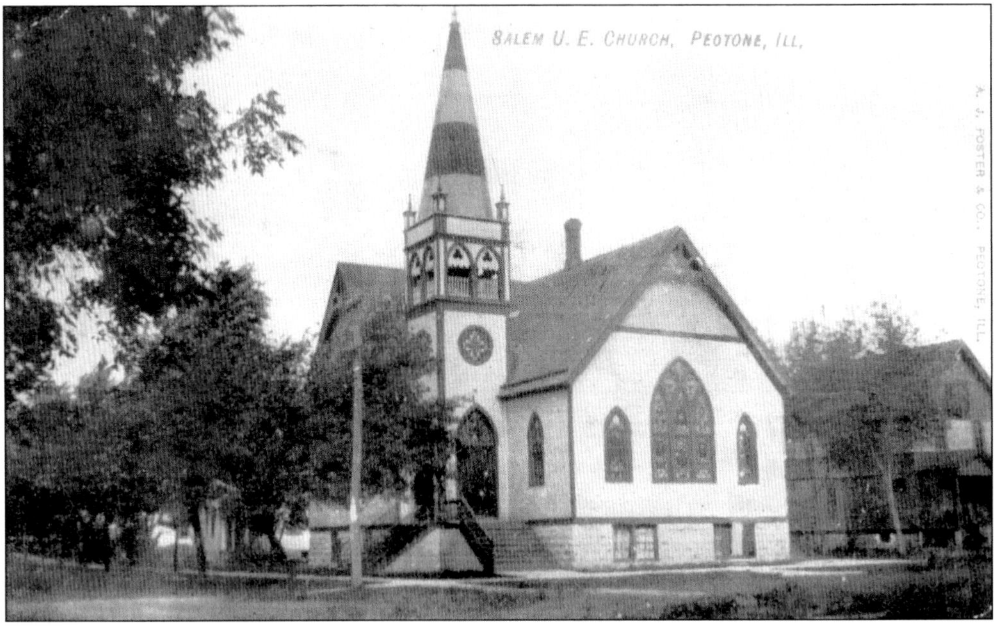

In 1890, the Zion Evangelical Church separated into two congregations, reflecting a split in the denomination at the national level. The Zion Evangelical Church continued at Wilson and Third Streets, and a new church named Salem United Evangelical Church began. Located at the corner of West and North Streets, the Salem United Evangelical Church was erected in 1899 to serve the new congregation.

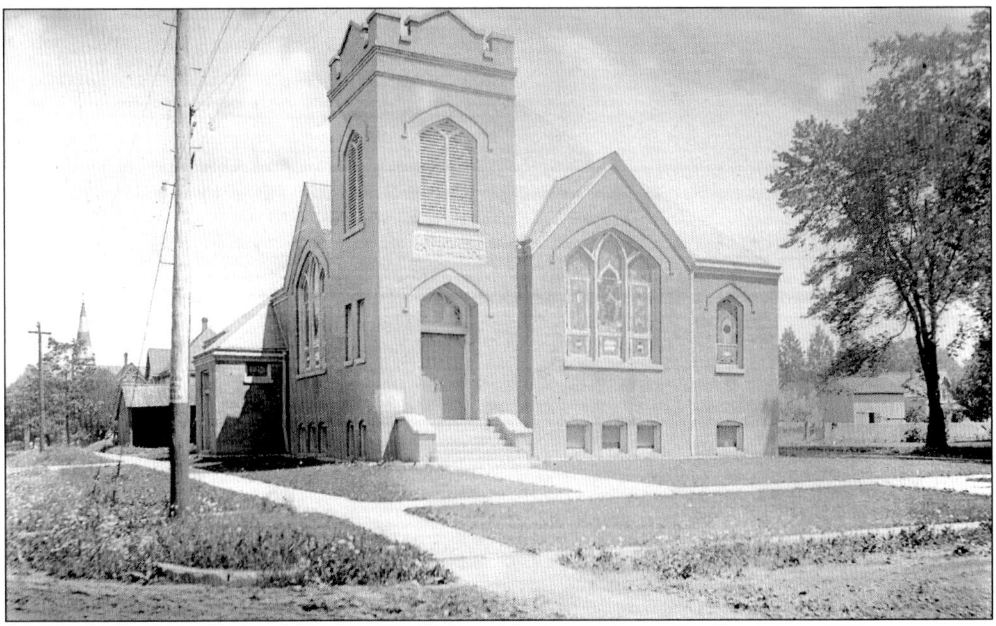

The Peotone United Methodist Church represents the oldest continuous church congregation in Peotone. In 1858, John Hitchins organized a Methodist society in Peotone with 10 members. As the congregation grew, a church was built in 1867 on the corner of West and Main Streets. In 1906, the old church was razed, and a new one, shown in this postcard, was built, and in 1914, a new parsonage was added to the east of the structure.

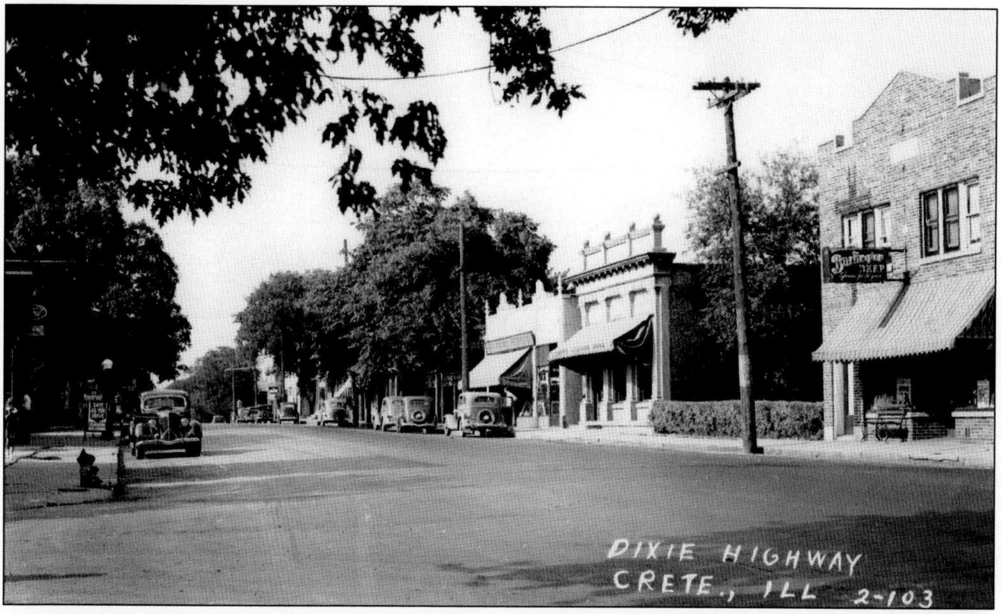

By 1925, the official map of the Dixie Highway consisted of 5,786 miles of improved roadway. The highway started in Chicago, traveling through Blue Island, Harvey, Homewood, and Chicago Heights, and then followed what is today Route 1 through Crete, Beecher, Grant Park, Momence, St. Anne, Watseka, Hoopston, and Danville, where the road turns east into Indiana. This postcard photograph shows a section of the Dixie Highway through downtown Crete.

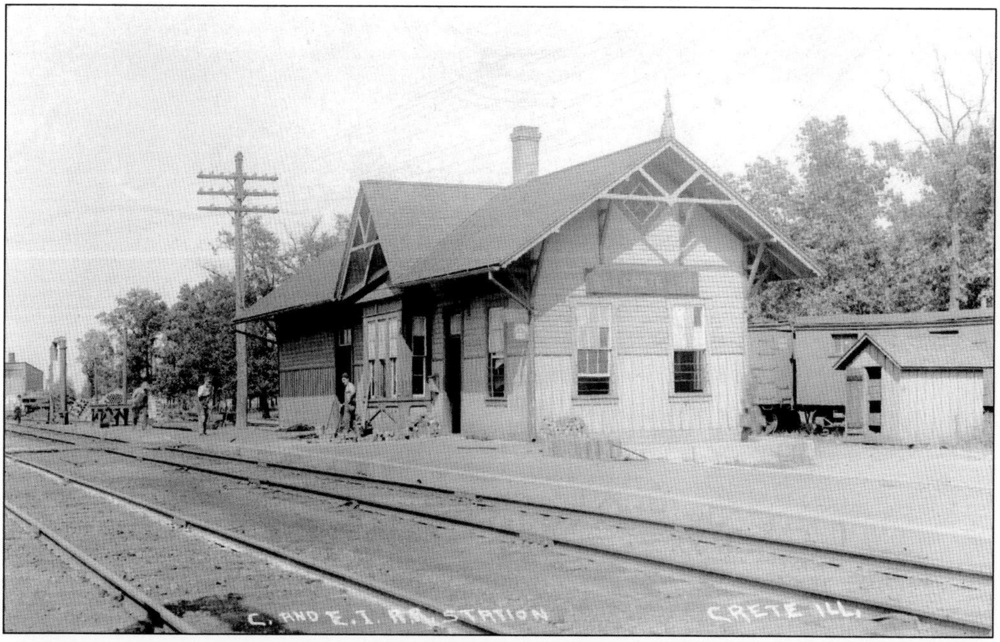

The first railroad station in Crete was built in 1869 when the railroad came through town. The first depot was located on the east side of the tracks about 100 feet north of First Street. This picture postcard looking northeast across the tracks shows the second railroad depot built soon after the 1880 fire destroyed the first one. The grain elevator and roundhouse are located out of view just north of the station.

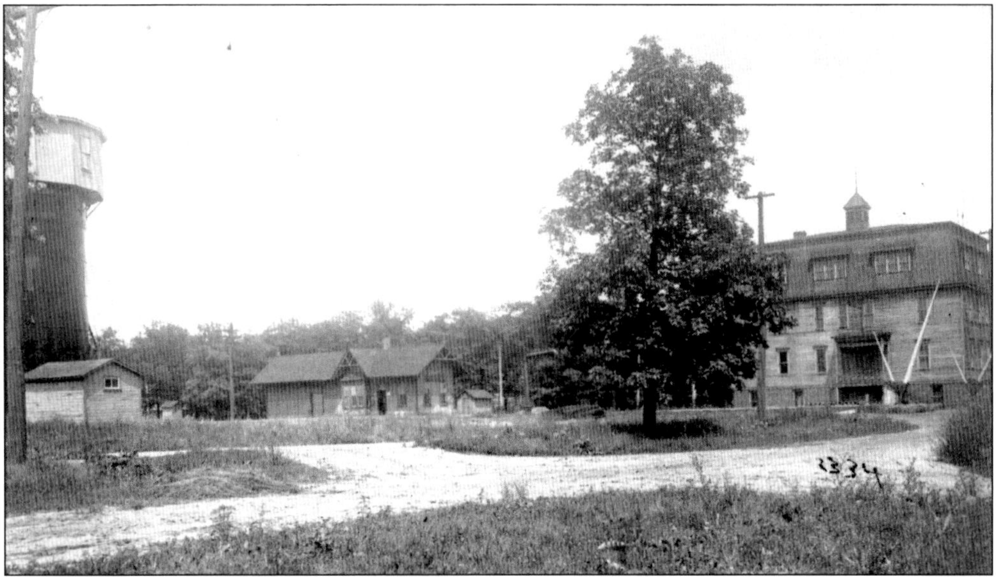

Looking east toward the Chicago and Eastern Illinois Railroad tracks, the second Crete railroad depot built in 1880 can be seen in the center of the photograph postcard. To the right and south of the depot, the three-story Hattendorf Hotel is visible. Originally built for visitors to the 1893 World's Columbian Exposition in Chicago, the fancy and spacious hotel had a large bar in the basement, a lobby, a dining room and kitchen on the first floor, 13 bedrooms and a bathroom on the second floor, and a ballroom on the entire third floor.

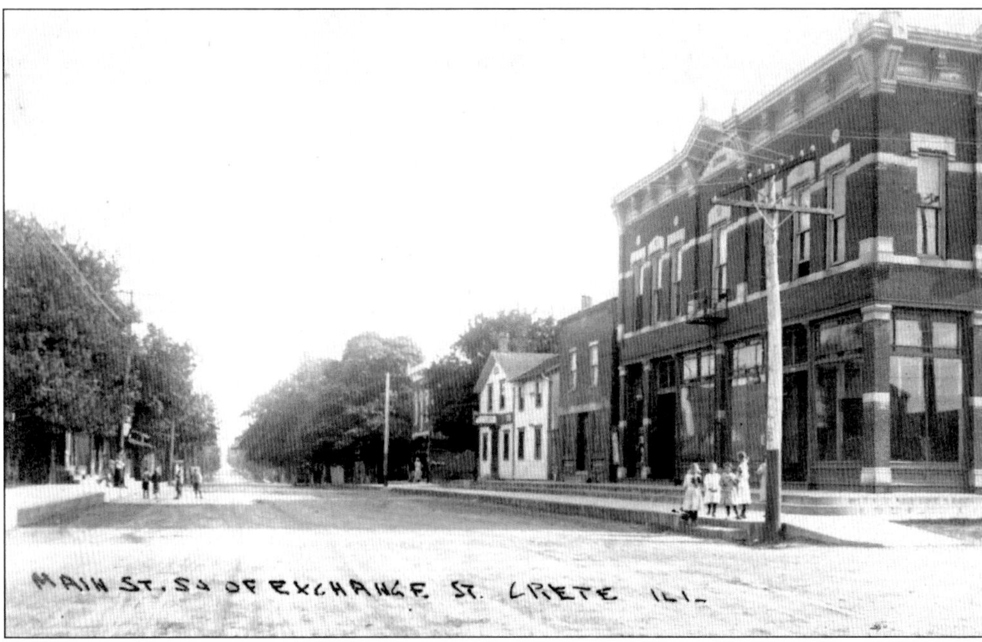

In 1880, Conrad Wilkening, one of Crete's leading merchants, purchased a building and lot on the southwest corner of Main and Exchange Streets and opened a dry goods store called C. Wilkening and Company. The company was so successful that, in 1886, the small brick store was moved south off the edge of the lot, and a new two-story brick, stone, and iron building was constructed. In 1960, the original Wilkening building and the Wilkening Block were razed.

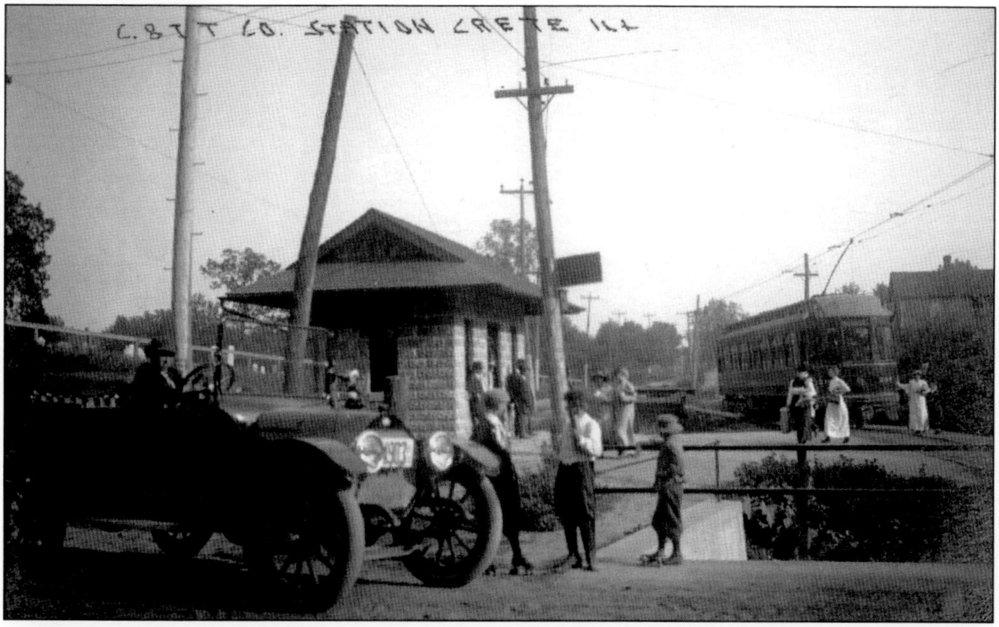

In 1907, the Chicago and Southern Traction Company began electric car service from Chicago to Kankakee. By 1912, the line became known as the Chicago Interurban Traction Company. A wooden depot was originally built on the southwest corner of Exchange and Vincennes Streets and was replaced in 1914 with the new concrete block structure seen in the postcard above. The interurban served the needs of Crete residents for many years, but the growing popularity of the automobile caused the company to lose customers. In 1927, the Chicago Interurban Traction Company ceased operations, and by the following year, the trolley tracks were removed. In the picture postcard above, passengers can be seen arriving on the interurban in Crete. Notice the automobile at the lower left of the picture. The postcard below shows a trolley car coming down the line toward Exchange Street. The old trolley line tracks through Crete ran down Columbia Street.

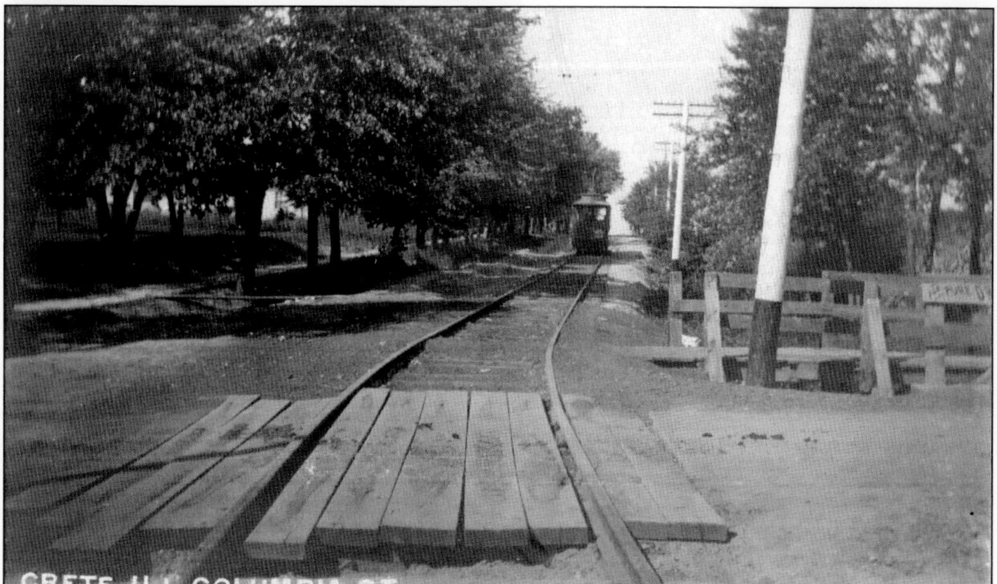

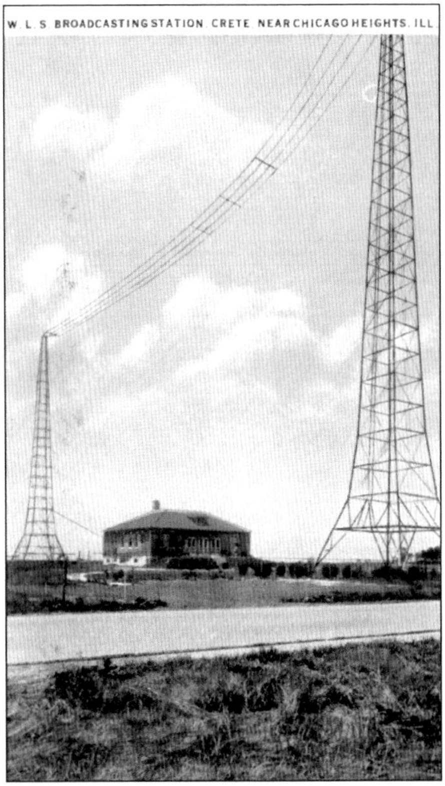

In the early 1920s, Sears and Roebuck began reaching the lucrative farm market by broadcasting on the radio. Using the call letters WLS (World's Largest Store), Sears officially began broadcasting from its own small studio in the company headquarters on Homan Avenue in Chicago. In 1925, a station with two large 200-foot-tall towers was constructed just south of Crete on the Dixie Highway. The transmitting station was closed in Crete in 1938, and its operation moved to the current location just northeast of I-80 and U.S. 45 in Tinley Park.

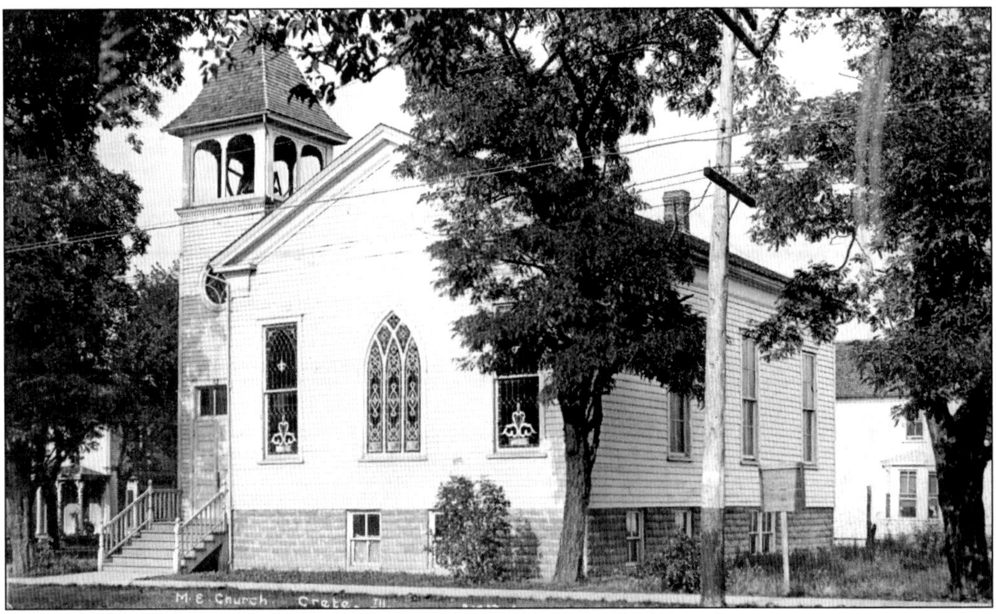

The first Methodist service in Crete was conducted by a circuit rider in 1836, and five years later, the Methodist Episcopal Church of Crete was organized and founded. In 1851, a lot on Main Street was purchased and a church was built. In 1906, the church building was moved one lot north to the northeast corner of Exchange and Main Streets where it still stands today.

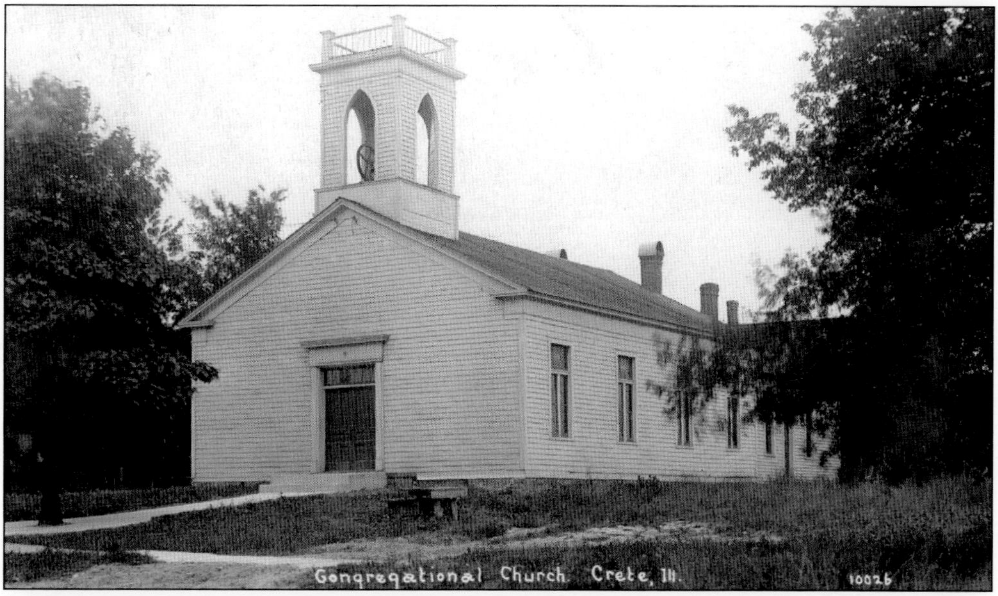

In 1853, the Societies of Bebbe's Grove Congregational and the Thorn Grove Congregational united as one church. A lot was purchased on West Exchange Street to build a new church. It was formally named the First Congregational Church in Crete, Will County. In 1869, when the Chicago and Eastern Illinois Railroad came through Crete, the church was moved to the west to clear a right-of-way. After 119 years, the First Congregational Church in Crete closed its doors.

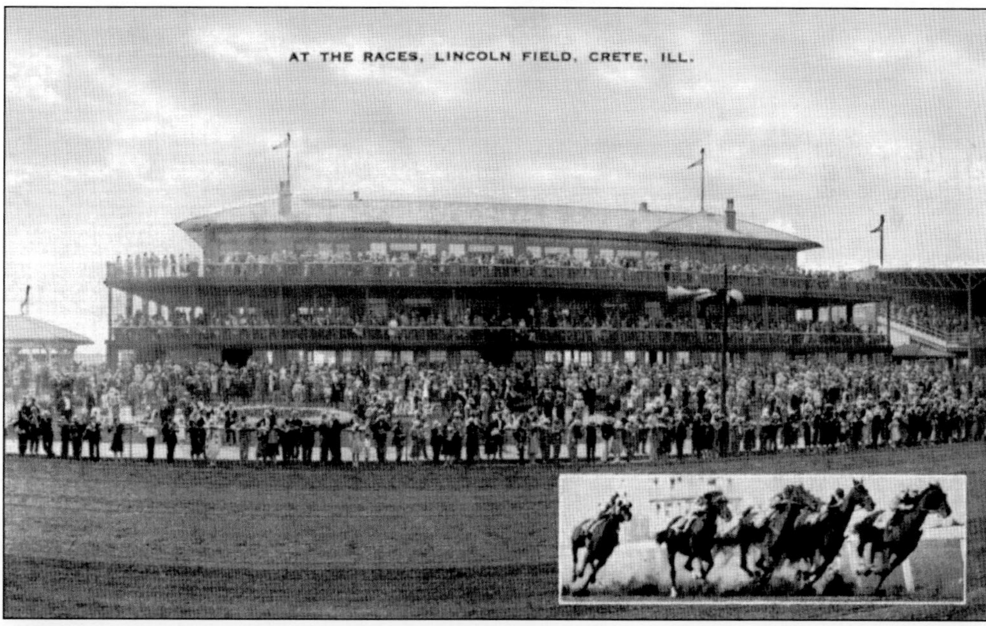

In 1925, Col. Matt J. Winn, manager of Churchill Downs in Kentucky, and his associates purchased 1,050 acres along the Dixie Highway just south of Crete and built a new racetrack named Lincoln Fields. Lincoln Fields was a favorite racing venue for many spectators because of its natural beauty, rolling hills, background forest, and flower gardens. In 1955, Benjamin Lindheimer formed the Balmoral Jockey Club, purchased Lincoln Fields, and changed its name to Balmoral Park.

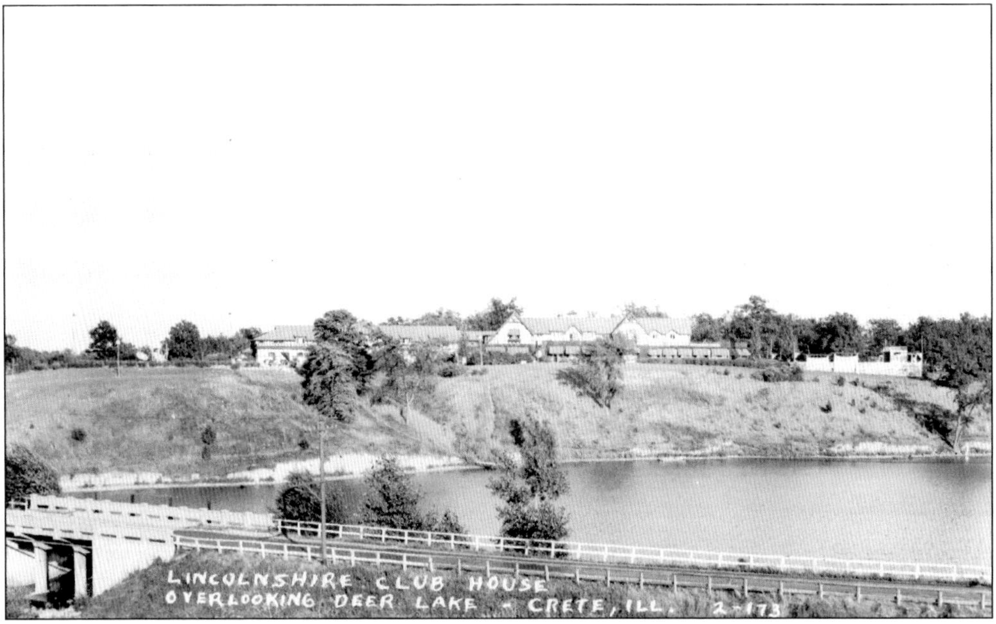

During the 1920s, a group of investors led by Sam Homan purchased nearly 1,200 acres of farmland in Crete for a unique land development, which was to include a country club, four golf courses, tennis courts, trapshooting pits, a swimming pool, 10 miles of bridle path, a large lake, and parcels of land for summer homes. The developers named the adventure Lincolnshire to link it to the racetrack, Lincoln Fields, being constructed south of town. Lincolnshire Country Club celebrated its 75th anniversary in 2002. Since its beginning in 1927, the country club, with its scenic beauty and wooded and wetland areas, has been an important part of the community of Crete. The postcard above shows a view of the Lincolnshire clubhouse overlooking Deer Lake, and the postcard below is a view of the swimming pool at the club.

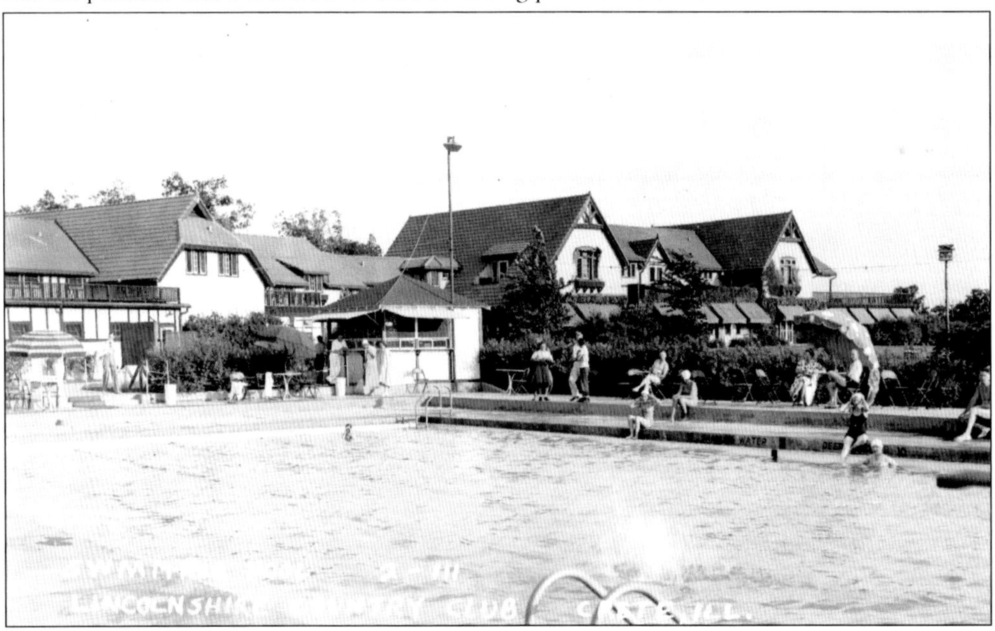

Bibliography

Adamsick, Tom. *Greetings from Peotone, Illinois, Pictorial History of Early Peotone, Illinois, the First 75 Years: 1856–1931.* Pediment Publishing, 2000.

Braidwood Centennial 1865–1965. Braidwood, IL: 1965.

Browning, Norma Lee. *Mokena, 1832–1845.* Mokena, IL: Mokena Civic Association, 1945.

Donna, Modesto. *The Braidwood Story.* Braidwood, IL: Braidwood History Bureau, 1957.

Genealogical and Biographical Record of Will County, Illinois. Chicago: Biographical Publishing Company, 1900.

Lamb, John M. "Early Days on the I & M Canal." *Chicago History* 3 (Winter 1974–1975): 168–170.

Lockport, Illinois: An HCRS Project Report. U.S. Department of the Interior, Heritage Conservation and Recreation Service, 1980.

Manhattan Memories. Manhattan, IL: Manhattan Township History Society, 2008.

Niemann, Judy, Richard Quizz, and Doris Sangmeister. *Mokena, 1880–1980, Century of Progress.* Mokena, IL: Mokena Centennial, 1980.

Pitman, Florence. *The Story of Mokena.* Mokena, IL: Mokena Women's Club, 1963.

Sterling, Robert E. *A Pictorial History of Will County.* 2 Vols. Joliet, IL: Will County Historical Publications Company, 1975–1976.

———. *Joliet: Transportation & Industry, A Pictorial History.* St. Louis, MO: G. Bradley Publishing, 1997.

Wilmington Centennial 1836–1936. Wilmington, IL: 1936.

Wilmington's 125th Anniversary 1836–1961. Wilmington, IL: Wilmington Chamber of Commerce and Industry, 1961.

Woodruff, George H. *Forty Years Ago! A Contribution to the Early History of Joliet and Will County.* Joliet, IL: Joliet Republican Stream Printing House, 1874.

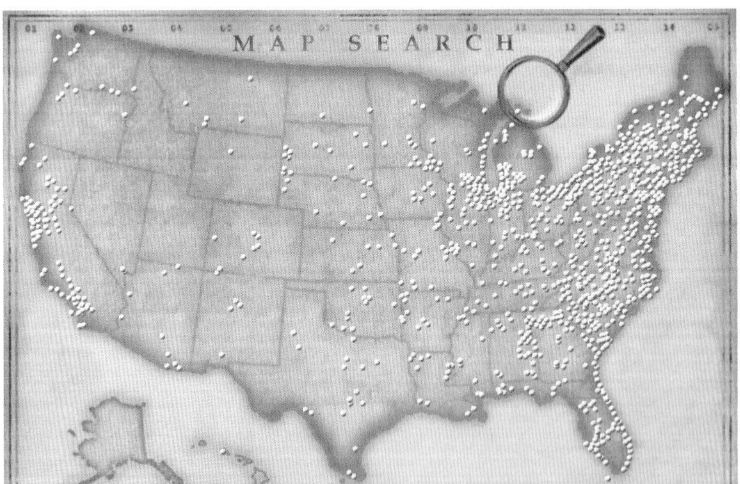
MAP SEARCH